*As a Christian, do you desire to live an exciting, rewarding, radical life-style that will definitely leave an impact on the lives of those around you?*

In *Lord, How Can I Ever Be Righteous,* Kay Arthur takes you into a practical study of Jesus Christ's Sermon on the Mount. She not only includes Chapters 5 through 7 of the Gospel of Matthew, but this exhaustive study also encompasses relevant passages of Scripture found in both the Old and New Testaments. Because the 18-week study provides you with provocative, searching questions, daily applications of biblical text, heartfelt prayers, admonitions, personal illustrations, and more, your serious involvement is certain to transform your Christian walk. Your path will go "from one that takes you from the valley of sin to the mount of blessedness." And you will learn how to follow Christ's example closely, so that you may truly become "the light of the world and the salt of the earth." You will receive God's blessings and see His promises come true as Kay Arthur teaches you the nuts and bolts of living sacrificially for the advance of the Gospel in today's society. You'll know the reality of living by faith as you learn how to follow Christ's commands to:

- *mourn over sin and evil, rather than tolerate it*
- *trust God to supply your daily needs*
- *hunger and thirst after righteousness*
- *seek the Kingdom of God*
- *be peaceful, even when persecuted*
*and rely upon the Holy Spirit within to lead you in the life-style of the Sermon on the Mount.*

# Kay Arthur

# Lord, How Can I Ever Be Righteous

Fleming H. Revell
A Division of Baker Book House
Grand Rapids, Michigan 49506

Permission to quote from the following is gratefully acknowledged:
*The Sermon on the Mount* by D. A. Carson. Copyright © 1978 by Baker Book House.

*Pastor Hsi* by Mary Geraldine Taylor. Published by OMF Books.

*A Bible for Russia,* published by A Bible for Russia, Inc., Corona, Calif.

*Samuel Morris, the March of Faith* by Lindley Baldwin. Copyright © 1969 by Bethany House Publishers.

"Finally Home" by Don Wyrtzen. Copyright © 1971 by Singspiration, Division of the Zondervan Corporation. All rights reserved.

This book was previously published under the title *How Can I Be Blessed*

Copyright © 1985 by Kay Arthur
Published by Fleming H. Revell
a division of Baker Book House Company
P.O. Box 6287, Grand Rapids, MI 49516-6287
All rights reserved

ISBN: 0-8007-5378-X

Fourth printing, January 1993

*Printed in the United States of America*

To those in Chattanooga who have patiently waited for me to grow—in love, in gentleness, in the knowledge of Him and His likeness . . .

To those in Chattanooga who have understood my impassioned heart and therefore, with His love that hopes, endures, and believes, wait patiently for me to mature . . .

To those in Chattanooga who have come alongside our ministry with your love, prayers, presence, and financial support . . .

To those Chattanooga churches, pastors, and ministries that have so graciously accepted us in the unity of the Spirit and the bond of peace . . .

And to the men and women of our city's own special Foundation which has given generously to so many Christian ministries, ours included, in monies for buildings and equipment . . .

My husband and I dedicate this book.

Truly God has blessed us abundantly through you. We love you, and as bondservants of Jesus Christ, our hearts' desire is to serve you, and in serving you, to serve Him.

# Contents

# Preface

You are hungry to know more about your God? You have a longing for greater intimacy with Jesus Christ?

You have seen it in others, and you're not satisfied with where you are in your relationship with your heavenly Father.

You want to know more about Him and His Word for yourself—to have meaningful quiet times with your God—to come away different, to have absolutes you can share with a hurting world.

*Lord, How Can I Ever Be Righteous* is a study that captures not only the head, but the heart. It is a study that involves you in the learning process so you can see truth for yourself—

- a study that can be done in the privacy of your home or in the fellowship of other believers
- a study that is more than "fill-in-the-blank"
- a study that will search your heart and set you free from chains of mediocrities
- a study that will plunge you beneath the surface of the Sermon on the Mount to the hidden wonders of its depth.

*Lord, How Can I Ever Be Righteous* is an eighteen-week study divided into five days of study for each week. It uniquely combines scholarly, yet practical teaching with a personal involvement in studying the subject at hand. The appendix (C) of the book includes discussion questions for each chapter, giving the book added practical value as it then becomes either a means for reviewing truth or an exciting and enlightening study book for church or home use.

How can you be blessed? The answer is within these pages, waiting for your commitment to a study such as this.

# 1 - Are We Condemned to Be Locked Behind a Mask of Hypocrisy?

Most religion is hypocrisy. Deep down inside we know it. It's hypocrisy because it's not changing lives. People say they have come to believe—but what they believe hasn't changed what they are.

The church of Jesus Christ is supposed to be salt and light. Salt stops the spread of corruption. It's a preservative. Light dispels darkness. But look about you. Sin and immorality blatantly parade before our eyes, walking the streets without shame or blushing. They are comfortable with the company they keep. After all—they walk with men, women, and teens who warm church pews Sunday after Sunday.

A sinful society is quite comfortable when corruption is at home in the pews. And when corruption finds comfort in the pews it has been welcomed in the pulpit as well. Hollywood and television love to portray it. And men watch, comforting themselves with the devil's theology—"After all, we're all only human!"

Are we only human? Are we, at best, only hypocrites of one degree or another? Is Christianity merely "the opiate of the people," something to drug us so we live now anesthetized from life's pain by the promise of a sweet by and by? Must our religion, our Christianity, be nothing but a frustrating ideal that everyone knows can't be attained? Are we, because we are merely human beings, condemned to be locked behind the mask of hypocrisy? Jesus says no. And who should know better than Jesus, the God-man!

Religion, or Christianity, as I prefer to call our faith experience, need not be hypocritical. There is another, a higher life-style. One that takes you from the valley of sin to the mount of blessedness; from the depths of destitution to the heights of God's approval; from the instability of building on sand to the security of a foundation on rock. There is a life-style that can endure all the torrential storms of life and stand *unshaken.* Where is it? It's all in seed form in Matthew 5, 6, and 7—Jesus' Sermon on the Mount. A teaching that rips off the mask of hypocrisy! A teaching that shows you how you can live!

## DAY 1

At the back of this book you will find Matthew 5, 6, and 7. Keeping in mind what you have just read, now read through those chapters without interruption. Don't get caught up in the intricacies; simply read to gain the general message of Jesus' Sermon on the Mount. When you finish, briefly note your first impressions.

## DAY 2

"We live in a time when many who claim to know Christ undermine the Gospel by short-circuiting the radical implications of a life of discipleship as set forth by Jesus the Christ." When I read this statement in Robert Guelich's commentary on the Sermon on the Mount I thought, "How true that is, and how typical!" We want heaven, life, eternity! Who doesn't?

We hear the good news about eternal life through Jesus Christ. It's free, so we take it, tuck it under our arm, and walk away. We're relieved. We have the problem settled! No hell now; heaven's our home. Now we can get back to the living of our own lives.

But can we? Does true Christianity allow us to go back to the living of *our own lives?* I would like to switch on a worldwide intercom and shout one loud, resounding NO! You cannot belong to God and live any way you please! True Christianity is discipleship. It's the willingness to turn around, to leave everything, and to let Jesus Christ be all in all. It's the willingness to follow Him wherever He leads and to do whatever He says. True Christianity is a total commitment of oneself to the lordship of Jesus Christ. Some of you may disagree. That's fine. Just don't stop studying until you see what the Sermon on the Mount has to say—lest you short-circuit the radical implications of the gospel of Jesus Christ.

Read Matthew 7:13–29. Then, from what you have read, answer the following:

1. Describe the way that leads to life.

2. Whose words are you reading in this passage? If you have trouble answering this, look at Matthew 5:1, 2 and 7:28, 29.

3. According to Jesus, how many are there who find the way to life?

4. Who is going to enter the kingdom of heaven?

5. How do those who are going to heaven respond to Jesus' words?

6. Why do you think the people were amazed at Jesus' teaching in Matthew 5–7?

**7.** According to what you have just read, do you think a person can live any way he pleases and still go to heaven? Explain your answer.

8. Now, let's get personal. How do you live?

## DAY 3

The next time you go to church, take a few minutes to look at the congregation. How many do you think are going to heaven? What percentage do you think have chosen the narrow way that leads to life? How many hear God's Word and live accordingly? As you saw yesterday, the way to eternal life is narrow; few walk that way. It's the way of obedience, for only those who do His will will enter His kingdom. Just calling Jesus "Lord, Lord" doesn't get you to heaven. Here were people who thought heaven was their destination, but instead went to hell. Sobering, isn't it?

Today I want us to look at the main theme of the Sermon on the Mount. What's this message all about? What point is Jesus making?

Two key words that help us grasp the theme of this Sermon are *righteousness* and *heaven*. Read through the Sermon on the Mount at the back of this book and mark every reference you find to *heaven* and *righteousness*, or their synonyms. *Heaven* or *heavenly* is used twenty-one times; *righteous* or *righteousness* appears five times. When you have finished marking each reference, fill in the appropriate spaces below. Note the chapter and verse of each mention of heaven or righteousness and record what you learn in each passage.

## *HEAVEN*

| Chapter and Verse | What I Learned about Heaven |
|---|---|
| 1. Matthew 5:3 | It belongs to those who are poor in spirit. |
| 2. | |
| 3. | |
| 4. | |
| 5. | |
| 6. | |
| 7. | |
| 8. | |

9.

10.

11.

12.

13.

14.

15.

16.

17.


18.


## *RIGHTEOUSNESS*

| Chapter and Verse | What I Learned about Righteousness |
|---|---|
| 1. Matthew 5:6 | Those who hunger and thirst for it are blessed. |


2.


3.


4.


5.

What is the theme of the Sermon on the Mount? It is: **The Righteous Life-style of Those Who Belong to the Kingdom of Heaven.** We will look at it more tomorrow. However, let me ask you one question. What did you learn today that you didn't know before?

## DAY 4

From looking at the words *heaven* and *righteousness* you may have noticed that those who will enter the kingdom of heaven fulfill four basic requirements. Let's summarize them.

Those who enter the kingdom of heaven:

1. Are poor in spirit (5:3).
2. Are persecuted for righteousness' sake (5:10)
3. Have a +R (a righteousness that surpasses the righteousness of the scribes and Pharisees, 5:20).
4. Obey God's will (7:21).

The bottom line of Jesus' message was the fact that righteousness is an absolute necessity for those who are going to enter the kingdom of heaven. It is for this reason that I believe the Key Verse for the Sermon on the Mount is Matthew 5:20, "For I say to you, that unless your righteousness surpasses that of the scribes and Pharisees, you shall not enter the kingdom of heaven."

Was it any wonder the multitudes were amazed at Jesus' teaching! A righteousness that exceeded the righteousness of the scribes and Pharisees! How could it ever be? These were the religious leaders of the day. None were more respected than they!

Understanding the scribes and Pharisees will give you deeper insight into Jesus' message in the Sermon on the Mount.

There were scribes long before the Pharisees entered the stage of history. The Old Testament has various references to them. But they really did not come into prominence until Judah was restored to its land following the Babylonian captivity. The office of scribe came out of the priesthood. The scribes were experts in the Law of Moses. Their responsibilities fell into two general categories: preserving the Law and teaching the Law.

The scribes seem to have been the originators of the synagogues. Synagogues were gathering places where the Jews went to worship and to study God's Word. They came into being as a result of the Babylonian exile. Cut off from the ruined temple of Jerusalem, the Jews created the synagogue as a place where God's people could meet and be instructed in the Law.

By the time of Jesus' birth, the synagogue was one of the Jews' most important religious institutions. There the scribes and Pharisees were in authority, teaching not only the Law, but their traditions and interpretations of the Law as well. The people did not have their own copy of the Law, therefore they had to depend upon the teachings of the scribes and Pharisees.

The Pharisees were a religious party which came into being during the intertestamental period. By Jesus' time, they had supreme influence among the people. They believed in the resurrection, angels, spirits, and the coming of the Messiah, but their forte was the Law of God! As a matter of fact, they had reduced God's Law to a code of 365 negative commandments and 250 positive commandments, making many additions to God's Word. They claimed that these additions came from direct inspiration and were God-given interpretations of the Law. As a result, when the people heard the Word, they heard a distorted version of it. This is why Jesus really takes the scribes and Pharisees to task about their interpretations and traditions (*see* Mark 7:13).

As a result of the scribes' and Pharisees' interpretation of the Law, sin had become only an external act rather than a matter of the heart. Something was declared right or wrong because an external condition was absent or present. If a Jew gave alms to the poor on the Sabbath, he could do so only if the beggar put his hand through the door to receive the alms. If the Jew extended his hand out the door to give alms to the beggar, he was considered to have broken the Sabbath.

Knowing this, you understand what Jesus means in Matthew 5 when repeatedly He says, "You have heard . . . but I say to you." They had heard a distortion of the Law from the scribes and Pharisees teaching in the synagogues, but they didn't know any better because they didn't know God's Word!

Isn't that the way it is today? Sometimes as I watch "Christian" television I shudder, for I know that thousands are listening to some teachings which just are not biblical. Yet, they don't know better because they don't know God's Word! And they will never know it in its purity and its authority until they study it for themselves. This is why someday I long to get you into one of our Precept courses so you can learn to study God's Word inductively!

## DAY 5

Hypocrisy is an age-old problem. It certainly was common in Jesus' day. Jesus used the word frequently, particularly for two groups of people. Take a few minutes and read Matthew 23. Then write below who Jesus called hypocrites and why He called them that.

*Hypocrite* was the word used for a stage actor. In the Greek and Roman theater actors customarily wore large masks to indicate a particular mood or emotion. No matter how the actor himself might feel, the mask was what everyone saw. Thus, a hypocrite would be one who wears a mask or who is a stage actor.

From your reading of Matthew 23, why do you think Jesus used the term *hypocrites* to describe the scribes and Pharisees? What were they doing? Write out your answer below.

Now, stop and think. Are you a hypocrite in any way? Do you speak words that your life does not back up? For instance, when you sing in church "I surrender all . . . ," have you really surrendered all?

— 20 —

When you pray the Lord's Prayer and say "Lead us not into temptation, but deliver us from evil . . . ," do you really desire to stay away from temptation? When you pray "Forgive us our trespasses as we forgive those who trespass against us . . . ," are you willing to forgive others as God has forgiven you? Do you pray at prayer meetings to be seen of men, but not at home shut up alone with God?

Do you ever wear a mask? Do you behave one way at church and another way at home or in your business? Does your attitude toward your mate or your children change when you get out of the car in the church parking lot? Do you exchange that angry scowl for a pleasant smile?

Do you see what I am saying? It was the religious ones whom Jesus called hypocrites. They were the ones who claimed to know God, not the prostitutes, the drunks, the thieves, the liars, and the adulterers.

Perhaps at this point you are asking: "Is it possible not to be a hypocrite? Is it possible for my heart to match what I portray on the outside? Can I truly be righteous inside and out?" You can—or Jesus would not demand it. Just remember, what He demands, He supplies. How? By coming to live inside you. By giving you the Holy Spirit who will lead you into all righteousness. Be patient, Beloved. You will see it all in the weeks to come.

Phillip Keller, in his autobiography, *Wonder O' The Wind* wrote:

> It was not that we neglected the church, the Word of God, or our daily devotions. We did not. Quite the contrary. Like other millions of modern-day Christians, we went through the regular routine of religious rituals, but they were dry as the dust in my sheep corrals, and just about as barren.
>
> Almost by default I concluded subconsciously that my joy in life could come from the earth and need not come from Christ.
>
> Yet the strange irony of my inner spiritual stagnation was that deep down within my spirit there was an intense hunger to really know God. There persisted an insatiable thirst to commune with Christ. But how?

How? We will see in the Sermon on the Mount.

# 2 - What Is the Kingdom of Heaven? When Is It? Whose Is It?

## DAY 1

> Just think of stepping on shore and finding it heaven,
> of touching a hand and finding it God's,
> of breathing new air and finding it celestial,
> of waking up in glory and finding it home!

### *from Finally Home by Don Wyrtzen*

It seems that generally the kingdom of heaven is thought of as some future possession. Yet according to the Sermon on the Mount it is the present possession of "the poor in spirit."

When, and what, is the kingdom of heaven? This is the theme of our study this week. It will be exciting—and I pray, convicting.

Remember what you saw last week as you looked up every reference to heaven in the Sermon? For the sake of continuity, let's review.

*Kingdom of heaven* implies a realm of rulership. Where there's a kingdom, there's a king! This king is none other than our heavenly Father (Matthew 5:45, 48; 6:9, 14, 26, 32; 7:11–21), for His throne is there (5:34).

One of the other things you should have seen is that not everyone will enter heaven—only those who are poor in spirit and those who are persecuted. Such people, because of obedience to God's will, have a righteousness that exceeds the righteousness of the scribes and Pharisees (Matthew 5:3, 10, 20; 7:21).

Will it be the same for everyone in the kingdom of heaven? Not according to Matthew 5:19. Some will be called "least" while others will be called "great." And what will make the difference? How each man has responded to God's holy commandments. I think we sometimes forget that there is a day of accounting, even for Christians (2 Corinthians 5:10 and Romans 14:10 present this very clearly).

1. Look up 2 Corinthians 5:10 and Romans 14:10 and then record what you learn about "being recompensed" or rewarded for our deeds.



2. From Matthew 6:20 it is apparent that we can lay up treasures in heaven. Matthew 5:12 refers to rewards in heaven. Can you see any possible relationship between these two verses and the judgment seat of Christ?



Have you ever thought about all this before—your accountability to God even as a Christian? Have you considered that you could miss some rewards or some treasures because you did not walk in obedience and dedication? Sobering thoughts aren't they? When I first heard about the judgment seat of Christ, I didn't like it! I wanted to believe it would be the same for every child of God. However, as I have studied I've seen that it is not! There are least and greatest in the kingdom of heaven!

In the light of this truth, how are you going to live?


## DAY 2

Before we progress any further in our review of the kingdom of heaven as seen in the Sermon on the Mount, let's talk a little more about our accountability and rewards.

As we have seen, every Christian will "appear before the judgment seat of Christ, that each one may be recompensed for his deeds in the body, according to what he has done, whether good or bad" (2

Corinthians 5:10). Whenever I teach this, one of the first things my students ask is, "What about our sins? Are we going to be judged for our sins?" No. Jesus was judged for your sins when God "made Him who knew no sin to be sin on our behalf . . ." (2 Corinthians 5:21). Since Jesus purged us from our sins, "having offered one sacrifice for sins for all time," there is therefore "no condemnation for those who are in Christ Jesus" (Hebrews 1:3, 10:12; Romans 8:1). We cannot be judged for what Jesus has already paid for!

However, when a Christian walks in sin for a period of time, that time is lost as far as being profitable for the glory of God and His kingdom. It is wasted, for ". . . apart from Me [Him] you can do nothing" (John 15:5). This, I believe, brings a loss of reward, because it was a deed that was bad.

Let's look at one more passage that deals with a Christian's accountability. Read 1 Corinthians 3:10–15 and answer the questions that follow.

1. What is the foundation?

2. What types of building materials are used for building upon this foundation?

3. What is to be tested and how?

4. What happens to the man whose:
   a. work is burned up?

   b. work abides?

I believe, because of its context, this passage is primarily an admonition to teachers. However, it certainly can have application in others' lives. Here is a warning regarding accountability—be careful how you build! Basically, there are two types of materials: those which can be grown by man—wood, hay, and straw—and that which can be discovered by man—gold, silver, and precious stones. God created the latter when He made the earth. Man only discovers and appropriates what is already there. But wood, hay, and straw are the fruits of man's labor. They are temporal, and can be destroyed by fire.

What is God saying in all of this? Simply that whatever man produces in and of himself has no eternal value; he will not receive a reward for it. However, what God produces through man has value. It's a good deed—eternal in value and therefore worthy of reward. Think about these things. If you believed they were true, would it change the way you are living? How? Be specific in your answer.

# DAY 3

If you were to do a thorough study on the kingdom of heaven you would see that basically it is referred to in four different ways. I want to share these with you and then will do a short study on each. What is my purpose? If you are going to fully appreciate the teaching of the Sermon on the Mount, then you need to know as much as possible about the kingdom of heaven. After all—the theme of Jesus' sermon is the righteous life-style of those who belong to His kingdom. We need to know what we belong to!

# THE FOUR ASPECTS OF THE KINGDOM OF HEAVEN

1. God's literal abiding place in the third heaven. This is where God dwells and where saved men go at their death. This also is the eternal dwelling place of the sons of God.
2. God's universal and eternal dominion over the heavens and the earth.
3. The invisible spiritual rulership of Jesus Christ within the lives of men. This aspect of the kingdom began with Jesus' first coming and continues as men believe on and receive the Lord Jesus Christ as their redeemer.
4. Jesus' millennial reign upon earth. This will begin at Christ's second coming to earth and will last one thousand years on the earth as we know it now, and then take us into eternity.

For the sake of clarity, examine the simple graphic drawing below, matching the numbers with those given above. These illustrate where each is and when it occurs in history.

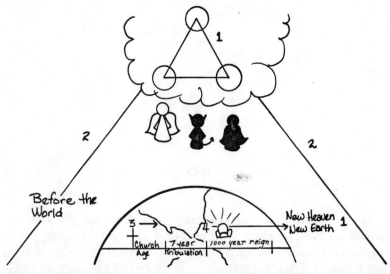

This is enough information to absorb in one day. Tomorrow we will begin a progressive study of each aspect of the kingdom of heaven. In the meantime, review what you have learned. At the back of the book there is a chart that gives an overview of God's plan for the ages. Basically, it is a larger, more complete presentation of what is printed on the world in the preceding diagram. Take a minute to look at it.

As you read about different aspects of the kingdom of heaven, where did you find yourself in relationship to each one? Could you relate to any of them? Has God ever taken up His residence as King in your life? Do you long for His kingdom to come, His will to be done?

## DAY 4

Have you ever stretched out flat on your back in the grass on a warm summer day and gazed at the heavens and wondered what it's like beyond all that your eyes can take in? Or have you ever flown above the clouds, with the earth obscured from your view, and felt drawn to go even higher—to see God? Sometimes I've stood embraced by the night and looked at the brilliance of the stars displayed on the black velvet background of heaven, thinking of the time when Jesus will come to take me home. Home—heaven—what is it like where God is?

Revelation 4 and 5 give us the best description that I know of. Take time to read these two awesome chapters and then list everything you learn about God's dwelling place.

Now join those around His throne and worship the Father:

Worthy art Thou, our Lord and our God, to receive glory and honor and power; for Thou didst create all things, and because of Thy will they existed, and were created.

*Revelation 4:11*

Now worship the Lamb:

Worthy art Thou to take the book, and to break its seals; for Thou wast slain, and didst purchase for God with Thy blood men from every tribe and tongue and people and nation. And Thou hast made them to be a kingdom and priests to our God; and they will reign upon the earth.

*Revelation 5:9, 10*

## DAY 5

The apostle Paul longed for heaven. His heart's desire was "to depart and be with Christ," the One for whom he had suffered the loss of all things, counting them but dung (Philippians 1:23; 3:8). He groaned, longing "to be absent from the body and to be at home with the Lord (2 Corinthians 5:8).

"At home with the Lord"! Where is "at home with the Lord"? Paul says it's in the third heaven, paradise (2 Corinthians 12:2–4).

Is it through the empty space in the north of the heavens (Job 26:7)? It could be! Wherever it is, I know that is where home is!

What security this brings when things on this earth seem so temporal—and so shaky! God's children have a New Jerusalem awaiting them, a heavenly city where they will dwell forever in the very presence of God and His Son.

Would you like to know more about your eternal city?

1. Read Revelation 21:1–22:5.
2. List the five things that impressed you the most from this passage of Scripture.

The New Jerusalem is the eternal destiny of every true child of God. It is as certain as God Himself, therefore:

> See to it that you do not refuse Him who is speaking. For if those did not escape when they refused him who warned them on earth, much less shall we escape who turn away from Him who warns from heaven. And His voice shook the earth then, but now He has promised, saying, "Yet once more I will shake not only the earth, but also the heaven." And this expression, "Yet once more," denotes the removing of those things which can be shaken, as of created things, in order that those things which cannot be shaken may remain. Therefore, since we receive a kingdom which cannot be shaken, let us show gratitude, by which we may offer to God an acceptable service with reverence and awe; for our God is a consuming fire.
>
> *Hebrews 12:25-29*

# 3 - When Jesus Comes in the Glory of His Kingdom

## DAY 1

In 1983, millions sat by television sets to watch "The Day After," a television production that dealt with the results of a nuclear holocaust. Special interviews followed its showing as "experts" discussed the purpose for such a program, the probability of the occurrence of such an event and what effect "The Day After" might have on those who viewed it.

In all the discussions, no one ever considered the fact that there is a God who sits in the heavens controlling the affairs of mankind. Never once did they mention the fact that God is in control of history and that what was proposed in "The Day After" did not synchronize with God's plans for the future.

For the most part, mankind is ignorant of God's universal dominion over the heavens and the earth. This is as true today as in the time of an ancient king, Nebuchadnezzar. How well his story illustrates God's sovereign rule over the universe from His throne in heaven.

Look up Daniel 4:34, 35 and write out the part that shows His realm of rulership. These verses have brought such assurance to my life.



Nebuchadnezzar is speaking. God had taught him a very hard, but very powerful lesson he would never forget. Nebuchadnezzar was the king of Babylon and there had never been an empire like Babylon. The only problem was that Nebuchadnezzar thought that he had built great Babylon by the might of his own power and for the glory of his own majesty (Daniel 4:30). He forgot that there is a God in heaven who changes the times and the epochs; who removes kings and establishes kings; who gives kingdoms power, strength, and glory (Daniel 2:21, 37). Therefore, God had to teach Nebuchadnezzar a lesson so he would recognize " '. . . that the Most High is ruler over the realm of mankind, and bestows it on whomever He wishes' " (Daniel 4:32).

Through God's chastening but gracious hand Nebuchadnezzar came to his senses. He saw clearly that God's "dominion is an everlasting dominion, and His kingdom endures from generation to generation. . . . He does according to His will in the host of heaven and among the inhabitants of the earth . . ." (Daniel 4:34, 35). God's kingdom is the supreme kingdom ruling over all others whether they be visible or invisible, earthly or spiritual.

God is in charge. Don't worry about "The Day After"; seek first His kingdom and His righteousness, and you will have an eternal place in His kingdom.

## DAY 2

In his Sermon on the Mount when Jesus makes reference to entering the kingdom of heaven, obviously He is not talking about it in the sense of its universal dominion. His reference instead is to His spiritual, invisible kingdom which will some day guarantee entrance into the third heaven of God's throne.

Today we want to take a careful look at the kingdom of heaven, or as it is sometimes referred to, the kingdom of God, to which only the redeemed of Jesus Christ belong. Let's begin with the familiar story of the rich young ruler. Read Mark 10:17–27 and answer the questions that follow.

1. What did the young man want to know?

2. What were Jesus' instructions?

3. If the young man followed them what would he have?

4. How did the young man respond?

5. According to these verses, what does all this have to do with the kingdom of heaven or of God?

The young man wanted eternal life, yet he never entered the kindom of God because he wanted it on his own terms! He loved his riches more than he loved God! I say that because the first time Jesus quoted the commandments, He deliberately skipped over the first and foremost commandment—"Thou shalt have no other gods before me . . ." "Thou shalt love the Lord thy God with all thy heart, and with all thy soul, and with all thy mind, and with all thy strength . . ." (Exodus 20:3; Mark 12:30 KJV). Little did the young man realize that this was the one commandment he had not kept. Not until Jesus told him to sell all that he had and follow Him did his idol become visible. Riches superseded God!

"Jesus felt a love for him" but He could not let him enter His kingdom. The way is narrow, the gate small, and the number few who enter His kingdom. What about you? Is there anything keeping you from forsaking all to follow Him? Is it worth missing the kingdom? Give it serious thought.

## DAY 3

On Day 1 we did a brief study of God's kingdom from the aspect of His univeral dominion. Yesterday we looked at the kingdom as it pertains to those who are saved and who are sons of the kingdom. They belong to His invisible, spiritual kingdom—known to God, but not necessarily recognized by man.

Matthew 13 brings to light both of these aspects of God's kingdom in the parable of the wheat and the tares. Read verses 24–30 and 36–43, noting carefully the references to the two aspects of the kingdom.

1. Who are the wheat?

2. Who are the tares?

3. From where are the tares gathered?

4. What is done to the tares?

5. What happens to the righteous (wheat)?

6. Who are the reapers?

7. When does all this happen?

It's interesting isn't it, that "the wheat" are referred to as righteous! Do you see how this parallels with the Sermon on the Mount which clearly teaches that only the righteous will inherit the kingdom of heaven?

Are you wheat or tares? You know, it's very hard to distinguish the two until it comes to fruit-bearing time. Only by their fruit can you really distinguish which is which. What does the fruit of your life bear witness to? Wheat or tares?

Talk to God about it—He knows. Ask Him.

## DAY 4

Jesus' first coming inaugurated His invisible spiritual reign within the hearts of mankind. The King had come and with Him, His kingdom. Yet the kingom he brought did not meet the Jews' expectations. They wanted that visible kingdom where Messiah would deliver Israel from the bondage of her oppressors, where Messiah would sit upon His throne ruling with a rod of iron, where all nations would come yearly to Jerusalem to give homage to the Jewish Messiah.

In Matthew's Gospel, he takes his Jewish readers from the invisible kingdom to the visible kingdom, from salvation to the millennium, showing how King Jesus fulfills the Law and the Prophets by bringing the kingdom of heaven to earth.

The purpose of Matthew's Gospel was to present Jesus as the Christ, *the King*. Matthew wanted to show that Jesus the King had come and therefore the kingdom of heaven was at hand. Thus Matthew is very careful to show us how Jesus fulfills the Old Testament promise of a king and a kingdom. This is why Matthew takes Jesus' genealogy back to Abraham so we can see that Jesus is the seed promised to Abraham and therefore, He is the Christ (or Messiah).

The word *kingdom* is used fifty-six times in Matthew—more than in any of the other Gospels. The first reference is Matthew 3:2, and the last is Matthew 26:29. The word *king* is used twenty-three times. The first reference to *king* is Matthew 1:6 where Matthew is very careful to show Jesus' genealogy through David. From the tribe of Judah and the line of David would come the One who was to rule over all the earth. The last reference to *the king* is Matthew 27:42, where we read that the priests, the scribes, and the elders mockingly said, ". . . He is the King of Israel." Of the first eight words of Matthew's Gospel, four of those are Jesus—Christ—David—Abraham. Who else could be the Messiah, the King, to establish the kingdom of God?

It is interesting to note that Matthew gives Jesus' legal descent through Joseph, showing His right to rule. Luke gives Jesus' descent through his mother, Mary. Both genealogies include Abraham and David. In his *Survey of the New Testament,* Irving Jensen gives a beautiful outline of the Gospel of Matthew. Let me share it with you.

Matthew 1:1–4:11
The King's Presentation
Behold Him

Matthew 4:12–16:20
The King's Proclamation
Understand Him

Matthew 16:21–28:20
The King's Passion
Follow Him

Jesus' message in Matthew 4:17 is, "Repent, for the kingdom of heaven is at hand." Salvation had come at last. Here was the Lamb of God that would take away sin. Here was the One who would begin His reign in the hearts of men although His time had not come to reign upon the earth.

Matthew 12:28 shows us the same truth. "But if I cast out demons by the Spirit of God, then the kingdom of God has come upon you." Had the kingdom of God come? How? Spiritually, invisibly, yet they knew it was there because He was casting out demons!

In Matthew 24 and 25, Jesus tells His disciples of His second coming, for at that time He will set up His throne and begin His millennial reign. Turn in your Bible to these chapters and read verses 29–31 in chapter 24 and verses 31–46 in chapter 25.

1. Who is going to come on the clouds of the sky with great power and great glory? Note what He is called.

2. Now, compare that title with Daniel 7:13, 14. Who was given dominion, glory, and a kingdom "that all the peoples, nations, and men of every language might serve Him"?

3. According to Matthew 24:29,30, when will this occur?

4. Who will see it happen?

5. How does Matthew 25:31 parallel with Matthew 24:29, 30? Read the verses carefully, noting the similarities and listing them below.

6. In Matthew 25:31–40 the Son of Man comes to sit on His glorious throne. In Matthew 25:34, what title does this Son of Man bear?

7. What does He offer those sheep whom He puts on His right?

8. Do you think that this passage speaks of a spiritual kingdom or a literal kingdom? Why?

9. According to Matthew 25:37, what does He call those on His right?

10. How does this description fit with the description of those in the Sermon on the Mount who inherit the kingdom of heaven and the earth?

Beloved, Jesus is coming again. We do not know the day, the hour, or the year, but we can know with absolute certainty that Jesus *will* come to reign as King of kings and Lord of lords. The secret of the zeal of the early church was that they lived as if He might come at any time. They knew that their citizenship was in heaven (Philippians 3:20).

Let me leave you with one question to meditate upon. How similar is your life to those in Thessalonica who ". . . turned to God from idols to serve a living and true God, and to wait for His Son from heaven, whom he raised from the dead, that is Jesus, who delivers us from the wrath to come" (1 Thessalonians 1:9,10)?

## DAY 5

Some think that the Sermon on the Mount describes a life-style that is impossible to live except in the Kingdom Age. By that term I mean the Millennium, the thousand-year reign of Jesus Christ upon earth.

Possibly some of you are like me. I wasn't saved until I was twenty-nine. I had never even heard about Jesus Christ returning to earth and setting up a literal kingdom. I must admit that when I heard about prophecy and began a study of it I was so excited that I didn't want to study anything else. That happens to a lot of us, doesn't it?

Now, in all fairness I have to tell you that some do not believe in a literal, millennial kingdom where Jesus Christ will rule and reign for a thousand years. They are called amillennialists, the *a* before a word denoting "without." I personally believe in a literal, thousand-year reign of Jesus Christ upon the earth. However, I do not believe that the Sermon on the Mount is for that time; it is for today.

Turn to Appendix B, a chart entitled, God's Plan of the Ages. Find the thousand-year reign on the chart. It begins with the Second Coming of Christ and happens at the end of the Tribulation (also called "Daniel's Seventieth Week").

The whole purpose of this chart is not to teach you eschatology (the study of last or final things), but rather to familiarize you with the context of our passage. In this way you'll know what I'm talking about when I say that some people believe that the Sermon on the Mount belongs to the Kingdom Age. The reason they believe this is twofold:

> **First,** they believe that the Gospel of Matthew was directed to the Jews.
>
> **Secondly,** they believe that the life-style called for in the Sermon is impossible. They believe it can be lived only by those who are no longer encumbered by their sinful flesh.

Let's examine this view. We know several things about the Millennium. We know that Jesus Christ will rule as King of kings. We know that He will rule with a rod of iron; He will not allow any disobedience whatsoever. We know also that we will rule with Him. In the light of the truths we know about the Millennium, we need to examine the Sermon on the Mount to see if it could possibly pertain to the Millennium. The answer is found within the Sermon itself.

Matthew 5:5 says that the meek shall inherit the earth. At the time of the Millennium, we will already have inherited the earth, right? Therefore, poverty of spirit (which gives us the kingdom) and meekness (which will give us the earth) would have had to occur in our lives prior to this time. Keeping this in mind, let's reason together. If I have already inherited the earth, would I, during the Millennium, be persecuted for the sake of righteousness? Of course not! And yet Matthew 5:10–12 says: "Blessed are those who have been persecuted for the sake of righteousness . . . blessed are you when men revile you, and persecute you, and say all kinds of evil against you falsely, on account of Me." Will the saints be persecuted and insulted when Jesus Christ comes in all of His glory to reign over the earth and we rule and reign with Him? No. Then the Sermon on the Mount cannot refer to the Millennium.

Let me show you another reason why the Sermon on the Mount is for today rather than the Millennium. Matthew 5:39–41 talks about turning the other cheek when someone slaps you on the cheek; about men being able to force you to go one mile; about loving your enemies and those who persecute you. During the Millennium will the children of God be slapped about, forced to go a mile, and be persecuted by their enemies? No. Therefore, the Sermon on the Mount does not belong to the Kingdom Age.

There are other views on the Sermon on the Mount that we will have to leave for those who want to study Precept Upon Precept (*See* back of book for information.) The question that we need to deal with is: Is the Sermon on the Mount for today? Yes, Beloved, it is. Robert A. Guelich, in his book, *The Sermon on the Mount, A Foundation For Understanding,* answers the question quite succinctly I believe. He says, "As did his predecessors, Augustine viewed the Sermon to be 'the perfect measure of the Christian life' and 'filled with all the precepts by which the Christian life is formed.' For him the Sermon applied to all Christians and was without question applicable to life."

The Sermon on the Mount is not a new law or an impossible standard to be reached for but never obtained until the Millennium. Rather, it is a teaching given by Jesus Himself on the new relationship with Him that is ours through the New Covenant.

The first seven beatitudes (Matthew 5:3–9) show the *character* of those who enter into this relationship. The next two beatitudes (verses 10–12) show the *conflict* that such character brings in a world that does not recognize Jesus' lordship. The remainder of the Sermon (5:13–7:27) shows the *conduct* of those who belong to Jesus. Therefore the conduct shows the presence of God's sovereign rulership in the life of the child of God.

So, what is our outline of the Sermon on the Mount?

### THE RIGHTEOUS LIFE-STYLE OF THOSE WHO BELONG TO THE KINGDOM OF HEAVEN

| | |
|---|---|
| Matthew 5:1, 2 | Prologue |
| Matthew 5:3–9 | Their Character |
| Matthew 5:10–12 | Their Conflict |
| Matthew 5:13–7:27 | Their Conduct |
| Matthew 7:28, 29 | Epilogue |

The Sermon on the Mount is only an impossible life-style for those who have not bowed their knees to the King nor yielded up the throne of their hearts to His right to reign as King of kings and Lord of lords!

If you will but bow—
    if you will yield—
        the kingdom of heaven, in all its fulness
        will be yours.

# 4 - Blessing Begins with Poverty of Spirit

## DAY 1

"All I want is to be happy!" You've heard those words before, haven't you? As a matter of fact, it's what your heart has told you over and over again. "Well, all I want is to be happy!"

Can you remember? Think back. When was the last time you felt really happy? Maybe it was because you woke up and the sun was shining. Perhaps it was one of those "Sound of Music" days when you wanted to dance across the mountaintops, twirling and singing. Things were going your way. No storm clouds were hanging over your head. It wasn't going to rain on your dreams. No, there was a gentle breeze that would catch the sails of your dream ship and take you to the land of happiness. Then, all of a sudden, from nowhere, a storm blew up. Suddenly your happiness was washed away in a downpour of horrible circumstances. Now you knew that you would never reach your destination. Happiness was only an illusive emotion that the circumstances had blown away.

Does happiness depend upon circumstances? To most people, it does. As a matter of fact, happiness means different things to different people. Generally it is a feeling of satisfaction and pleasure, a feeling of contentment. Note I said "feeling," for feelings are usually determined not only by our circumstances, but also our emotions. By emotions I mean feelings either of well-being because our bodies are in good health, our chemistry is working right, everything is going well, and we have a good self-image, or feelings of depression that come when our health is threatened, our chemistry or our circumstances have gone haywire and our self-image has been marred.

Happiness comes in all forms. All you have to do is listen to what people say and you can find out what will make them happy. For instance:

"I'd be happy just to have this cold go away."

"If I got this job, I'd be happy."

"If he would ask me to marry him, I'd be the happiest woman alive!"

"I'd be happy if it weren't for all these rules. I can't even do what I want to do!"

"I'd be happy if I could only have a new home."

Well,

. . . the cold went away—but you have a toothache!

. . . you got the job—but your boss is horrible!

. . . he asked you to marry him—but now you're miserable.

. . . you got around the rules—but you suffered the consequences.

. . . the house was built—but you're unhappy because you didn't build it the way you should have.

Have any of these "showers" rained on your circumstances? Has happiness been a fickle friend to you, a fair weather friend who won't take the storms and stand by your side, but who leaves you the minute the going gets rough?

I understand, but let me tell you one thing, Beloved: that kind of happiness is never a true friend. And it's not the kind of happiness that you're looking for. That's the world's version of happiness. Real happiness is not an illusive dream. It's something that you can have only if you know where to find it. And in the weeks to come I guarantee you, if you will listen carefully and apply what you learn, you will find true happiness—a friend who is not fickle nor fair-weathered, a friend who will be closer than a brother, a friend who will stick with you through all sorts of adversity.

How can I be so confident in what I am sharing with you? It's simply because I know the truth of God's Word. The Sermon on the Mount has the key that will unlock the door to an estate of true happiness.

Happiness is disguised in the Word of God under the term "blessed" or "blessedness," from the Greek word, *makarios*. In it the Greeks saw a moral element. Of course, it left God out, but they did see that you have to behave or fate would punish you. From there, the word *blessed* moved to an inward correctness as an essence of happiness. Until finally in the Word of God *makarios* blossomed into truth. Blessedness meant "a sense of God's approval." It comes from being right with God, from doing what is right before God. "It was a happiness that came from pure character (which saw) sin as the fountainhead of all misery and holiness as the effectual cure for every woe."[1]

This, then, is true happiness: a state of blessedness that comes not from circumstances but from a right relationship to God. This, Beloved, is why you see so many whose circumstances are so unbelievable and yet they have a peace, a contentment, a quietness, a confidence. They seem happy in the midst of the storm.

Look at these three Scriptures that use the word *makarios* in one form or another. As you look them up, keep in mind that the word *blessed* is God's word for true happiness. Write down the insights that you glean from each.

1. John 13:17

2. John 20:29

3. 1 Timothy 1:11

When you looked up 1 Timothy 1:11, undoubtedly you saw that God is a blessed God, a happy God. Therefore, wouldn't happiness be found in being like God or in having godlike qualities? And do you ask, "But, Kay, how can I ever be like God? You don't know what I am like." Oh, yes, Beloved, I do know what you are like because I know what I am like apart from God. We'll look at it tomorrow, for the answer is in being poor in spirit.

## DAY 2

When you stop and think about it, aren't you thankful that true happiness comes from within and not from without? That it is found in character and not in circumstances? As He begins the Sermon on the Mount, the Lord Jesus Christ tells us eight times in nine verses that happiness is found in who we are. It's a blessedness that comes from being poor in spirit, mourning, being meek, hungering and thirsting after righteousness, being merciful, being pure in heart, being peacemakers, and being persecuted. It seems strange, doesn't it—especially the one that says we can be happy because we are persecuted. How opposite is this to what the world equates with happiness!

Is it any wonder that Jesus' teaching in the Sermon on the Mount literally amazed His listeners to the point of losing self-control! Here was a man who spoke with authority, a man who was God in the flesh. The Creator speaking to the created, telling them that the wellspring of happiness was found in a sense of His approval. Loved ones might ridicule, but what does it matter as long as God continually whispers, "I know who you are, My child, and it brings Me pleasure." Man was made for God's glory, for God's pleasure—how then can man be complete or satisfied until he achieves that for which he was created?

Keeping all this in mind, let's look at the Beatitudes. Surely as you read them you were aware that they were not natural qualities. They couldn't be because a man could never achieve these attributes on his own when his heart is deceitful and desperately wicked (Jeremiah 17:9).

Those who would say that this Sermon is not for today surely have never understood what it means to be poor in spirit. This first beatitude is the foundation stone upon which all the others are built. It's the "alpha" of the Christian life and the "omega" to self-achievement. The sum of life truly is hidden in this verse: " 'Blessed are the poor in spirit, for theirs is the kingdom of heaven.' "

What does it mean to be "poor in spirit"?

The word for *poor* means "one who crouches and cowers." It comes from a word which means "to cower down" or "to hide one's self for fear." It means to be poverty-stricken, powerless, utterly destitute. Destitute of what? Destitute of the spirit.

John 4:24 says, " 'God is spirit, and those who worship Him must worship in spirit and truth.' " When Adam and Eve sinned in the Garden of Eden, they died. And yet they did not die physically nor did they die in their souls. They were still living souls. Therefore, they must have died another way, for God said that " 'In the day that you eat from [that tree] you shall surely die' " (Genesis 2:17b).

What caused Adam to hide from God, to suddenly be aware of his nakedness, to have that knowledge of good and evil? What caused him to clothe himself with fig leaves? Why was he no longer able to have communion with God? Why did God banish him from the Garden?

I believe that man was created body, soul, and spirit. Some people hold that man is a dichotomous (two-part) being rather than a trichotomous (three-part) being. And yet, in 1 Thessalonians 5:23, we see that Paul refers to a three-part being. "Now may the God of peace Himself sanctify you entirely; and may your *spirit* and *soul* and *body* be preserved complete, without blame at the coming of our Lord Jesus Christ" (italics added). When man sinned, he lost God's Spirit. When man returns to God and receives Jesus as his Savior, then the Holy Spirit comes to live within—man becomes a partaker of the "renewing by the Holy Spirit" (Titus 3:5). What then is man apart from God? He is poor in spirit; he is utterly destitute; he lacks the Spirit who can commune with God, who can satisfy God, for who but God alone can satisfy God? Who alone can even understand the things of God except the Spirit of God (1 Corinthians 2:11)?

Therefore, to be poor in spirit is to be conscious of your total impotence before God, your total inability to please Him or to serve Him. To be poor in spirit is to acknowledge your total dependence upon God for vindication from your sins. To be poor in spirit is to cry out with the apostle Paul, "I know that nothing good dwells in me, that is, in my flesh ..." (Romans 7:18).

Poverty of spirit is beautifully illustrated for us in Luke 18:9–14. Read this passage; then in your own words explain how this parable illustrates poverty of spirit. Also, note Jesus' reason for telling this parable.

Let me ask you a question, Beloved. Have you ever really seen your poverty of spirit? Have you seen yourself as a sinner? Have you realized your total inability to please God? Think on this and write your insights below.

## DAY 3

I was reared in a church-going family and yet it wasn't until I was twenty-nine that I was truly saved. Oh, if you had asked me if I were a Christian I would have told you yes without question. After all, I was baptized and confirmed. I had taught Sunday School. I could even pray without a prayer book! My father became a clergyman, and my first husband, who is now deceased, even studied for the ministry. "Me? A Christian? But, of course! After all, I live in the United States of America and I go to church! Besides, I think God is very lucky to have me on His team! Here I am, this sweet young thing serving on the Ladies Auxiliary with all these old ladies!"

This was exactly the way I viewed myself. I really thought God had good taste in choosing me. Poverty of spirit? I didn't know what it was. Until my late twenties I really didn't have any great consciousness of sin. Primarily this was because I was in a religious environment where I did not really hear the Word of God expounded in power, under the conviction of the Holy Spirit. I was like the Pharisees. I had a set of rules. I obeyed them, practicing my righteousness before men to be seen of men. Yet my heart was not right.

Then, when I was twenty-six, I divorced my husband, took my two sons, and moved to the Washington, D.C. area. I stood in my living room, shook my fist at God and said, "To hell with You, God. I'll see You around town. I'm going to find someone to love me." I put on a low-cut dress, threw my mink stole over my shoulders, and went out to find someone who would love me as my husband had not loved me—unconditionally—whether I was pretty or ugly, sick or well, happy or sad. In the process I became what I had vowed I would never become—an immoral woman. I went from one man to another, looking for the ideal man. "Mommy, is he going to be our daddy?" my two little boys asked over and over as I found myself caught in a snare of sin.

Psalms 9:15 says that the heathen have sunk down into a pit that they have dug with their own hands. More and more I became aware of the pit that I was in, the mud in which I was wallowing. I hated being dirty. I wanted to be free, so I tried to climb out of the pit. I would say to myself, "I'm never going to do that again. It's wrong." But I would do it again. Digging my fingers into the walls that surrounded me, I would seek again to pull myself out of that miry clay. And then in an evening, I would lose my grip. The mud was there to welcome me. Try as I might, all the will power, all the resolve could not get me out. I was trapped in sin. How well I understand Paul's words, "For that which I am doing, I do not understand; for I am not practicing what I would like to do, but I am doing the very thing I hate" (Romans 7:15). Finally I knew that nothing good dwelt in me, that is, in my flesh; for the wishing was present in me, but the doing of the good was not. The good that I wanted to do, I did not do; but I practiced the very evil that I did not wish to do (see Romans 7:18,19).

Where once I thought God was lucky to have me on His team, now I wondered how He could bear the sight of me. I knew that if I were to stand before Him, in justice He would have to say, "Depart from me." I wanted to be good, but I couldn't. I was utterly destitute . . . a beggar before God. I did not know these words of Paul then, but some-day, when I would read them, I would understand them fully: "Wretched man that I am! Who will set me free from the body of this death?" (Romans 7:24).

On the morning of July 16, 1963, I ran to my room and flung myself at His feet, and cried out, "Oh God, I don't care what you do to me. I don't care if you paralyze me from the neck down. . . . or if I never see another man for as long as I live. . . . I don't care what you do to my two sons, if You'll just give me peace." And there, finally poor in spirit, I received His Spirit. I fell to my knees, an adulteress; when I arose I felt like a brand-new virgin—pure! I had worn the attire of a harlot. But when I got off my knees, somehow I knew that God was going with me wherever I went, and I would have to dress in a way befitting to Him.

> The cords of death encompassed me,
> And the terrors of Sheol came upon me;
> I found distress and sorrow.
> Then I called upon the name of the LORD:
> "O LORD, I beseech Thee, save my life!"
> Gracious is the LORD, and righteous;
> Yes, our God is compassionate.
> The LORD preserves the simple;
> I was brought low, and He saved me.
> Return to your rest, O my soul,
> For the LORD has dealt bountifully with you.
> For Thou hast rescued my soul from death,
> My eyes from tears,
> My feet from stumbling . . .
> What shall I render to the LORD
> For all His benefits toward me?
> I shall lift up the cup of salvation,
> And call upon the name of the LORD.
> I shall pay my vows to the LORD,
> Oh may it be in the presence of all His people. . . .
> Oh LORD, surely I am Thy servant,
> I am Thy servant, the son [the daughter] of Thy handmaid,
> Thou hast loosed my bonds.
>
> *Psalms 116:3–8, 12–14, 16*

I had become poor in spirit! The kingdom of heaven was mine! God's Spirit had come within. Now my body was His temple.

What is poverty of spirit? It is an absence of self-assurance, of self-reliance, of pride. It is the deepest form of repentance. It is turning from your independence to total dependence upon God. It is brokenness. Therefore, open your arms and welcome anything that will break you, that will bend your knees, that will bring you to utter destitution before your God.

1. For whom is the gospel? Whom did Jesus Christ come to call? Read Matthew 9:10–13 and write your answer below.

2. Now read Luke 4:18. What do you think it meant when Jesus read this passage from Isaiah and said, " '... he anointed me to preach the gospel to the poor ... to proclaim release to the captives' "?

## DAY 4

D. A. Carson, in his excellent little book, *The Sermon on the Mount: An Evangelical Exposition of Matthew Five Through Seven,* says: "In much contemporary evangelism, there is little concern for whether or not God will accept us, and much concern for whether or not we will accept him. Little attention is paid to whether or not we please him, and much to whether or not he pleases us." Carson continues, "I would argue that the reason we are currently seeing such an embarrassingly high percentage of spurious conversions to Christ is precisely because we have not first taught people their need of Christ."[2]

Until people come to see their utter poverty of spirit, they are not ready for the kingdom of heaven. Is this not what John the Baptist was doing when he cried out, "Repent, for the kingdom of heaven is at hand," and told the scribes and Pharisees to bring forth fruit worthy of repentance (Matthew 3:2, 8)? Surely he had seen that they were not willing to leave behind their pride, their self-reliance, and their self-assurance. In all probability they, too, thought that God was very lucky to have them on His team. Their self-righteousness kept them from seeing the righteousness that comes by faith.

What kind of a gospel are we preaching? A gospel that brings men under the conviction of sin? A gospel that causes men to beat their breasts and cry out, "God, be merciful to me a sinner!"?

In one of his letters to a young man who wanted to know how to preach the gospel, John Wesley shared a very biblical approach—one from which we can learn much.

> He says that whenever he arrived at any new place to preach the gospel, he began with a general declaration of the love of God. Then he preached "the Law" (by which he meant all of God's righteous standards and the penalty of disobedience) as searchingly as he could. This he kept up until a large proportion of his hearers found themselves under deep conviction of sin, beginning even to despair of the possibility of forgiveness from his holy God. Then, and only then, did he introduce the good news of Jesus Christ. Wesley explained the saving significance of Christ's person, ministry, death, and resurrection, and the wonderful truth that salvation is solely by God's grace, through faith. Unless his audiences sensed that they were guilty, and quite helpless to save themselves, the wonder and availability of God's grace would leave them unmoved. Wesley adds that after quite a number had been converted he would mix in more themes connected with law. He did this to underline the truth that genuine believers hunger for experiential righteousness, and continue to acknowledge poverty of spirit, recognizing constantly that their acceptance with God depends always and only on Christ's sacrifice.[3]

Poverty of spirit is not to be just a one-time event in the life of a child of God. Rather, it is a whole way of life. It is the life of total dependence upon God, realizing that in and of yourself you could never please God; you could never meet His standards of righteousness. Only by God's gift of His Spirit and by walking in the Spirit can we please God.

Pause now and consider a few things that keep us from recognizing our poverty of spirit. Tomorrow we examine the walk of the poor in spirit.

1. Read Romans 10:1–3 and answer the following questions.
   a. What kept many in Israel from seeing their poverty of spirit?

   b. Were they saved or not? Support your answer from these three verses.

   c. Do you see this happening today? If so, where? Illustrate your answer.

2. Read 1 Corinthians 1:18–22.
   a. What is keeping men from seeing their poverty of spirit?

   b. Do you see how this could happen today? If so, explain your answer.

3. Remember Mark 10:17–25, the story of the rich, young ruler? If not, read it again.
   a. According to this passage, what would keep men from the kingdom of heaven, from seeing their poverty of spirit?

   b. Can you see why this would happen then and even today? If so, write out your insights.

4. Read 1 Corinthians 1:26–31.

  a. How does this passage relate to poverty of spirit?



  b. What do you boast in before God?



Have your own righteousness, your intellect and worldly wisdom, your wealth, or your great ability kept you from seeing your poverty of spirit? If so, Beloved, you can know that they will also keep you from the kingdom of heaven because only the poor in spirit possess the kingdom of heaven. Think upon it and then we will talk about it more tomorrow.


## DAY 5


The Sermon on the Mount describes the righteous life-style of those who belong to the kingdom of heaven. The question is: "How can one attain such a righteousness?" The Beatitudes are certainly not qualities that are naturally ours.

The humanly impossible demands of Matthew 5:21–7:12 can only be fulfilled by Jesus Christ. Thus Jesus begins His Sermon on the Mount with the beatitude that is foundational to all that follows: "Blessed are the poor in spirit, for theirs is the kingdom of heaven." How do you become poor in spirit? I believe it begins with getting a glimpse of God—seeing Him in His holiness, recognizing that He is not a God who is to meet our standards. We are to meet His. The Word of God and the Law of God both show us His holiness. The Law tells us what God demands, and rightfully so, and the Word reveals God to us as He really is. When I catch a vision of God, I begin to see my own sin. When I see the high standard that He holds before us, I find that I fall short of the glory of God. I miss His standard of righteousness or holiness. Is this not what happened to Isaiah in the year of King Uzziah's death?

Read Isaiah 6:1-8; then answer the following questions.

1. When did Isaiah see himself as he really was?



2. When did Isaiah know God's forgiveness?



3. When was Isaiah ready to do what God wanted him to do?



God shows us our poverty of spirit when we try, in our own strength, to walk in a way pleasing to God, and yet continually fail. This is the testimony the apostle Paul gives of his own experience in Romans 7.

Humility came only when he fell on his face and cried out, "Wretched man that I am! Who will set me free from the body of this death?" (Romans 7:24). Then God gave him the Spirit, and with the gift of the indwelling Holy Spirit came the right to be called a son of God (Romans 8:1-17). The Spirit of God is the key to the Christian life. One does not only *attain salvation* by being poor in spirit; he *lives* the Christian life by remembering that apart from God's Spirit he can do nothing.

In all of the Beatitudes you will find Jesus Christ as our glorious example, the Author or Leader of our faith (Hebrews 12:2). Therefore, stop and fix your eyes on Him. In doing so, see how He walked in total poverty of spirit. Remember, Jesus was God. He lacked nothing. His character was everything that the Father is. And yet, when He lived this life as a man, He lived in total dependence upon God.

Read the following Scriptures and next to each note the ways that Jesus depended upon the Father.

1. John 8:26, 28, 29



2. Luke 6:12, 13

It's interesting to note in Matthew 3:16, 17 that before Jesus Christ ever began His public ministry, He was baptized because He wanted to fulfill "all righteousness." It was at His baptism that the Spirit of God descended upon Him as a dove. Here is our example. As Jesus walked in total dependence upon the Spirit, so are we to walk even as He walked. The words we speak are to be God's words. We are not to give man our own wisdom, our own thoughts, or even to think apart from God's truth. The works that we are to do are to be His works. They are to be directed by the Spirit of God. Ephesians 5:15 and 18 say that we are to be careful how we walk, and that we are to be filled with the Spirit, to be under His control. The Holy Spirit was not given to us merely as a guarantee of our salvation, but also to be our Comforter, our Helper, our Teacher, and our Guide (Ephesians 1:14; John 14:16, 26; 16:13). To live in poverty of spirit is to let the Holy Spirit be to us all that He was to Jesus.

To walk in poverty of spirit means to abide in the Vine and to allow the life of the Vine, by God's Spirit, to flow through us so that we might bear fruit. For apart from Him we can do nothing (John 15:5).

To walk in poverty of spirit is to live out Philippians 2:12, 13: "So then, my beloved, just as you have always obeyed, not as in my presence only, but now much more in my absence, work out your salvation with fear and trembling; for it is God who is at work in you, both to will and to work for His good pleasure." To "work out your salvation" means to carry out to completion that which God desires to do in you—for He will not only give you the will to do it but also the ability. Thus, to walk in poverty of spirit is to allow God to have full rein within your life, to control you, to do what He wants you to do, to be what He wants to be in you. The poor in spirit walk in total dependence upon God.

In the summer of 1983 I had the privilege of teaching a short quarter at Columbia Bible College. During that time, Howard Ball from Churches Alive was also teaching a course, and I enjoyed sweet fellowship with him. As we sat and talked, he shared how God had brought him up short one day with the question: "If God withdrew from you, from your church, from your ministry, what difference would it make?" He said, "I realized then that I had lost my dependency upon God."

O Beloved, have you lost that which you once gained—that which laid the kingdom of heaven at your feet? Poverty of spirit is not to be a one-time affair; rather, it is a whole way of life. What is your prayer to God? Write it out below.

If you abide in Me,
and My words abide in you,
ask whatever you wish,
and it shall be done for you.
*John 15:7*

# 5 - When Was the Last Time You Wept Over Sin?

## DAY 1

There I was, sitting in the dingy basement of a Reformed Presbyterian Church. Only a few of us had gathered for the Wednesday night prayer meeting, but that didn't matter to me. I was so hungry. As a brand-new child of God, I could not get enough of His Word. On Sunday mornings, I sat in the sanctuary, elbows on the pew in front of me, eagerly drinking in the words of life. Now I wanted more, and that is why I was back.

The minister stood at the little, wooden podium and asked who would read the Scripture. Nobody moved. Nobody volunteered. Suddenly I was embarrassed for this man of God. It must be awful to stand up there and have no one respond. Finally, when I could stand it no longer, although I was a stranger to the church, I volunteered. "I'll read it," I said. I rose from my chair, went to the podium, and opened my Bible to read at Luke 7:36.

Now one of the Pharisees was requesting Him to dine with him. And He entered the Pharisee's house, and reclined at table. And behold, there was a woman in the city who was a sinner; and when she learned that He was reclining at table in the Pharisee's house, she brought an alabaster vial of perfume, and standing behind Him at His feet, weeping, she began to wet His feet with her tears, and kept wiping them with the hair of her head, and kissing His feet, and anointing them with the perfume. Now when the Pharisee who had invited Him saw this, he said to himself, "If this man were a prophet He would know who and what sort of person this woman is who is touching Him, that she is a sinner." And Jesus answered and said to him, "Simon, I have something to say to you." And he replied, "Say it, Teacher." "A certain moneylender had two debtors: one owed five hundred denarii, and the other fifty. When they were unable to repay, he graciously forgave them both. Which of them therefore will love him more?" Simon answered and said, "I suppose the one whom he forgave more." And He said to him, "You have judged correctly." And turning toward the woman, He said to Simon, "Do you see this woman? I entered your house; you gave Me no water for My feet, but she has wet My feet with her tears, and wiped them with her hair. You gave Me no kiss; but she, since the time I came in, has not ceased to kiss My feet. You did not anoint My head with oil, but she anointed My feet with perfume. For this reason I say to you, her sins, which are many, have been forgiven, for she loved much. . . ."

*Luke 7:36–47*

I could read no further. I broke down in tears. There, before this handful of people who had come to hear from God, I wept openly. Never before had I read this passage, but suddenly I was there washing His feet, kissing them, adoring the One who had radically transformed my life.

Empathy for this woman flooded my soul. How well I understood her love for the Lord. How I rejoiced with her in having her sins forgiven. Almost two thousand years stood between us. We came from different cultures, different worlds, yet our sins were the same. And there He stood. Jesus Christ, the same yesterday, today, and forever granting both of us pardon. I was overwhelmed with love and at the same time, grief. How could I ever have sinned so grievously? How could I ever have hurt the One who loved me so much. Tears paraded my grief as they rolled in constant procession down my face. The people sat in silence, watching, and, I imagine, wondering what had caused this outburst. Little did they realize how fresh my forgiveness was.

Finally words came again. I had only three verses to go. Surely I could get through them.

> ". . . but he who is forgiven little, loves little." And He said to her, "Your sins have been forgiven." And those who were reclining at table with Him began to say to themselves, "Who is this man who even forgives sins?" And He said to the woman, "Your faith has saved you; go in peace."
>
> *Luke 7:47–50*

"Go in peace." It was peace that I had cried out for on July 16, 1963. "Oh, Lord, if you'll only give me peace." He had given me the Prince of Peace, the God of all comfort, because finally I had seen my sin as God had seen it. I had abhorred it as God abhorred it. In His mercy He had heard my cry and had forgiven my sin.

"Blessed are those who mourn, for they shall be comforted" (Matthew 5:4). Do you understand, Beloved, what it means to mourn? Take a few minutes and read again Luke 7:36–50 then write out below what you learn about Jesus, about the Pharisee, and about the woman. Note how each responds to the other and then in a sentence or two write out to which one you relate and why.

**Jesus**

**Pharisee**



**Woman**



I relate to:



# DAY 2


When was the last time you mourned—not because of something someone did to you or because of something that happened to you, but because what you did was wrong and it hurt God? When was the last time that you cried over the sins of others? When was the last time you hurt because God hurt? Is it hard for you, Beloved, to imagine a God who sits remotely in the heavens and, yet, truly hurts? When was the last time that you wept in intercessory prayer—mourning, lamenting over the awful degradation of man? Or because of the persecution of our brothers and sisters in Christ? Or because God's holy name had been blasphemed by man's independent, rebellious behavior?

It's time for tears, Beloved. It's time to cry. Will you not pray with me?


"Oh God, break my heart with the things that break Your heart."


Of all the "blesseds," "Blessed are those who mourn" is the one that is probably the most difficult to understand. How could anyone who is mourning consider himself blessed, spiritually prosperous, or approved of God? Do tears, grief, and mourning really go with happiness? Yes—in God's economy. For only those who mourn shall be comforted. The blessedness does not come in the mourning; it comes in the results of the mourning—knowing the comfort of His intimacy, the surety of His arms about you, hearing the beat of His heart as He draws you close to His all-sufficient breast.

The word for *mourn* in the second beatitude means "to mourn for or to lament as a way of life." The way that the word is used here means that we are never to be hardened or inoculated to sin or to sorrow. We are never to lose our ability to grieve, to weep, to mourn. We are never to become so calloused that we can look at sin or at pain and remain unmoved—or even worse, laugh.

"But," you may ask, "why are we to mourn? Doesn't the Scripture say 'the joy of the Lord is [our] strength'?" Yes, that is what Nehemiah 8:10 says, but we must never take that verse out of context.

The children of Israel had returned from captivity and rebuilt the temple and the walls of Jerusalem. Now they were hearing the Word of God, the Word they had so neglected. They knew that it was neglect that had taken them into captivity. But now the day of chastening was over. The seventy years of captivity had passed. It was no longer time to mourn or weep. It was time to receive the comfort of the Lord. Hence, the joy of the Lord could be their strength.

Let me ask you a question. Look around and what do you see? What do you see as reality in our world?" Look at the condition of men. Look at the complacency, the apathy in the church. Do you see men and women wholly consecrated to God? Do you see them hungering and thirsting after righteousness? Do you see them pursuing holiness? Do you see Peters and Pauls, or scribes and Pharisees? Tell me, is it a time for rejoicing or for mourning?

If Jesus were here again in bodily form, do you think He would be mourning or rejoicing? If we are to be as He was in this world, we need to know the mind and the heart of God in regard to a society like ours.

1. Read Isaiah 53:1–6 and as you read it, think about the second beatitude. Then write out how you think Jesus would respond to a society like ours, and why.

2. Read Genesis 6:1–12.
   a. List what you learn about the state of man during this time.


   b. How did the state of man affect the heart of God? Record your answer and note the verse from which you find your answer.


3. Read Ezekiel 6:9a.
   a. What is the condition of God's people as described in this verse?


   b. How has it affected God?


4. Is it a time to mourn? Why, or why not?


   Would you be willing to pray, "God, break my heart with the things that break Your heart"?


## DAY 3


As we have seen from the second beatitude, mourning is not to be just a one-time thing. It is to be a habit of life while we are here upon the earth. We must not think this strange. If you remember the life of Jesus, you know that at times He wept. He wept over Jerusalem because they did not know their day of opportunity (Luke 19:42–45). He wept at the tomb of Lazarus. There He stood—the Resurrection and the Life—and yet He was touched with the feeling of our infirmities. He wept with others as they stood enshrouded in death, for sin once again had paid its wages (John 11:33–38; Romans 6:23). He lamented over the blindness of Israel and the fate of Jerusalem, for there He stood with outstretched arms and His own people would not come to Him that they might have life (Matthew 23:37–39).

Surely it was grief that drove Him to a lonely place by Himself when He heard how John the Baptist's head was delivered on a platter to Herod and Herodias. Sin had seemingly silenced righteousness by cutting off the head of the one who had said, " 'It is not lawful for you to have her' " (Matthew 14:4). If only they had listened to John, they could have had forgiveness. John could have had his head! No wonder Jesus had to be by Himself (Matthew 4:12).

Yes, Jesus was a Man of Sorrows. Righteousness could not laugh in the presence of sin. He mourned. And if He mourned, then my heart must break with the things that break God's heart. I must mourn.

But over what are we to mourn?

I would like for us to cover three things in these next three days on this beatitude. First, we are to mourn over sin in our own lives; second, we need to mourn over sin in the church; and third, we need to mourn over sin in the world.

There is a specific progression to the Beatitudes. As I have mentioned, the foundation is poverty of spirit. All else finds its footing there. Sin is independence from God; therefore, sin is not being poor in spirit. But when that true poverty of spirit comes, then walls of mourning will go up on its foundations. Mourning and repentance go together. Remember, repentance is the deepest form of poverty of spirit.

We are going to look at 2 Corinthians 7:6–13. However, before we read these verses, consider the setting of this book. The church at Corinth had sinned grievously. Because of that sin, which we will look at tomorrow, Paul had chastened them by means of a letter—1 Corinthians. Now, in 2 Corinthians, he expresses the sorrow that he felt in having to write that first letter. However, his sorrow has turned to rejoicing because of their repentant response. In the midst of all this, God gives us an insight into two kinds of sorrow and the fruit of each.

Read 2 Corinthians 7:6–13. In the following space note the two kinds of sorrow and what each leads to.

Note how many times the word *comfort* is used and when the comfort came. Write it out.

What kind of sorrow do you have over your own sin? There is a worldly sorrow, a sorrow that says, "I'm sorry I got caught. I'm sorry I have to pay the price for my sin." This is the sorrow that looks upon itself and simply moans over the consequences of its own sin. It is so totally self-centered that it never thinks about how sin affects the heart of God. And where does this sorrow lead? It leads to death because it does not lead to repentance.

The other sorrow mentioned is godly sorrow, which leads to repentance. Remember that repentance is a change of mind that results in regret and thus a change in direction. This kind of sorrow brings salvation. The salvation that Paul is talking about in this passage is not a salvation that saves us from hell and takes us to heaven. Rather, it is salvation from the snares of sin. Godly sorrow causes us to run to the arms of God, weeping, confessing our sin. "If we confess our sins, He is faithful and righteous to forgive us our sins and to cleanse us from all unrighteousness" (1 John 1:9). The comfort of God awaits us because we have mourned as God would have us mourn.

In 2 Samuel 11, God gives us a vivid illustration of sin's consuming passion. Apparently this was a time of apathy, for David had not gone to war and it was time for kings to go to war. David found himself caught in a whirlpool of sin that spun him round and round, taking him deeper and deeper into the waters of iniquity. He would have all but drowned if not for the obedient boldness of Nathan, the prophet. David would not have recovered himself. I'm sure you know the story well, for Hollywood has flaunted David's sin upon its giant screen, glorifying iniquity and minimizing the retribution of God.

David had stayed in Jerusalem. He should have been on the battle-front, but he was in bed and it was evening. From his rooftop, David saw a beautiful woman bathing and he did not turn away! He knew Bathsheba was married, but he took her anyway. What was one man's wife when he had many wives of his own? When the news came that Bathsheba was pregnant, instead of running to the throne of mercy, he plotted how to bring her husband Uriah home from battle so that Uriah would sleep with Bathsheba and think that the child was his. David did not know what nobility he was dealing with, for Uriah would not consider sleeping with his wife while his fellow soldiers were still on the field of battle! Even though David made Uriah drunk, still Uriah stood—a man of principle. Surely David winced in the presence of such righteousness.

Still David did not mourn, but went deeper into sin. His intention for Uriah was obvious when he wrote a letter to his commander, Joab: "... place Uriah in the front line of the fiercest battle and withdraw from him, so that he may be struck down and die" (2 Samuel 11:15). The whirlpool was getting smaller, tighter, stronger. When Joab sent the news of the loss of lives—including that of Uriah—sin merely put its tongue in cheek and said, "Thus you shall say to Joab, 'Do not let this thing displease you, for the sword devours one as well as another; make your battle against the city stronger and overthrow it' " (2 Samuel 11:25).

Bathsheba mourned for her husband, but David had a new wife. He didn't mourn. He had resolved his own sin. Little did he realize that things would soon be out of his control as fourfold retribution would come upon him. Apparently David had forgotten that a holy God cannot overlook sin, even the sin of a king of God's anointing.

In his message on 2 Samuel 11, Pastor Wayne Barber of Woodland Park Baptist Church in Chattanooga, Tennessee, makes three points. I wrote them in my Bible:

Sin will take you farther than you ever thought you would stray.

Sin will keep you longer than you ever thought you would stay.

Sin will cost you more than you ever thought you would pay.

If you have ever been drawn into the whirlpool of sin, you know how true these statements are.

It wasn't until God finally confronted David through the prophet Nathan that David began to mourn with a godly sorrow. How thankful I am that God not only shares with us the victories of His saints, but also their defeats. "For whatever was written in earlier times was written for our instruction, that through perseverance and the encouragement of the Scriptures we might have hope" (Romans 15:4).

Read through Psalms 51:1–17 and write in your own words a short statement telling how David repented.

"The sacrifices of God are a broken spirit; a broken and a contrite heart, O God, Thou wilt not despise" (Psalms 51:17). Finally, David could be comforted by God.

We look now at James 4:7–10. As we do, keep in mind James's purpose in writing this epistle. He states his purpose in James 5:19, 20: "My brethren, if any among you strays from the truth, and one turns him back, let him know that he who turns a sinner from the error of his way will save his soul from death, and will cover a multitude of sins." James is showing us what the truth is and what it means to stray from that truth.

Those of you who have done our Precept course on the Book of James know the conviction that a study like this brings; yet it is a conviction that brings great liberation. In James 4:7–10, James is calling the people to repentance. They were caught up in a friendship with the world—a friendship that had made them proud, had led them into spiritual harlotry, and had broken the heart of God.

What is the solution? It is to stop laughing at sin. Carefully read James 4:9. "Be miserable and mourn and weep; let your laughter be turned into mourning, and your joy to gloom." Look around you. What do you see? You see people who laugh, who snicker, who howl over sin. There is hardly a comedian today, a story on television, or a play on Broadway that in some way does not entice us to laugh at sin.

Recently, I was skimming an article in *Reader's Digest* by George Burns, the comedian. It was on how to stay young. (At fifty, articles like this catch my eye!) Remember how we used to listen to George Burns and Gracie Allen on the radio? Their jokes were clean then—whether by choice or because of broadcasting restrictions I do not know—and the laughter hearty. In this article, however, George Burns tainted his comments with sexual innuendoes. Can you imagine that coming from a man in his eighties?

What is God's word to us? "Cleanse your hands, you sinners; and purify your hearts, you double-minded. Be miserable and mourn and weep . . ." (James 4:8, 9). How can we laugh over sin when sin nailed Jesus to the cross?

Have you sinned? Can you be comforted? Note I said "can." Is God able to comfort you? It all depends on whether or not you have God's heart on the matter. It all depends on whether or not you have mourned!

## DAY 4

The second object or cause for our mourning is sin in the church. I want you to stop and to think for a few minutes. How does your church deal with sin? When sin is discovered in the church—a man is committing adultery—someone is verbally abusing others—a person has been seen drunk—members of the church are swindling others through their businesses—does your church take action against such sin?

When I ask you this, how do you answer? Do you feel that you would be judging and that God tells us in Matthew 7:1 that we are not to judge? Or you may reason in your heart, "Well, after all, we're all sinners! Besides, what would we do with someone who was openly sinning?"

These are legitimate questions and they are fine to ask as long as we seek biblical solutions.

Read 1 Corinthians 5 and then write out your answers to the questions that follow.

1. What was the problem in the church at Corinth? Why was Paul upset with them?

2. What were his instructions to them? List them one by one after reading the whole chapter.

3. Whom were they to judge?

4. Whom would God judge?

As you saw in 1 Corinthians 5, the thing that upset Paul the most was not the son's incest, but the church's arrogance! The church had not mourned over the sin. They had not had a godly sorrow that led to repentance. (Remember 2 Corinthians 7 and your study on worldly sorrow versus godly sorrow? Sin had been tolerated instead of judged, until Paul wrote 1 Corinthians!)

"But," people have said to me, "if we put people out of our fellowship, they will just go deeper into sin! We have to show them the love of God! The forgiveness of God!"

Oh, are we wiser than God? Do we know the ways of man better than the One who created man? Our responsibility, Beloved, is not to turn to human reasoning. Rather, our responsibility is to be obedient to God. What does God say? He says, "Remove the wicked man from among yourselves" (1 Corinthians 5:13). Give him up to Satan for the destruction of his flesh. Don't have anything to do with him. Don't even eat with him. Yes, the guilty party may go deeper into sin. That's what God means when He says, ". . . deliver such a one to Satan for the destruction of his flesh" (1 Corinthians 5:5).

Why does God tell us to do this? So that man might come to know the awful wages of his sin and, feeling the just judgment of God, be brought to a godly sorrow and to repentance. Did it work? Yes, it did. Read 2 Corinthians 2:5–11. The church repented, the man repented, and the church was to forgive the man, comfort him, and reaffirm their love for him. We must never forget, Beloved, that God cannot forgive what we will not confess. And God cannot comfort us when we walk in rebellion.

Your next question may be, "But how do you approach a person? How do you deal with a person who is living in sin?" The answer is found in Matthew 18:15–20. There you will find the steps you are to take when your brother sins.

1. Go to him and reprove him in private.
2. If he does not listen to you, then take one or two more with you, and bring it before the church.
3. If he refuses to listen to the church, then you are to treat him as a Gentile and a tax-gatherer. In other words, you are to have nothing to do with him.

When you do this you are binding on earth what has already been bound in heaven. You are carrying out the will of God on earth. And when two of you are in agreement on this you can come to the Father and ask for His judgment and it will be done for you because He is there in your midst.

Isn't it interesting to see Matthew 18:18, 19 in the light of its context? So often these verses are misquoted and used out of context because people don't know the Word of God. And they don't know it because they haven't taken the time to study. May I commend you for taking the time to study and to grow so that you might fulfill God's commandment to study to show yourself approved unto Him so that you might not be ashamed, because you have learned to handle the Word of God accurately (2 Timothy 2:15).

I want to show you one last passage, to acquaint you with the heart of a man who deeply mourned over the sin of God's people. The man is Jeremiah, often referred to as "the weeping prophet."

"Harvest is past, summer is ended, and we are not saved." For the brokenness of the daughter of my people I am broken; I mourn, dismay has taken hold of me. Is there no balm in Gilead? Is there no physician there? Why then has not the health of the daughter of my people been restored? Oh that my head were waters, and my eyes a fountain of tears, that I might weep day and night for the slain of the daughter of my people!

"For the mountains I will take up a weeping and wailing, and for the pastures of the wilderness a dirge, because they are laid waste, so that no one passes through, and the lowing of the cattle is not heard; both the birds of the sky and the beasts have fled; they are gone."

Thus says the LORD of hosts, "Consider and call for the mourning women, that they may come; and send for the wailing women, that they may come! And let them make haste, and take up a wailing for us, that our eyes may shed tears, and our eyelids flow with water. For a voice of wailing is heard from Zion, 'How are we ruined! We are put to great shame, for we have left the land, because they have cast down our dwellings.' "

*Jeremiah 8:20–22, 9:1, 10, 17–19*

Should we not join Jeremiah in weeping over the sins of those who call themselves children of God? Let us call for mourners. Let us take up a weeping and wailing. The Lord may hear us and attend to the words of our cry. Is not God's desire for His Son to have a chaste virgin as a bride rather than a harlot (2 Corinthians 11:2)?

## Day 5

We are to mourn over our own sin, sin in the church, and sin in the world.

It was the summer of 1983, and Jack and I were having our annual time of rest and relaxation in the home of our dear friends, Chuck and Barb Snyder. I think taking care of us has become a ministry with them! Evenings are spent in wonderful fellowship lingering over delicious meals as we honestly communicate with two people who understand us and give us valuable insights. August is one of the rare times during the year when Jack gets to go fishing in the ocean and I get to do those fun "girl things" with Barb.

As Barb and I came out of Nordstrom's after having hit a big and unbelievable shoe sale, we noticed that the musical "Chorus Line" was playing. Seeing the show seemed like such a fun thing to do that we never paused to seriously consider whether it would be offensive. We bought tickets for the following night's performance.

The musical opened with some great choreography that reminded me of how out of shape I was. Talk about stamina—they had it! All went well until the singing and dancing stopped and the dialogue began. One by one, each performer in the chorus line stepped forward to tell a little bit about herself. I could not believe what my ears were hearing. The words were not just crude. They were perverted, rash, and blatant. They mocked everything that was holy and righteous and pure. They recked with filth. Their blatant innuendoes set off a ripple of snickering across the audience. It was not that good, wholesome, belly-shaking laughter, but an insidious, sick, "I can't believe I'm hearing what I'm hearing" snicker. It was filled with guilt.

I jammed my fingers into my ears and cried out, "Oh, Father, I am so sorry, so sorry." Barb and I turned to one another and agreed that we had to get out of there.

As we stood up to leave I wanted to shout to everyone in the theater, "Why are you laughing? You know it's wrong! Why do you laugh? Why do you listen to such filth? This is what is destroying America. You know that it's wrong!" I wanted to tell them about a holy God who sees and knows all that we do and all that we think.

I wanted to, but I didn't.

Oh, Jeremiah. I know why you wept. Did I leave you standing alone? I honestly don't know what I should have done. All I know is that I didn't do what I wanted to do. A verse (Matthew 12:19) sometimes restrains me in situations like that. It tells us that Jesus did not cry or raise His voice in the streets. Maybe I would have been casting my pearls before swine, giving what is holy to dogs. Or maybe, in my flesh, I was simply too weak to be a watchman on the walls warning the people to flee their sin (Ezekiel 33).

One thing I do know: My heart broke with the things that broke God's heart. And more and more as my heart draws closer to His, I feel, I weep, and I mourn over sin in the world.

One Sunday afternoon my attention was caught by a science film that Jack and our son David were watching on television. The camera peered down through a microscope, showing two different pieces of heart tissue that had been removed from two bodies. Each was beating; but their rhythms were different. Then a pair of hemostats picked up one piece of heart tissue and laid it beside the other. The minute the two came into contact, they started beating simultaneously. Why can

God comfort those who mourn? Because our hearts touch His and they beat as one!

Your last assignment for this week is to read Ezekiel 9, a very short chapter containing only eleven verses.

The Book of Ezekiel was written during the time of the Babylonian captivity of Judah. God had permitted the Southern Kingdom of Judah to go into captivity because they were breaking God's holy commandments. Through His prophets, God had constantly tried to call the people to repentance, but they would not listen. At the time of Ezekiel 9, Jerusalem had not yet been totally destroyed; therefore, some Jews were still living in the land. God had yet to bring about a full execution of judgment upon the sacred city. This is the context of Ezekiel 9. Read the chapter carefully and then answer the following questions.

1. Why did the Lord summon the executioners? What was His purpose?

2. What were the executioners to do?

3. What was the man clothed in linen with the writing case to do?

4. Why was he to do this?

5. Who was exempt from the judgment of the executioners?

Unless America repents, Beloved, God is going to have to judge us, and His means of judgment may be the same with us as with Jerusalem. He may bring another country to take us captive. If He were to do this, and if He were to send a man with a writing case to put a mark (a *tau,* which was the form of a cross) on the foreheads of those who sigh and groan over all the abominations committed in the United States of America, would he put a *tau* on your forehead? In that day God will be no respecter of persons. As in Israel He started from the temple and moved out to the people, so in America He will start in the churches and move from the leaders to the people. None will be exempt. It will be a *tau* or a sword. Only the mourners will be spared.

> The Spirit of the Lord GOD is upon me,
> Because the LORD has anointed me
> To bring good news to the afflicted;
> He has sent me to bind up the brokenhearted,
> To proclaim liberty to captives,
> And freedom to prisoners;
> To proclaim the favorable year of the LORD,
> And the day of vengeance of our God;
> To comfort all who mourn,
> To grant those who mourn in Zion,
> Giving them a garland instead of ashes,
> The oil of gladness instead of mourning,
> The mantle of praise instead of a spirit of fainting.
> So they will be called oaks of righteousness,
> The planting of the LORD,
> That He may be glorified.
>
> *Isaiah 61:1–3*

Yes, Beloved, it's a time for tears. It's a time to cry, "Oh, God, break my heart with the things that break Your heart."

# 6 - Meekness: Knowing God, His Character, His Sovereignty

## DAY 1

As you study the Sermon on the Mount, you cannot help but realize that the Beatitudes are not natural qualities. They are, rather, the in-wrought character of the indwelling Holy Spirit as He molds us and makes us into the image of God. Having seen our total poverty of spirit, and having mourned over our independent life-style which brought such grief to the heart of God, in meekness we bow our knees in total submission to God. The realization finally comes to us—if we were to serve Him the rest of our lives, we would still be unworthy and unprofitable servants! Having embraced those nail-pierced hands of love, we can bow before the sovereign God and in purity of trust say, "What pleases Thee, Father, pleases me."

It's the meek who will inherit the earth. Tell this to the Alexander the Greats, the Napoleons, the Hitlers, the Stalins, the Khrushchevs, and they will laugh and call you insane and "take counsel together against the LORD and against His Anointed" (Psalms 2:2). They march on, seeking to conquer the earth and forgetting that they are men and that their "... days are determined, the number of [their] months is with [God], and [their] limits [God] has set so that [they] cannot pass" (Job 14:5). They know not that the Lord rules, "In whose hand is the life of every living thing, and the breath of all mankind" (Job 12:10).

Meekness—what is it: How does it fit with the sovereignty and character of God? These are the quetions that we want to answer this week as we go on to maturity.

Let's look at the word *meek*. Oftentimes, *meek* or *meekness* is trans-lated "gentle" or "gentleness" in the New American Standard Bible. In the Old Testament it is translated "humble" or "afflicted." Over the years of study I have gathered so many notes on the definition of meekness that I'm not sure that I will give all my teachers proper credit. I pray that somehow, should this book fall into their hands, they will understand if I inadvertently quote them and yet have failed to credit them.

W. E. Vine says of meekness:

> Meekness is an inwrought grace of the soul; and the exercises of it are first and chiefly towards God. It is that temper of spirit in which we accept His dealings with us as good, and therefore without disputing and resisting.[4]

Meekness is used of a submissive and trusting attitude toward God that accepts all of God's ways with us as good and therefore does not murmur, dispute, or retaliate. It realizes that what comes to us from man is permitted and used by God for our chastening and our purifying. Meekness is a trusting attitude that looks beyond circumstances and beyond man to the sovereign God and, bowing the knee, says, "Lord, what pleases Thee pleases me."

I am convinced, Beloved, that if we are to walk in meekness we must know our God. We must understand that He is sovereign. We must know the character of this One who rules over all the affairs of man and all the host of heaven. Therefore, what I want to share with you this week is a glimpse into the character and sovereignty of God. Of all the truths that I have ever learned, none has brought me such assurance, boldness, calmness, devotion, equilibrium, gratitude, and humility as has the sovereignty of God. I pray that it will do the same for you.

Once again we must return to Daniel 4:34, 35. To me this is the keystone to all the Scriptures on God's sovereignty. When I speak of God's **sovereignty**, I am referring to the fact that God rules over all; God is totally, supremely, and preeminently over all His creation. There is not a person or a thing that is not under His control or in His foreknown plan. Let me diagram Daniel 4:34,35 for you.

You will notice that Daniel 4 says that God rules over "the armies of heaven." What do these armies include? (See diagram on next page.) There are a host of good angels who do the bidding of God, and there are a host of fallen angels who do the bidding of Satan. I have diagrammed Satan between the good and the bad angels. He is referred to in Ephesians 2:2 as the prince of the power of the air, the spirit that works in the sons of disobedience. His realm of authority is not only over fallen angels, but also over men who do not know the Lord Jesus Christ, who are "by nature children of wrath" (Ephesians 2:3). At this point a very legitimate question may arise in your mind: "If God is sovereign and in control over everything, where does that leave the free will of man?" That is a good question. The sovereignty of God does not negate the free will of man nor does man's free will rule out the sovereignty of God. "But, if one is true," you may ask, "how can the other be true? Do they not contradict each other?"

In man's mind, they seem contradictory, incongruous. Yet we must remember that one of the attributes of God is the fact He is **incomprehensible**. This means that because God is God, He is beyond our understanding. His ways, His character, and His acts are higher than ours. We can only understand Him to the depth that He chooses to reveal Himself to us. God's Word does not reveal to us how His sovereignty and our free will fit together. He only says to us, as in Isaiah 55:8, 9, " 'For My thoughts are not your thoughts, neither are your ways My ways.' declares the LORD. 'For as the heavens are higher than the earth, so are My ways higher than your ways, and My thoughts than your thoughts.' "

Faith steps into the picture at this point. Because we are finite human beings with limited understanding, we cannot seek to rationalize the truth of the Word of God. Rather, if God says it, we must accept it. Not to do so is to go to extremes in doctrine. Understand or not, we must always keep the balance of revelation. God has revealed enough truth so that we can know how we are to live. Beyond that we must say with Paul, "Oh, the depth of the riches both of the wisdom and knowledge of God! How unsearchable are His judgments and unfathomable His ways! For who has known the mind of the Lord, or who became His counselor? Or who has first given to Him that it might be paid back to him again? For from Him and through Him and to Him are all things. To Him be the glory forever. Amen" (Romans 11:33–36).

So what is the bottom line of what I have just said? It is this: God is sovereign and is in absolute control. God's sovereignty does not annihilate the free will of man, nor does it cease to make us accountable. Matthew 18:7 clearly shows our accountability, " 'Woe to the world because of its stumbling-blocks! For it is inevitable that stumbling-blocks come; but woe to that man through whom the stumbling-block comes!' "

Stumbling-blocks can only be permitted by a sovereign God. Yet God tells us that we are fully accountable if we cause these stumbling-blocks. We see the same truth of the accountability of man and the sovereignty of God when Jesus says to Pilate, "You would have no authority over Me, unless it had been given you from above; for this reason he who delivered Me up to you has the greater sin" (John 19:11). God knew all along that Judas Iscariot was going to betray Jesus. Jesus knew it also. God used it to accomplish His plan of redemption, and yet Judas was totally accountable before God!

But you might say, "Kay, it's not fair. It doesn't fit. It doesn't seem right. It's hard for me to believe." I understand, but I have to tell you that such statements are from biblical immaturity. You are uttering the cries of one who is still on milk and has not yet gone to meat. Let's press on to know our God and then we will never say that anything He does is unfair, because unfairness is contrary to His character. God is just.

What will be your prayer today? Do you need wisdom, revelation, understanding? Or if you already know these things, is your heart's cry for a greater degree of meekness? I understand. That is my heart's cry also. Cry, Beloved. Cry out to your God. He never turns a deaf ear to the sincere cry of His child who hungers and thirsts after righteousness.

## DAY 2

"The LORD of hosts has sworn saying, 'Surely, just as I have intended so it has happened, and just as I have planned so it will stand ... For the LORD of hosts has planned, and who can frustrate it? And as for His stretched-out hand, who can turn it back?" (Isaiah 14:24, 27.)

Let me ask you a question. Has there ever been even one single time when you looked at your mate and wondered if you married the wrong person? Be honest now. I think the majority of us would say yes. I would have to say yes and I'm sure that my husband would say the same. Thoughts like that panic you, don't they? You wonder if you've missed the will of God.

Or possibly you are single, and your friend excitedly introduces you to a man or a woman who seems made for *you* instead of *your friend*—yet they are the ones that are engaged. Do you panic and wonder, *Oh, God, why didn't I get there first? Was this the one You meant for me?*

As a single person, have you run hither and yon, trying to be at the right place at the right time so that God could bring along the mate of your dreams? Have you traveled from church to church surveying the prospects, then absolutely panicked that you're going to miss God's will for you?

If you have lived with the torment of wondering if you have missed God's will and God's best, you know that it's torture. Yet what you don't realize is that this is a tactic of the enemy that is as old as the Garden of Eden.

"God's holding back on you. God's keeping you from having what you really need. Surely you're an exception. This attraction must be from God. It's so pure, it's so lovely; why, it's even drawn you closer to God. Take it. Eat it." Oh, please don't!

Run to the sovereignty of God. Know that, as Isaiah 14:24, 27 says, "just as [He] has intended so it has happened, and just as [He has] planned so it will stand. For the LORD of hosts has planned, and who can frustrate it? And as for His stretched-out hand, who can turn it back?" If you are married, the will of God is your mate—nothing else, no one else.

"But I'm not happy! I'm not fulfilled! I've missed what I've always wanted," you say. O Beloved, you have not missed it. Meekness bows the knee and realizes that everything is permitted and used by God for our chastening, our purifying. Meekness says, "Not my will, but Thine be done." Meekness bows before the throne and realizes that the God who sits upon that throne is an all-wise (omniscient) God. The things that God has planned, in His wisdom are based on His character which allows Him to choose righteous ends and to make fitting plans to achieve those ends. Meekness knows that the God who sits upon that throne is a good God. He is inclined to bestow blessedness and He takes holy pleasure in the happiness of His people. He is kind, benevolent, and full of good will toward men. Therefore, if neither happiness nor fulfillment comes through your marriage, God will see that even that will work together for good. So bow your knee and say, "I will give Thee thanks forever, because Thou hast done it, and I will wait on Thy name, for it is good . . ." (Psalms 52:9). Because He is God, He will satisfy your thirsty soul. He will fill your hungry soul with what is good (Psalms 107:9).

So many books have been written, and so many seminars given painting such a beautiful picture of marriage. They make it seem that the chief aim of man is to be happily married! I can't buy that. I must agree with the Westminster Confession that the chief aim of man is "to glorify God and to enjoy Him forever."

Despite all the seminars, the Marriage Encounters, the seemingly biblical formulas for a happy marriage—despite all the books that give the hows, the why, and the wherefores—some people still live in their own little hell. They have tried it all, done all they were told to do, and it still hasn't worked.

If the person to whom you are married will not comply, then what will you do? Will you break God's holy covenant? Will you get a divorce? Will you say, "Surely God doesn't expect me to endure this, to be miserable for the rest of my life"? Or will you in meekness bow the knee and say, "As the Lord has planned, so it has come to pass. If it seems good to Thee, Father, it seems good to me. Now Father, perfect that which concerns me. Work it all to Your glory and to my good."

I don't know where you are, Beloved, but I know as surely as I write this that God is speaking to some of you very directly. I pray that you will listen.

Your assignment for today is to write down what you have learned about your God.

## DAY 3

If God is a sovereign God, how do you explain the injustices, the holocausts, the rapes, the incests, the abuses, the murders? How do you explain suffering, pain, and cruelty? How could God be a God of love and let these things happen? I think most of us, at one time or another, have wanted to doubt the sovereignty of God, because we couldn't understand how a loving God could permit such things.

I understand. I will never forget the night that I sat on my bed and read a murderer's detailed explanation of how he sexually assaulted a little girl and eventually killed her. As he sought to violate her sexually in the back seat of a car, she said to him, "God doesn't like what you're doing. It's wrong." It so angered the man that he killed the girl. When I finished reading the deposition, I put it down, threw my head back and clamped my eyes shut, but to no avail. Tears coursed down my cheeks as I sobbed, "Father, I don't understand, I don't understand."

And I didn't understand. I know that God is sovereign and I know that this sovereign One Who sits upon the throne is a God of **love**. I know that the very essence of His being is love. I know that He holds me in His **omnipotent**, all-powerful hand and that no one can touch me, say a word to me, or even look at me without His permission. God had taught me this in my first days of infancy as His child. Then I thought: *All I know is what happened to the little girl from the murderer's point of view. I don't know what happened to her from Your point of view. I do know, Father, that You are faithful and truthful—I will cling to that. All that You say is reality because You are truth. Your promise to us in Your Word is that all things work together for good to those who love You, who are the called according to Your purpose. You promise us, Father, that no temptation, trial, or testing overtakes us but such as is common to man. You will never permit us to be tried above that which we are able. With every trial or testing or temptation, You will make a way of escape that we might be able to bear it.*

In the attributes of God I found my comfort and my understanding. God is a God of **truth**. Jesus is truth. What He says is reality. And because God is **faithful** to His promises, I knew that somehow and in some way this little girl was given the grace of God to bear the perversion of that man. "But she lost her life!" Oh? I thought that Jesus was the resurrection and the life and that those who believe in Him shall never die. Her life was not taken from her. Deuteronomy 32:39 says, " 'See how that I, I am He, and there is no god besides Me; it is I who put to death and give life. I have wounded, and it is I who heal; and there is no one who can deliver from My hand.' " Revelation 1:18 tells us that Jesus has the keys of death and of Hades.

Take a few minutes and summarize what you've learned today about God's character and His sovereignty. Then talk to God about these things and if you're having difficulty understanding them, tell Him about it. He knows it anyway, but He wants to hear it from your lips so that He can take the things that belong to Him and reveal them to you by His Spirit.

## DAY 4

As we saw yesterday, one of the things that makes it difficult to accept God's sovereignty is the fact that God apparently permits adversity or evil. And that's true, He does. Isaiah 45:6, 7 says, "That men may know from the rising to the setting of the sun that there is no one besides Me. I am the LORD, and there is no other, the One forming light and creating darkness, causing well-being and creating calamity; I am the LORD who does all these (things)." The word *calamity* is also translated "evil"; it means adversity.

Ecclesiastes 7:13, 14 says. "Consider the work of God, for who is able to straighten what He has bent? In the day of prosperity be happy, but in the day of adversity consider—God has made the one as well as the other so that man may not discover anything that will be after him."

One reason we have problems with God's sovereignty in the face of adversity, evil, or calamity is that we are temporal beings. Our vision is temporal and we cannot see beyond the limits of our vision. Before I entered my late forties and had to resort to contacts I had twenty-twenty vision. Yet, once I grew older, I could read things far away, but couldn't see things close to me; my vision would blur. However, my contacts give me an entirely new perspective. This is the way it is with many of us. We are so focused on the future that we can't understand the things that are happening to us now. They don't seem to be taking us in the direction we think we should be going. The immediate is blurred and indistinguishable.

This is why some people have problems with the sovereignty of God. They look at the future, thinking they see it very clearly. Therefore, because of their expectations, the immediate and difficult occurrences of life are hard to distinguish as coming from God. They need spiritual contacts that will give them a proper perspective of the eternal. Only faith will do. For those who come to God must believe that He is (*see* Hebrews 11:6). And what is He? God is **eternal**. This God who creates prosperity and adversity has no beginning and no end. He is not confined to the finiteness of time or to man's reckoning of time. He is, in fact, the cause of time. Meekness then, when faced with adversity, bows the knee knowing that God is eternal. It says with the psalmist, "But as for me, I trust in Thee, O LORD, I say, 'Thou art my God.' My times are in thy hand . . ." (Psalms 31:14, 15).

Meekness looks "not at the things which are seen, but at the things which are not seen; for the things which are seen are temporal, but the things which are not seen are eternal" (2 Corinthians 4:18). Meekness remembers that it is finite and that God is **infinite**. The realm of God has no limits or bounds whatsoever.

Do you have another "but" for me? That's fine. You need to look at every "but" that would throw doubt on the sovereignty of God or His impeccable character.

"But it doesn't seem fair for God to let these things happen," you may be saying. "Look at all the murderers who are running around free. Look at all the Christians who love God and are locked up in Communist lands in prisons and psychiatric institutions. How can a just, sovereign God allow a Hitler to carry out his holocaust, or let the Chinese crucify, behead, and mutilate millions? How can a just and holy God let Idi Amin live unpunished in a quiet resort after he and his men barbarically dismembered their enemies before the very eyes of their loved ones? How can a merciful God allow countless numbers of little boys and girls to be molested and their assailants go undetected? How?! It's not fair! There's nothing right about it!!!"

When you want to cry out, "It's not fair," you need to go back again to the character of God. God is righteous. He is always good. It's essential to His character that He be so. Ultimately, since He is God, whatever He does is right—He is the absolute. His actions are always consistent with His character, which is love. So, remember that the God who sits on His throne can never divest Himself of His love or His righteousness or His holiness or His justice. He cannot take off any one of His attributes and lay it aside and act independently of it. It is part of His being to be just. In all of His actions, God acts with fairness. Whether He deals with man, angels, or demons, He acts in total equity by rewarding righteousness and punishing sin. Since He knows all, every decree is absolutely just.

Please don't think I am saying that God decrees or orders men to do evil. This would be contrary to His nature. "Let no one say when he is tempted, 'I am being tempted by God'; for God cannot be tempted by evil, and He Himself does not tempt any one" (James 1:13). It is hard to explain to those who want everything to be logically understood within the realm of their comprehension. This is where faith and meekness come in. Faith says, "God, I don't understand, but I know You are sovereign, loving, and just. I may not understand but I will not accuse You, nor alter Your word to fit my theology."

Moses had given God forty years of consecrated obedience. Then, in one moment of pressure, he broke. He struck the rock a second time when God had told him to speak to the rock. Moses failed to sanctify God in the eyes of His people. So, God, in His justice, told Moses that he could never enter the Promised Land. He would see that land of Canaan from Mt. Nebo, but he would never enter into it.

And what did Moses say after God pronounced this judgment upon him? Never taking his eyes off God, he said "For I proclaim the name of the Lord; ascribe greatness to our God! The Rock! His work is perfect, for all His ways are just; a God of faithfulness and without injustice, righteous and upright is He "(Deuteronomy 32:3, 4). O Beloved, meekness does not accuse God of being unrighteous or unjust. Meekness realizes that God is **holy**. He is a morally excellent, perfect being, pure in every aspect. So meekness bows the knee and says, "God, I trust You. I know that You are holy. I know that You are righteous. I know that You are just. I accept everything that comes into my life without murmuring, without disputing, without retaliation. I know, God, that You are a God of wrath. I know that within You is a hatred for all that is unrighteous—an unquenchable desire to punish all unrighteousness. I know, God, that whatever is inconsistent with You must ultimately be consumed. And I wait for that day when You, in righteousness and justice, will move with wrath."

For after all it is only just for God to repay with affliction those who afflict you, and to give relief to you who are afflicted and to us as well when the Lord Jesus shall be revealed from heaven with His mighty angels in flaming fire, dealing out retribution to those who do not know God and to those who do not obey the gospel of our Lord Jesus.

*2 Thessalonians 1:6–8*

But why does God wait so long? Why does He let unrighteous men live? Why is God's judgment not quick and swift? Because, Beloved, God is **merciful and longsuffering.** God is an actively compassionate being. In His mercy He acts in a compassionate way toward those who have opposed His will in pursuit of their own way. God is longsuffering. His righteous anger is slow to be kindled against those who fail to listen to His warnings or to obey His instructions. The eternal longing for the highest good for His creatures holds back His holy justice. "The Lord is not slow about His promise, as some count slowness, but is patient toward you, not wishing for any to perish but for all to come to repentance" (2 Peter 3:9).

There's another question in your heart, isn't there? "If God is not willing that any should perish, what about the heathen? Why are the heathen, who have never heard about God, going to perish? How can God be fair and just and let men go to hell who have never heard about Jesus Christ?"

Can we wait until tomorrow to answer that question? I think that we have had enough for today, don't you? Stop once again and meditate upon all that you have learned about the sovereignty and character of God. Write your insights below. It will be good review.

# DAY 5

What about the heathen? If God is not willing that any should perish, then how could He permit men who have never heard about Jesus Christ to die and enter a Christless eternity? Let me answer this question by way of illustration. I will never forget the day a young man stood in chapel, weeping. One of the men whom he had worked with had suddenly died. Heartbroken, he said, "Because of me, that man is in hell today. I did not witness to him."

Is that man in hell because a young friend failed to witness to him? If so, where does that leave the sovereignty of God and the eternal destiny of man? The man's remorse was not off-key, but his theology was. We are accountable. We are our brother's keepers. We are to give the gospel to others so we can say with Paul, "I am innocent of the blood of all men" (Acts 20:26, 27). However, no man's destiny rests on one man's faithfulness or unfaithfulness. What is true in the United States of America is true for the heathen who have not yet heard the name of Jesus Christ.

The God who sits upon the sovereign throne of all the universe is **self-sufficient**. Within Himself, God is able to act and to bring about His will without any assistance. Although He may use assistance, it is because He chooses to, not out of need. God can and has revealed

Himself without any human instrument. The story of Samuel Morris illustrates this point.

Samuel Morris—or Kaboo, as he was named at birth—the eldest son of a chieftain of West Africa, knew absolutely nothing about God.

In those regions it was the custom for a chief who was defeated in war to give his eldest son as a pawn or hostage to insure the payment of war indemnity. If payment lagged, he was often subject to torture. Such was the fate of Kaboo.[5]

When fifteen, Kaboo, became a pawn of war for the third time—only this time his father was unable to pay off his debt of war. Furious, his captor began to torture Kaboo.

The flesh of his back hung in shreds. Soon he became so exhausted from loss of blood and the fever induced by the poison vine that he could no longer stand or even sit up. A cross-tree was then erected and he was carried out and thrown over it while he was again beaten over his raw back.

### The Miraculous Escape

Kaboo hoped that death would release him before he met the awful fate of an unredeemed pawn. A number of Kaboo's tribesmen had been taken as ordinary slaves by this brutal chief. Several of them had been accused as bewitchers. Kaboo had seen them literally torn to pieces by drunken and frenzied men. But he was now faced by an even more diabolical fate.

Already, they had dug a pit in anticipation of the possible failure of his father to return. If his final beating induced no further payment, he was to be buried up to the neck. His mouth would then be propped open, and smeared with a sweet mixture to attract the ants from a nearby anthill. The resulting torment would merely prepare for the final act when another type of insect—the dreaded driver ants—would be permitted to devour his living flesh bit by bit. After the ants had cleaned his bones of every particle of flesh, his white skeleton would then be placed in front of his execution hut as a gentle reminder to all future debtors.

As Kaboo was flung upon the cross-tree for his final beating, all hope as well as physical strength left him. He longed only for the boon of death.

Then, suddenly something very strange happened. A great light like a flash of lightning broke over him. The light blinded all about him. An audible voice that seemed to come from above commanded him to rise and flee. All heard the voice and saw the light but saw no man.

At the same time there occurred one of those instantaneous healings which science can neither deny nor explain. In the twinkling of an eye Kaboo found his strength restored. He had had nothing to eat or drink all that day. Yet he felt neither hunger nor thirst nor weakness. Leaping up, he obeyed the mysterious voice and fled from the astonished natives with the speed of a deer.

What was the source of the mysterious light that had brought him new strength and freedom? Kaboo did not know or suspect. He had never heard of the Christian God. He knew nothing of special acts of Divine Providence. He had never heard of a Savior who had once been put in pawn, a ransom for many. The earthly prince who had just hung over a cross-tree of torture did not dream of a heavenly Prince who had been mocked and beaten as a prisoner and had suffered a degraded death by slow torture upon a tree.

But Kaboo did know that some strange and invisible power had come to his rescue. At one moment he had been too ill to sit erect and now he was runing away at top speed.

It was on a Friday that he made his escape. Kaboo never forgot that day. He called it his Deliverance Day, and as long as he lived he always celebrated the day of the week by fasting, taking neither food nor water.[6]

After fleeing from his enemies, Kaboo finally found his way to a coffee plantation.

His Kru companion had been listening to the missionaries and had learned to pray. Kaboo saw him on his knees, both hands lifted up and face upturned. When Kaboo asked him what he was doing, he replied, "I am talking to God."

"Who is your God?" asked Kaboo.

"He is my Father," answered the boy.

"Then you are talking to your Father," said Kaboo. Ever afterward he called praying "talking to my Father." To his childlike faith, prayer was as simple and as sure as conversing with an earthly parent.

The next Sunday Kaboo was invited to attend church. He found a crowd gathered around a woman who was speaking through an interpreter. She was telling them about the conversion of Saul; how a light from heaven suddenly shone upon him and a mysterious voice spoke from above.

Kaboo cried out: "That's just what I saw! I have seen that light! That is the same light that saved me and brought me here!" Kaboo had been wondering all the time why he had been so marvelously saved from death and guided through the forest. Now, in a flash he began to understand.

God cannot save a soul until that soul has knowledge of Him and exercises conscious faith. But the Providence of God often spares the lives and heals the bodies of those who are yet strangers to Him, either in answer to the prayers of believers or for His own good purposes.[7]

Perhaps you are saying, "I know that you have told me all this about God, but what if He changes? I know that He is a different God in the New Testament then He is in the Old Testament. In the Old Testament He required Joshua to put to death all the inhabitants of Jericho. But in the New Testament He won't even allow the scribes and the Pharisees to stone a woman caught in the very act of adultery. So what if He changes again?"

God can't change. He is **immutable**. God is always the same in His nature, His character, and His will, and He can never be made to change. Malachi 3:6 says, "For I, the LORD, do not change . . ." Hebrews 13:8 says, "Jesus Christ is the same yesterday and today, yes and forever." There are not two Gods—a God of the Old Testament and a God of the New Testament. Jesus is not a new, updated version of God—kinder, more compassionate, full of **mercy** and **longsuffering**. No, these have always been the attributes of God. When He slaughtered the children and adults of Jericho, He was acting in His just wrath, for they had had years to repent and they did not. The children of Israel could not have even taken possession of Canaan until the iniquity of the Amorites was "full." This is what God told Abraham in Genesis 15:16.

One more "What if?" "What if God ceases to be? What if man proves that God does not exist?"

Man will try to prove that God does not exist. Man will give you all sorts of arguments, but you can know that God is **self-existent.** There is nothing upon which God depends for His existence except Himself. The whole basis of His existence is within Himself. There was a time when nothing existed but God Himself. He added nothing to Himself by Creation. Man will never blot out the knowledge of God from the face of this earth. He is the great I AM: " 'I AM WHO I AM.' . . . This is My name forever, and this is My memorial-name to all generations" (Exodus 3:14, 15).

In the light of all you have learned, let's reason together. When confronted with all this, some would still say God is not sovereign. So, let's suppose for a minute that God is not. Who then *is in control?* Would it not have to be man, the devil, or fate?

If man is in control, then he is as great or as powerful as God. He can usurp the will of God and do whatever he wants to do. Would you accept this teaching?

If the devil can do things without God's permission, then the devil can foul up God's plans. If this is so, then Satan is as powerful as God. Can that be? Can one who was created by God set his throne above the Most High? No. He tried and found himself condemned to the lake of fire (Isaiah 14:12–15).

But then, if neither man nor the devil is in control, are we in the hands of fate? If that's so, then some power or force, whatever it may be, is determining our destiny rather than God. God is not transcendent; He is not above His creation, but has been usurped from His sovereign throne by that which He brought into being.

The facts are clear, aren't they. Meekness bows its knee and says, "My Lord and my God, if it pleases Thee, it pleases me."

On this final day on the character and sovereignty of God, I urge you to rehearse what you have learned. Then, write it below and in prayer, work into your heart the things that you have taken into your mind. In prayer, submit your will to His. What a harvest of untold peace you will reap!

# 7 - Meekness: How Does It Behave Toward God and Man?

## DAY 1

Meekness is an elegant gem with many facets. As each of these facets catches the light of God's truth, we discover that this is indeed a magnificent and rare jewel—a jewel fit for His crown.

But before we talk about that, I want to encourage you. Since I cannot come alongside you in person and put my arm around you, I want to do it on paper. I want to thank you for being among the minority who are willing to discipline themselves to go on to maturity. Should you be weary, I want to tell you that I understand. But persevere. We're almost across the halfway mark. I would not ask you to run where I have not run. I would not say, "You can do it!" if I did not know that it could be done. I would not promise you rewards "exceedingly abundantly beyond all that we ask or think" if I had not experienced and known for a fact that those rewards are there. So take my hand and let's go!

Meekness was one of the great words of Greek ethics. Aristotle defined it with great care. He said meekness is the mean between excessive anger and the inability to show anger at all. Therefore, meek is the man who is angry on the right occasion with the right people at the right moment for the right length of time. In his book *Kingdom Living,* an outstanding exposition of the Beatitudes, John MacArthur puts it this way: "Meekness . . . is anger under control." But because meekness is not self-centered at all, it is not anger at what is done to oneself, but a righteous anger at what is wrongly done to others.

Some have thought that all anger is sin; yet what does Ephesians 4:26 say? Look it up, write it down, and then according to this verse tell me whether or not all anger is sin. Make sure that you explain your answer.

Meekness has also been used to describe domesticated animals who have learned to accept control by their masters and therefore are properly behaved ("broken"). From there it was extended to people who are properly behaved. The meek are those of gentle behavior, soft and loving. Submission is always a facet of meekness.

But it is in the Word of God that the gem of meekness is cut and polished. Meekness accepts all of God's ways with us as good and therefore does not murmur or dispute. Psalm 37 shows us four ways that meekness responds: it trusts, commits, rests, and waits. Trust is a facet of meekness because meekness trusts in the Lord, delighting in Him (verses 3 and 4). Because of this trust it can commit its way to the Lord (verse 5), resting in Him and waiting patiently for whatever is God's pleasure (verse 7). It does not fret at the prosperity of the wicked (verses 7 and 8), but waits upon the Lord, knowing that it will inherit the land. It is confident that "the humble [meek] will inherit the land ..." (verses 9 and 11). There it is—a direct Old Testament parallel to Jesus' words in the Sermon on the Mount: " 'Blessed are the [meek] for they will inherit the earth.' "

Meekness is humble submission to the will of the Father. It does not fight or struggle or contend with God.

An example of meekness is Joseph's love and acceptance of his brothers—the very brothers who, out of jealousy, plotted against him to put him to death, and then sold him into slavery. Meekness caused Joseph to look beyond the acts of his brothers to the sovereignty of God and accept all of God's dealings with him without bitterness. We see this in Joseph as he says to his brothers, ". . . Do not be afraid, for am I in God's place? And as for you, you meant evil against me, but God meant it for good in order to bring about this present result, to preserve many people alive" (Genesis 50:19, 20). Meekness is walking under the control of the Holy Spirit, "always giving thanks for all things in the name of our Lord Jesus Christ to God, even the Father" (Ephesians 5:20).

Meekness also manifests itself in its reaction to evil men by turning the other cheek, by loving its enemies, and by praying for those who persecute it (Matthew 6:39, 44). Meekness can do this because it realizes that the insults and the injuries which man may inflict are only permitted and used by God for its chastening and purifying. Meekness is not weakness, but the fruit of power. It is "equanimity of spirit that is neither elated nor cast down, simply because it is not occupied with self at all."[8]

Where does meekness come from? It is part of our inheritance as children of God. It is part of the fruit of the Holy Spirit as we shall see later. It has its birth in poverty of spirit when we see that we are nothing, have nothing, and can do nothing in order to please God. When we see what a mess we have made out of our lives, what else can we do but submit in meekness to God's sovereignty and cast ourselves upon His all-sufficient breast? Apart from Him there really is no life!

Spend some time, Beloved, in prayer. Review what you have learned about meekness. In the space below, list the way it behaves. Ask God to show you where you are lacking meekness. Then commit your way to Him and trust in Him, and He will bring it to pass.

## DAY 2

Look at the Beatitudes and you will see the character of Jesus Christ. In Matthew 11:28–30 we read:

> "Come to Me, all who are weary and heavy-laden, and I will give you rest. Take My yoke upon you, and learn from Me, for I am gentle (meek) and humble in heart; and you shall find rest for your souls. For My yoke is easy, and My load is light."

From these verses it is obvious that meekness is acquired. It comes from walking in Jesus' yoke, or, to put it another way, from walking in the Spirit. Today I want to look at meekness as seen in the Lamb of God.

We said that meekness was used of domesticated animals who have learned to accept their masters' control and who are properly behaved. We saw it was a submissive, trusting attitude toward God. If anyone manifested this, it was the Lamb of God. He was the One Who said, "My food is to do the will of Him who sent Me, and to accomplish His work" (John 4:34).

1. Do you remember John 8:28, 29? Read these verses again and then note below how they show us the meekness of Jesus Christ.

Second, we saw that meekness is anger under control. Meekness is not apathy; it is not a doormat mentality or existence. How does anger under control behave?

2. Read John 2:13–17. Was Jesus angry at the right time with the right people and for the right reason? Explain your answer from these verses.

It would have been apathetic to let the moneychangers stay in the temple and make His Father's house a den of thieves.

Finally, come with me to the Garden of Gethsemane and once again we will see the example of meekness as it submits to God's sovereign will, no matter what the cost!

Read Matthew 26:37–44, and then answer the questions that follow.

1. What is Jesus' request from the Father?

2. When He refers to "the cup," to what is He referring? Compare this with John 18:11 and write your answer.

3. How many times did Jesus pray this prayer?

4. How does this demonstrate meekness?

Well, Beloved, there is our example! The yoke is waiting. Will you take it and learn from Him? Believe me, it will be the only way that you will find rest for your souls for your day-by-day living. Do not be afraid. You will find that His yoke is easy. You will find that His load is light.

Write out your answer in the form of a prayer. If you're afraid, tell God you're afraid. Tell Him why; He'll meet you at the point of your fear if you will confess it to Him. Ask Him to show you His perfect love which casts out all fear (1 John 4:18).

## DAY 3

We have defined meekness and have seen it demonstrated in action through our Lord and Savior, the Author and Finisher of our faith. Now let's see how it is worked out in our own lives.

When God made the earth and put man upon it, it was His intention that man would rule as His vice-regent over all the Creation. All man had to do was to walk in submission to God, in total dependence upon his Creator. However, the submission needed to be voluntary, so God gave man the right to choose to walk independently. He put a test of man's will in that Garden. It was the tree of the knowledge of good and evil.

God's instructions were very clear. " 'From any tree of the garden you may eat freely; but from the tree of the knowledge of good and evil you shall not eat, for in the day that you eat from it you shall surely die' " (Genesis 2:16, 17). Man was not blind to the consequences of his sin. God tells us very clearly in 1 Timothy 2:14 that Adam was not deceived. Eve was, but not Adam. He knew exactly what he was doing when he listened to the voice of his wife rather than the voice of God. He ate of the fruit of the tree in willful disobedience. In the process, Adam chose to walk independently of God and lost the right to rule as God's vice-regent on earth. Man lost the earth because he was not willing to submit to God. Only meekness will regain that which was lost in the Garden, for " 'blessed are the [meek], for they shall inherit the earth.' "

We have seen it already, but it bears repeating. Meekness begins with poverty of spirit. It comes with salvation, for it is submission to God's authority over your life. I think the Scriptures are very clear in Matthew 7 as Jesus brings His message to conclusion. Those who call Him Lord but do not live as such will not enter the kingdom of heaven. Therefore, to call Him Lord, and yet fail to do His will, clearly shows us that we have never truly been born again. Meekness must be present to one degree or the other. If it's not, we can know for certain that neither heaven nor earth belong to us, but only the certain fearful condemnation and just judgment of God.

I have told you several times that meekness is a fruit of the Spirit. Read Galatians 5:22, 23; then write those two verses below. Note how many fruits there are. Put the number below.



There are _____ fruits of the Spirit. How many did you write down? The correct answer should be "one ninefold fruit." Did you notice that the subject is singular and so is the verb? "The fruit . . . is!" When you are under the control of the Holy Spirit, *all* these things will be manifest in your life. Remember when we said that the Beatitudes are not natural, inherent qualities, but they are the work of the inwrought grace of God? Is this not what we see in the fact that meekness, or "gentleness," is born of the Spirit?

Now turn to James 1:21. Write the verse below and then answer the following questions.

1. When it says "in humility receive the Word implanted," the word for *humility* is the same that is sometimes translated "meekness." According to this verse, what does meekness have to do with your growth?

2. If I receive the Word in meekness, how will I behave? As you answer this question, remember what the definition of meekness is.

Now look up Psalms 25:9 and write it below. Answer the questions that follow. Remember, in the Old Testament many times the word for *meekness* is translated "humble" or "afflicted."

1. According to this verse, whom does the Lord lead?

2. To whom does He teach His way?

Are you willing to be led? Are you teachable? Are you willing to receive with meekness the engrafted Word of God? When you become more than a hearer of the Word and walk in obedience as a doer of the Word, it will show.

Summarizing what we've learned today, if you are going to be meek, you will submit to God's authority over your life. You will walk circumspectly, filled with the Spirit. You will be that good soil that receives God's Word and bears fruit. How does your life measure up to what you have seen today? Think about it. Ponder these things in your heart. Ask God to reveal to you any way in which you have failed to be meek.


## DAY 4


How is meekness to be characterized in our dealings with others? Both Galatians 6:1 and 2 Timothy 2:24–26 use the word *meekness*. Therefore, it is essential for you to read both of these passages and note what you learn about meekness.

1. With what similar problem do these two passages deal?



2. Put down specifically what you learn from these two passages.




When I think of correction and how we are instructed to correct people in meekness, I cannot help but remember the night years ago when my husband brought to my attention my lack of gentleness in dealing with people. It was in the days of the barn loft. When we launched Precept Ministries, we renovated two barns—one a long, low cow barn and the second a two-story hip roof barn with a loft which we used as an auditorium. Those were precious days and we all look back on them with fond memories. They were also days of growth and maturing.

One night the barn loft was packed with about 250 young people. I had brought them a very strong message. That night as Jack and I crawled into bed, he said to me, "Kay, I didn't hear any love in your voice tonight."

"But those teens know that I love them!" I retorted rather quickly.

"I know, but I still didn't hear any love in your voice."

I didn't say another word. I simply turned to my side of the bed and thought, *What do you know about it anyway? You don't know how to work with teens.* I closed my eyes in disgust. Things were always better in the morning, but sleep wouldn't come. His words rang over and over in my mind. "I didn't hear any love in your voice tonight."

Finally despairing of sleep, I got up, got out my concordance, and looked up every reference to "gentle." I will never forget the verse I discovered that night: "Thy gentleness makes me great" (Psalms 18:35). How I wept before God. How I pleaded with Him, "O Father, just bring them back. I know that I don't deserve to teach them again, but, please, just bring them back so that I can tell them I was wrong, so that I can ask them to forgive me."

He brought them back. The barn loft was packed again. I stood before them and wept, asking their forgiveness and telling them what God had taught me. O Beloved, no matter how grievous the sin, no matter how strong the snare of Satan, we are not to correct anyone in any other way except meekness. All our righteous indignation must be brought under the control of meekness. Otherwise, when we seek to restore a brother and recover him out of the snare of the devil, he will never see the character of God and be drawn to Him.

Moses gives us another example of how meekness behaves in its dealings with others. Read Numbers 12:1–3 and 9–13. Now answer the following questions:

1. What do you learn about Moses and meekness from this passage?

2. How did Moses respond to Miriam and Aaron when they attacked him?

3. How did God respond?

4. How does Moses manifest meekness in Numbers 12:9–13?

Have you ever been unjustly attacked or falsely accused by any member of your family? How did you respond?

Did their unjust attack or accusation cause you to go into depression? If so, that's a sure sign that you did not respond in meekness. Remember, meekness is neither elated nor cast down, because it is not occupied with self at all. Meekness does not get angry at what is done to it, but meekness gets angry at what is wrongly done to others.

We need to look at one more passage from Moses' life. Remember what we have learned about Moses, that he "was very humble, more than any man who was on the face of the earth" (Numbers 12:3). Yet meekness is not weakness. It is power under control. This is clearly seen in Numbers 16:1–4 and 28–35. The sons of Korah challenged Moses' leadership. They were disobeying God and resisting Him, not Moses. But Moses went to his knees before God; as God's representative, Moses could not yield his God-given leadership and allow the sons of Korah to rebel against God. Therefore, in meekness, Moses called down the judgment of God and the earth opened and consumed the 250 men who were transgressing in offering incense upon the altar.

In Numbers 16:41–50 we also see meekness not caring to vindicate itself. When the congregation of the sons of Israel grumbled against Moses and Aaron, God in anger sent a plague. Moses interceded even as he interceded for Miriam. Never forget it, meekness is *not* weakness! It is *not* a "milk-toast" mentality. Meekness holds its ground when God's honor and glory are at stake. Meekness does not become a doormat for sin.

Does it help to share these things, to look at the different facets of meekness and see how they are to be reflected by us in the midst of a crooked and perverse generation? I do pray that you understand the balance of meekness, because it's vital.

"And so, as those who have been chosen of God, holy and beloved, put on a heart of compassion, kindness, humility (meekness), gentleness and patience; bearing with one another, and forgiving each other, whoever has a complaint against any one; just as the Lord forgave you, so also should you" (Colossians 3:12, 13).

Meekness is a sure cure for bitterness. As a matter of fact, if there is any bitterness in your life you can be set free today. What eats at the gut of your soul? What corrodes the beauty of His countenance? What torments you behind those closed-off doors of your mind? It can be done away with today if you will listen carefully to God's Spirit as He speaks to you through His Word.

Some of you do not have a problem with bitterness, but do you know how to help those who do? We are not only to be ministered to, but we are to become ministers to others, stewards of the mysteries of God. So study well and you will find that God will put someone in your path who is consumed with bitterness. When He does, you will have the balm of Gilead to heal their sinsick soul.

Carefully and prayerfully read Hebrews 12:1–17. When you come to the word *bitterness,* underline it or note it in some special way. Ask God to open the eyes of your understanding. Ask Him to take the veil off of His Word and speak to you in His own poignant, practical way. I want you to mark two other words: *endure* ("persevere" or "patience" come from the same word and mean endure) and *chasten* (or "discipline," depending on which version of the Bible you use).

Have you read it? It would do no good for me to discuss it with you until you have read it, so be faithful to use your own Bible, to secure God's Word in your heart by the use of your senses.

The theme of this passage is enduring discipline as God's children. This passage warns us against not enduring, giving up, growing weary, and losing heart. Why would we not endure? Because no discipline for the present time seems to be pleasant. Therefore, instead of responding to discipline, instead of seeing it as for our good so that we might share in His holiness, we are apt to become discouraged, to allow the discipline of God to wound us and therefore to be of no use to God. Another danger is the possibility of falling short of the grace of God when He disciplines or chastens us and thereby having a root of bitterness spring up in us, causing us trouble and defiling others. Look at Hebrews 12:15 again. "See to it that no one comes short of the grace of God; that no root of bitterness springing up causes trouble, and by it many be defiled."

May I ask you a question? How would meekness respond to the discipline of God? Meekness always responds to God in submission and trust. It does not fight or struggle. It does not contend with God. It realizes that the insults and injuries which men may inflict upon it are filtered through fingers of love, permitted and used by God for chastening and purifying. There it is: the key to bitterness! Bitterness comes when you do not bow in submission before God, when you resist His chastening hand, when you do not endure and persevere. Bitterness comes when you fall short of the grace of God. To endure means to abide under, not to run away. In meekness we can persevere because we see everything as coming from God and, therefore, having a divine purpose. O Beloved, are you enduring, or are you running away?

What does it mean to come short of the grace of God? First let's define *grace*. You have often heard the definition that grace is unmerited favor, and that it is. Grace is God's favor to us that we did not merit, earn, or deserve in any way.

But there is another definition of grace that I just love and I want to share that with you. "Grace is all that Christ is, made available to me." Therefore, Beloved, for you to fall short of the grace of God is for you to fail to appropriate all that God has for you. Romans 5:2 says that when you were saved you obtained an introduction by faith into the grace of God in which you stand. There it is! Everything that you will ever need, made available to you! You are standing in God's adequacy for every situation of life. To fall short then of the grace of God, is to fail to appropriate that in which you stand. It's just a matter of stooping down and in faith scooping it up because you stand with all the grace of God surrounding you. So stoop and scoop!

In 2 Corinthians 12:1–10 Paul tells about a time when the Lord disciplined him after he was caught up into the third heaven. Paul saw revelations that were so great that God did not want Paul to exalt himself beyond measure. Therefore, God gave Paul a thorn in the flesh, a messenger of Satan to buffet him. That thorn in the flesh was very hard to bear and Paul went to the Lord three times, asking Him to take it away. What was God's answer? "And He has said to me, 'My grace is sufficient for you, for power is perfected in weakness.'" (2 Corinthians 12:9). The perfect tense of the Greek verb "has said" shows us that what God was saying to Paul was, "Don't ask Me again to remove this thorn in the flesh. This is My answer and it stands. My grace is sufficient for you, Paul, for power is perfected in weakness."

O Beloved, do you see it? What God is saying to Paul, He is saying to you. When you come under the discipline of the Lord, when God takes you through the refining process to make you into the image of His Son, know this: His grace is sufficient. He will not give you more than you can bear. This is the promise of 1 Corinthians 10:13, "No temptation (trial or testing) has overtaken you but such as is common to man; and God is faithful, who will not allow you to be tempted beyond what you are able, but with the temptation will provide the way of escape also, that you may be able to endure it." You can endure it because His grace is sufficient!

When then does bitterness come? Bitterness comes when we fail to be meek, when we fail to submit to the chastening hand of our Father, when we fail to give thanks in everything, when we come short of the grace of God.

If you are bitter, it is because someone has disappointed you or hurt you and you failed to see that it had come into your life filtered through fingers of love. You failed to see that God in His sovereignty permitted it. You failed to bow the knee in meekness and say, "My Lord, if it pleases Thee, it pleases me." You failed to give thanks always for all things.

So how can you get rid of that root of bitterness? It's as easy as confession and forgiveness. But you say, "Kay, that's not easy." All right. Then it's as close as willful obedience to God.

Will you obey?

Will you confess to God that you have fallen short of the grace of God? Will you confess that you have allowed a root of bitterness to spring up in you? And will you call upon God and ask Him to remove that root of bitterness and to fill you with His Holy Spirit? For the fruit of the Spirit is what? "Love, joy, peace. . . ." Then you must forgive. In your heart you must fully forgive whoever has transgressed against you. You may even have to say, "God, I forgive You," because your complaint may be with God alone.

"But I can't!" you say? No, Beloved, it's not that you can't, but that you *won't*. There is a big difference. Know this: If you do not forgive others, God cannot forgive you. So you can forgive and you must forgive. The question is, will you?

Meekness—the sure cure for bitterness. What is the one thing that you have learned this week that has meant the most to you? Write out a prayer thanking God for that one precious insight.

# 8 - Hungering and Thirsting for Righteousness

## DAY 1

The Sermon on the Mount is a radical teaching that threw Jesus' listeners off their feet. Why? Because He called for a righteousness that exceeded the righteousness of the scribes and Pharisees (Matthew 5:20). He redefined true blessedness, happiness. Those who listened saw that it was not a happiness of circumstances, but a happiness that came because of who they were. It was not attained through self-righteousness. It was not for those esteemed independent, aggressive, or sure of themselves—but blessedness was for the poor in spirit, for the mourners, for the meek, for the hungry, for the merciful, for the pure in heart, for the peacemakers, and for the persecuted.

The Sermon on the Mount explains the true intent of the Law. It is a law that goes beyond external obedience to the heart. It cancels the natural responses of men and calls for supernatural behavior. That's why Jesus said, "Be ye therefore perfect, even as your Father which is in heaven is perfect" (Matthew 5:48, KJV).

As we move into the sixth chapter of Matthew we see that Jesus re-evaluated true piety and godliness. Godliness was not to be paraded before men. Acts of worship were for God's eyes and praise alone! He caused men to examine the thrust of their lives. What were true treasures? Who really was their master? They couldn't serve more than one. And to what were they giving themselves and their energies?

According to Matthew 7, Jesus knew that righteousness could lead to hypocritical judging. So He carefully warned His listeners to make sure that they took the beam out of their own eye before they sought to take the mote out of their brother's eye. He wanted them to know that those who have inherited the kingdom of heaven only need ask, seek, and knock. After all, God was now their Father and it was His delight to give what was good to them who ask Him. Finally in one short sentence, recorded in verse 12, Jesus gave them the true interpretation of the Law and the Prophets.

Then came the invitation to enter in by the narrow gate. They need not be amazed that few would find it, for most would go by the broad way that led to destruction. In a staccato process Jesus clearly set before His hearers two ways, two gates, two responses, two fruits. He showed them that the kingdom of heaven does not belong to those who call Him "Lord, Lord," but to those who live under His lordship. Hearing and obeying brings righteousness.

His statement created either disbelief and a walking away, or it aroused a genuine hunger and thirst for righteousness. This, Beloved, is our topic of study for the week. " 'Blessed are those who hunger and thirst for righteousness, for they shall be satisfied' " (Matthew 5:6).

What I have just given you is a brief overview of the Sermon on the Mount. It's important that you keep it continually in mind so that you look at each of the Beatitudes in the context of the whole Sermon. Your assignment today is to read through Matthew 5, 6, and 7. As you do, remember this overview and note how it capsulizes the content of the Sermon on the Mount. Then go to your Father and ask Him to show you what it really means to hunger and thirst after righteousness. Briefly write down what He shows you.

## DAY 2

What does it mean to hunger and thirst after righteousness?

Hunger and thirst are cravings of the body that must be satisfied if life is to be sustained. And there, Beloved, is the key. The Sermon on the Mount clearly shows us that unless we have a righteousness that surpasses the righteousness of the scribes and Pharisees, we shall in no way attain to eternal life. The Sermon on the Mount is all about the righteous life-style of those who belong to the kingdom of heaven.

To what degree, then, are we to desire this righteousness? To the same degree that we hunger after food, and thirst after water! If we are going to have a righteousness that will bring life, then we must crave it with the intensity of hunger and thirst. Are you thinking, *That sure does eliminate a lot of people, doesn't it?* Yes, it does. Now you can understand why Jesus says that the way is very narrow and the gate is very small!

The tense of the Greek verbs translated "hunger" and "thirst" shows us that this hunger and thirst for righteousness is not a one-time action; it is to be a continual habit of life. As one meal does not satisfy you for the rest of your life or even for the rest of the week, so one initial hungering and thirsting for righteousness cannot satisfy you for life. It is to be a day-by-day occurrence. Jesus chose the words *hunger* and *thirst* because everyone understands them.

Beloved, is there within you a hunger and a thirst, a craving for righteousness?

What is righteousness? The word for *righteousness* in the Greek is used of whatever is right or just in itself and therefore conforms to the revealed will of God. Further definitions will help you to have a fuller understanding of what God means. Righteousness is whatever God says is to be acknowledged and obeyed by man. Note: It is what *God says,* not what *man thinks!* Righteousness is the sum total of all the requirements of God. Righteousness is also used to refer to a man's religious duties. We see this in Matthew 6 where Jesus tells us to beware of practicing our righteous acts such as almsgiving, praying, and fasting, to be seen of men. Finally, as we have seen before, righteousness is an attribute of God. It is the very essence of God's being. To hunger and thirst after righteousness is to have an inherent, inbred longing to please God. Yet, when I say inherent, I don't mean that we're born with that longing, but it is a longing that God puts within our hearts to cause us to seek after Him. Finally, when we come to God, it becomes inherent and inbred through the new birth. To hunger and thirst after righteousness is to desire with all our being to live and walk the way God says to live and walk. It is to crave God. It is to crave holiness.

Now I will ask you again. "Is there within you a hunger and thirst after righteousness?" Your answer may be, "Kay, I'm not sure." Well, before this week is finished, Beloved, we'll be talking about how you can know for sure if it's there. If it is there, you'll find out what you can do to increase it. And if it's not there, I pray that God will show you how it can be.

In the United States of America it is hard for most of us to understand the intensity of these two words, *hungering* and *thirsting.* We live in a land of abundance. We have lots of drinking fountains and certainly an ample supply of soft drink machines. However, if we could go back to Jesus' day, we would see that those people really understood what it was to have an intense craving for food and an overwhelming thirst for water. Often, parched lips blessed God for wells that brought welcome relief from the intense heat of the Judean hills.

A marvelous biography that comes out of London is the story of Pastor Hsi who lived during the 1878 famine which almost devastated the provinces of North China. At that time he had not yet become a Christian. He had been a proud Confucian scholar who was highly respected in his community and often sought out for his wisdom. He was seized with a horrible illness which brought him great pain, and his friends urged him to try opium for relief. However, having witnessed the awful ravishes of the opium habit he resisted this temptation. He lived among men who had been literally destroyed by opium and were totally worthless to society. As his pain became greater and unending, his advisors pressed him, "You need not smoke it constantly; just take a little until you are better. It will then be quite easy to give it up." So Hsi yielded, and became an opium addict. When the famine hit in 1878 he only managed to survive because he grew opium and men would sell their very souls to support their habits.

In the famine, 70 million human beings were starving. "During that journey," one man recorded, "we saw scenes that have left an indelible impression of horror on the mind. . . ." He went on:

> We passed men, once strong and well-dressed, staggering over the frozen ground with only a few rags to shield them from the piercing wind. Their feeble steps, emaciated bodies and wild looks told only too plainly that they were about to spend their last night upon earth. As we passed along the road in the early morning we saw the victims of the preceding night lying dead and stiff where they fell. Upon that road we saw men writhing in the last agonies of death. No one pitied them; no

one cared for them; such sights had long ago become too common. There were hundreds of corpses lying by the roadside. . . . Families were broken up; the wife sold; the children sold or cast out on the mountainside to perish, while the men wandered about in the vain search for food. The whole district through which we passed (three or four hundred miles) was in the same condition.[9]

It was so bad that men did not go out in the streets alone lest someone attack them, kill them, and drag them home to eat them.

Early in 1878, *The London Times* carried this report, as quoted in *Pastor Hsi:*

It is stated on authority which cannot be questioned, that seventy millions of human beings are now starving in the famine-stricken provinces of North China. The imagination fails to cope with a calamity so gigantic. The inhabitants of the United Kingdom and the United States combined hardly number seventy millions. To think of the teeming populations of these lands, all crowded into an area very little greater than that of France, starving and eating earth, with no food to be had, and with no hope of succour, is enough to freeze the mind with horror.[10]

This, Beloved, is the intense hunger that God is talking about. A hunger that has to have food or it dies. Not a hunger that decides whether it wants a third helping or not.

Pastor Hsi is a living example to us of one who hungered and thirsted after righteousness. Under the direction of Hudson Taylor, the China Inland Mission sent missionaries into North China. In his desire to reach the Confucian scholars, one of these missionaries offered a goodly sum of silver as a prize to those who would propound six theses on various biblical subjects. Each contestant would be supplied a packet of Christian books and tracts so that they might thoroughly study the subject. The winner would have to appear in person in order to collect his prize of silver. Hsi won every prize! As a result, the missionary invited Hsi to become his translator and so Hsi was continually thrust into the Word of God. That, plus the fact that he lived in the missionary's house, was God's means of drawing Hsi into His kingdom.

I pray that you will not only read with your eyes but that you will listen with your hearts as I share directly from the book. Do you remember the first four beatitudes?

" 'Blessed are the poor in spirit ...' "
" 'Blessed are those that mourn ...' "
" 'Blessed are the meek ...' "
" 'Blessed are those who hunger and thirst for righteousness. ...' "

We have seen that there is a definite order to the Beatitudes; they show the progression of God's work in our hearts as we come to Him. As you read, note in the margin any manifestations of the Beatitudes you see in Pastor Hsi's life.

> Gradually as he [Hsi] read, the life of Jesus seemed to grow more real and full of interest and wonder, and he began to understand that this mighty Savior was no mere man as he had once imagined, but God, the very God, taking upon Him mortal flesh. Doubts and difficulties were lost sight of. The old, unquenchable desire for better things, for deliverance from sin, self, and the fear of death, for light upon the dim, mysterious future, came back upon him as in earlier years. And yet the burden of his guilt, the torment of an accusing conscience, and bondage to the opium-habit he loathed but could not conquer, grew more and more intolerable.

> At last the consciousness of his unworthiness became so overwhelming that he could bear it no longer and placing the Book [the Bible] reverently before him, he fell upon his knees on the ground, and with so many tears followed the sacred story. It was beginning then to dawn upon his soul that this wonderful, divine, yet human Sufferer, in all the anguish of His bitter cross and shame, had something personally to do with him, with his sin and sorrow and need.

> And so, upon his knees, the once proud, self-satisfied Confucianist read on until he came to "the place called Gethsemane," and the God man, alone, in that hour of His supreme agony at midnight in the Garden. Then the fountains of his long-sealed

heart were broken up. The very presence of God overshadowed him. In the silence he seemed to hear the Savior's cry—"My soul is exceedingly sorrowful, even unto death": and into his heart there came the wonderful realization—"He loved me, and gave Himself for me." Then, suddenly, as he himself records, the Holy Spirit influenced his soul, and "with tears that flowed and would not cease" he bowed and yielded himself, unreservedly, to the world's Redeemer, as his Savior and his God. . . .

He saw Him then, not only as his Savior, but as his absolute Owner, his Master, his Lord. . . .

Immediately upon his conversion the conviction came clearly to the scholar's mind that his opium-habit must at once be broken. There seems to have been no parleying about it. Ever since he first entered the missionary's household, his conscience had troubled him on the subject. . . .

But at that time he knew of no power that could enable him to cleanse himself from the degrading vice. Now all was different. He belonged to Christ, and there could be no doubt as to the will of his new Master. . . . Of course he knew well what leaving off opium-smoking would involve. But there was no shrinking; no attempt at half measures. He saw it must be sacrificed at once, entirely, and forever. Then came the awful conflict. . . .

As hour after hour went by, his craving for the poison became more intense than the urgency of hunger or thirst. Acute anguish seemed to render the body asunder, accompanied by faintness and exhaustion that nothing could relieve. Water streamed from the eyes and nostrils. Extreme depression overwhelmed him. Giddiness came on, with shivering, and aching pains, or burning thirst. For seven days and nights he scarcely tasted food and was quite unable to sleep. Sitting or lying he could get no rest. The agony became almost unbearable; and all the while he knew that a few whiffs of the opium-pipe would waft him at once into delicious dreams. . . .

At last, in the height of his distress, it seemed to be revealed to him that the anguish that he was suffering arose not merely from physical causes, but that behind it all lay concealed the opposition of some mighty spiritual force; that he was in fact, hard pressed by the devil, who was using this opium craving as a weapon for his destruction. . . .

Then how utterly did the helpless man cast himself on God. Refusing to be dragged away one step from his only refuge, he fought out the battle in the very presence of his new-found Savior. . . .

"Devil, what can you do against me? My life is in the hands of God. And truly I am willing to break off opium and die, but not willing to continue in sin and live!"

In his most suffering moments he would frequently groan out loud: "Though I die, I will never touch it again!"

At last, after many days of anguish, his attention was attracted by some verses in his open Bible telling about "the Comforter"; and, as he read, it was borne in upon his mind that He, the Holy Spirit of God, was the mighty power expressly given to strengthen men. Then and there, in utter weakness, he cast himself on God. . . . He did not understand much, but he had grasped the supreme fact that the Holy Spirit could help him, making impossible things possible, and overcoming all the power of the enemy. And there as he prayed in the stillness, the wonderful answer was given. Suddenly a tide of life and power seemed to sweep into his soul. . . . the Holy Spirit came, flooding his heart with peace.[11]

This, Beloved, is what it means to hunger and thirst after righteousness. It means that you just have to be right with God no matter what it costs! It is a craving that must be satisfied if life is to be sustained!

## DAY 3

As we come to this fourth beatitude, " 'Blessed are those who hunger and thirst for righteousness . . . ,' " it seems that we reach a pinnacle in our relationship with God. The first four beatitudes—poverty of spirit, mourning, meekness, and hungering and thirsting for righteousness—are certainly Godward. And it seems that this hungering and thirsting for righteousness then becomes the forward thrust for the beatitudes that follow: desiring to be merciful, pure in heart, a peacemaker, and as a result, being persecuted. I have drawn a little diagram below to illustrate what I am saying to you.

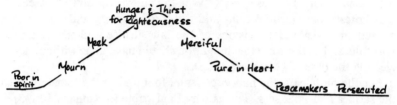

Dr. D. Martyn Lloyd-Jones in his *Studies in the Sermon on the Mount,* said this of hungering and thirsting after righteousness:

> This beatitude follows logically from the previous ones; it is a statement to which all the others lead. It is the logical conclusion to which they come and it is something for which we should all be profoundly thankful and grateful to God. I do not know of a better test that anyone can apply to himself or herself in this whole matter of the Christian profession than a verse like this. If this verse is to you one of the most blessed statements of the whole of Scripture you can be quite sure you are a Christian; if it is not, then you had better examine the foundations again.[12]

We need to be aware of the fact that there are two kinds of righteousness so that we do not get confused and think that we have the genuine when we do not, and thereby miss the kingdom of heaven. There is (1) a self-righteousness, and there is (2) a righteousness that comes from God.

Self-righteousness is living by your version of what you think is required of man. In the Sermon on the Mount, Jesus deals very pointedly with this kind of righteousness. He does it repeatedly in Chapter 5 when He says "You have heard . . . but I say unto you. . . ." They had heard from the scribes and Pharisees that there was a certain code of righteousness to which they must adhere if they would be granted entrance into the kingdom of heaven. Therefore, Jesus had to correct their thinking.

The righteousness of the scribes and Pharisees was a self-righteousness. God's righteousness went far beyond self-righteousness. That's why in Matthew 23, he constantly said, "Woe to you, scribes and

Pharisees," for they kept the Law only to the limit of their desires. Theirs was an external, not an internal righteousness. This couldn't be more clear than when Jesus says, "Woe to you, scribes and Pharisees, hypocrites! For you tithe mint and dill and cummin, and have neglected the weightier provisions of the law; justice and mercy and faithfulness; but these are the things you should have done without neglecting the others" (Matthew 23:23).

For the most part, the nation of Israel followed in the footsteps of the scribes and Pharisees. This is why Paul wrote in Romans 10:1-3, "Brethren, my heart's desire and my prayer to God for them is for their salvation. For I bear them witness that they have a zeal for God, but not in accordance with knowledge. For not knowing about God's righteousness, and seeking to establish their own, they did not subject themselves to the righteousness of God." Do you see the contrast, Beloved? They were depending on their own righteousness instead of God's righteousness.

What about you? What kind of righteousness do you have? Is it your own or is it God's? Do you live by a set of dos and don'ts, your own little code of righteousness? Because you do certain things, or because you don't do certain things, do you consider yourself righteous? And do you judge the righteousness of others by your code?

For example, in our area of the country, there are some who evaluate women according to the length of their skirts, and who judge men by the length of their hair. Some would not be caught in a movie theater. Others feel it's a sin to go "mixed bathing." (Let me explain that one—it means men and women in the same swimming pool.) Others measure their righteousness by the number of times that they attend church during the week. Every Sunday, in many churches, nickels and noses are counted. Now, whether a man deems these things right or wrong is not important. The issue is this: These things comprise an external code of righteousness. What's going on in the hearts of people that set up these various codes? Do they judge and criticize others? Do they cut them down or murder them with their tongues? What kind of thoughts are harbored in the mind, in the heart? If the heart does not match the outward performance, then it is a case of self-righteousness. It is a righteousness that is lived by the letter of the Law rather than a righteousness based on faith.

Self-righteousness is always man's interpretation or addition to the clear-cut teaching of God's Word. It's a problem of tacking on a whole lot of extra laws and then saying that if you are really going to be righteous, you must keep all these rules. It is judging others by your standard rather than God's. How deceptive it is! It becomes so external that it blinds us to the righteousness based on faith, a righteousness that transforms the heart. Let me say it again; self-righteousness is living by your version of what you think is required by God and then imposing that standard on others and judging their righteousness by whether or not they march to the same drumbeat as you.

And what about God's righteousness? That is a whole different story! God's righteousness begins with a dissatisfaction, a yearning. When sin's presence within is finally realized, one has an inner longing to be righteous. When a glimpse is gained of the holiness of God as it happened to Isaiah (Chapter 6), then comes an awareness of self. One sees where he really stands. God's standard of perfection has been missed. Things have been left undone which should have been done and things have been done which ought not to have been done. All of our righteousness is as filthy rags in God's sight. We are unclean!

Finally the realization comes: "God, You alone are righteous." And so a hunger and a thirst for righteousness is awakened. But where is that hunger and thirst to be satisfied? We know we cannot attain it, so we run to the fountain of living waters and we receive the gift of the indwelling Holy Spirit who alone can lead us into a life of righteousness by leading us into the truth.

It was not without purpose that Jesus made such a proclamation as on that last day of the Feast of Tabernacles. During this great feast the people went to the pool of Siloam each day for seven days and there they filled pitchers with water. As they walked to the temple, they sang Psalms 103 through 118. Upon arriving at the temple they would pour the water on the altar, symbolizing (1) the early and latter rains and (2) the pouring out of the Holy Spirit:

> Now on the last day, the great day of the feast, Jesus stood and cried out, saying, "If any man is thirsty, let him come to Me and drink. He who believes in Me, as the Scripture said, 'From his innermost being shall flow rivers of living water.'" But this He spoke of the Spirit, whom those who believed in Him were to receive; for the Spirit was not yet given, because Jesus was not yet glorified.
>
> *John 7:37–39*

It's very interesting to note that when Jesus said, "let him come to Me and drink" that the verbs *come* and *drink* are in the present tense. It literally means, "Let him keep coming to Me and let him keep drinking." Jesus is the fountainhead of God's righteousness. O Beloved, do you see it? You can be as righteous as you want to be. It is simply a matter of total dependence upon God and a matter of yearning more and more for Him.

Ours is to be an ever-increasing hunger and thirst. The more we get, the more we want; the more we want, the more we get. This is what Jesus was saying to His hearers as He told the parable of the sower in Matthew 13. " 'For whoever has, to him shall more be given, and he shall have an abundance; but whoever does not have, even what he has shall be taken away from him.' " (Matthew 13:12).

What did He mean? He had just told the parable. Only one type of soil—*good* soil—yielded a crop. Matthew 13:23 says, " 'And the one . . . brings forth, some a hundredfold, some sixty, and some thirty.' " What made the difference? It wasn't the seed, because Jesus tells us in Matthew 13:19 that the seed is the word of the kingdom, the truth of righteous living. It was the soil's receptivity to the seed that made the difference. Mark 4:20 makes it a little clearer: " 'And those are the ones on whom seed was sown on the good ground, and they hear the word and accept it, and bear fruit, thirty, sixty, and a hundredfold.' "

Did you notice the words "accept it"? Why don't you underline them. Obviously the more I accept, the greater the crop will be. That's why Jesus goes on to say in Mark 4:24,25, " 'Take care what you listen to. By your standard of measure it shall be measured to you; and more shall be given you besides. For whoever has, to him shall more be given; and whoever does not have, even what he has shall be taken away from him.' "

Do you want to be righteous? Then receive what God has for you. Be obedient to the revealed will of God, not just with an external obedience, but from the heart. God will give you more and more. But neglect it, refuse some of it, and you will have a meager harvest.

As we close today, I want you to read Psalms 63:1–5 and meditate on it in the light of this fourth beatitude, and all that you have learned thus far. Then pray those first five verses back to God, making them the very cry of your heart.

## DAY 4

How can you be sure that you have a genuine hunger and thirst for God's righteousness? First of all, you will be aware of a longing for God and His Word. Psalms 42:1,2 illustrates this well. Write out these two verses below.

1. Now turn to Psalms 27:4 and tell me what was the "one thing" that David desired above all else.

2. Read Psalms 119:1–8, 40, 123. The words *law, judgments, precepts, statutes, commandments,* and *testimonies* are all references to the Word of God. What do you note in these verses about the Psalmist and his relationship to God and His Word?

When you have a genuine hunger and thirst for righteousness, you will also long for God and His Word. You will also love righteousness and hate sin. You cannot love both righteousness and sin; they are incompatible. Therefore, you will hate wickedness because it keeps you from righteousness. Psalms 45:6, 7 say, "Thy throne, O God, is forever and ever; a scepter of uprightness is the scepter of Thy kingdom. Thou hast loved righteousness, and hated wickedness. . . ." Righteousness loves the things that God loves and hates the things that God hates.

Psalm 101 graphically sets before us in detail the standards of the righteous. Read Psalm 101 and then list on the next page six things that the Psalmist has determined to do because he wants to walk blamelessly before God.

1.

2.

3.

4.

5.

6.

The third and last evidence of the presence of righteousness is a longing to do God's will. If you are genuinely hungering and thirsting after righteousness, you must know and walk in obedience to the will of God. The highest example of hungering and thirsting for righteousness is seen in Jesus when He says, "My food is to do the will of Him who sent Me, and to accomplish His work" (John 4:34). What about you? What is your food? Calling Jesus "Lord" is not a guarantee of true righteousness, but treating Him as Lord, longing to do His will, is. This is why Jesus says, "Not everyone who says to Me, 'Lord, Lord,' will enter the kingdom of heaven; but he who does the will of My Father who is in heaven" (Matthew 7:21).

If the Holy Spirit is truly within, you will hunger and thirst for righteousness. You will know He is there because you will have a longing for God and His Word. You will love righteousness and hate sin. You will long to do His will. Now, where do you stand? Is the kingdom of heaven yours? Then you have seen your total poverty of spirit. There is a mourning over sin. You have submitted yourself in meekness to His lordship. And you hunger and thirst for righteousness. However, if this is not the case, then you need to see your poverty of spirit. You need to see the self-righteousness that is keeping you from the kingdom of heaven. You need to see your filthy rags. You need to fall prostrate at the feet of God and say:

God, I have no righteousness of my own. There is no way that I could ever please You in and of myself. God, I have walked in independence and have lived my own life. I abhor myself and my actions and I want to turn to You. I am a sinner.

Save me; make me a saint; set me apart for Yourself. Fill me with Your righteousness.

O Beloved, if that is your heart's cry, God will not turn you away. Walk into His open arms and record this as the day of your salvation. Write out your prayer of commitment.

## DAY 5

The last thing we want to look at this week, Beloved, is a list of seven things that you can do to increase your hunger and thirst for righteousness. As we begin, pray with the psalmist,

Search me, O God, and know my heart; try me and know my anxious thoughts; and see if there be any hurtful way in me, and lead me in the everlasting way.

*Psalms 139:23, 24*

If you are going to have an increasing hunger and thirst for righteousness, you must first get rid of the idols in your heart. An idol is anything that stands between you and God and keeps you from following Him fully—anything that usurps the rightful place of God so that God no longer has preeminence in your life. Idols do not necessarily have six heads and twenty-four arms. Idols are not only simple fetishes such as sticks and stones worshiped by bushmen. They can also be television sets, houses, golf clubs, a job, a man, a woman, a child, a hope, a dream, an ambition.

Note what Ezekiel 14:3 says, " 'Son of man, these men have set up their idols *in their hearts,* and have put right before their faces the stumbling block of their iniquity' " (italics added). An idol is a matter of affection; you love it more than you love God. Or you devote yourself to it more than you devote yourself to God. "If then you have been raised up with Christ, keep seeking the things above, where Christ is, seated at the right hand of God. Set your mind on the things above, not on the things that are on earth" (Colossians 3:1, 2). Are there any idols in your heart that are keeping you from hungering and thirsting after righteousness? If so, list them below and then, in prayer, smash them at the feet of God.

If you want to increase your hunger and thirst for righteousness, secondly you must watch very carefully what you put before your eyes. "For all that is in the world, the lust of the flesh and the lust of the eyes and the boastful pride of life, is not from the Father, but is from the world." Therefore, "do not love the world, nor the things in the world. If anyone loves the world, the love of the Father is not in him" (1 John 2:15, 16). As we will see when we study Matthew Chapter 6, the lamp of the body is the eye. We need to sing the same chorus that the little children sing in Sunday School, don't we?

Be careful little eyes what you see,
Be careful little eyes what you see;
For the Father up above is looking down in love,
So be careful little eyes what you see.

Why don't you pray Psalms 119:37, 38. "Turn away my eyes from looking at vanity, and revive me in Thy ways. Establish Thy word to Thy servant, as that which produces reverence for Thee."

Thirdly, count all things as loss for the excellency of knowing Jesus Christ. Take a minute and read Philippians 3:7–10. As you do, you will see that hungering and thirsting after righteousness is not just a matter of forsaking certain things. It is a matter of embracing others—primarily one thing, knowing your God.

This leads us to the fourth thing. You must be a pursuer of one thing. Take time (and I mean do take time) to read Luke 10:38–42. You must read it now, or you won't understand what I'm saying. For clarity's sake, let me ask you a few questions about this passage.

1. What was Martha's problem?

2. What was Mary doing?

Did you see that the very thing that Martha was doing for Jesus drew her away from the Lord? That's what "distracted" means. And this can happen to you. You can become so busy, so involved in the work of the Lord, that you lose your hunger and thirst for righteousness. Remember, *doing* is secondary in the Christian life. The primary thing is *being*. What you do will be worth only as much as who you are!

What was Jesus' word to Martha? " 'Martha, Martha, thou art anxious and troubled about many things: But one thing is needful.' " There we have it! "One thing is needful." As you see, it's a matter of choice. " 'Mary hath chosen that good part, which shall not be taken away from her' " (Luke 10:41, 42 KJV). If you want to increase your hunger and thirst for righteousness, you need to pursue one thing; to "know Him, and the power of His resurrection and the fellowship of His sufferings, [and to become] conformed to His death" (Philippians 3:10).

> I rise before dawn and cry for help;
> I wait for Thy words.
> My eyes anticipate the night watches,
> That I may meditate on Thy word.
>
> *Psalms 119:147, 148*

Fifthly, you need to watch the company you keep. First Corinthians 15:33 says, "Do not be deceived: 'Bad company corrupts good morals.' " Righteousness is living morally according to God's standard. What friends do you have who distract you from your pursuit of holiness? " 'Come out from their midst and be separate,' says the Lord . . . 'and I will welcome you. And I will be a father to you' " (2 Corinthians 6:17, 18).

Since Jesus is the fountainhead of all righteousness, the sixth thing we must do is keep coming to Him. We saw this in John 7:37. I want you to see it again in Isaiah 55:1–3.

> Ho! Every one who thirsts, come to the waters; and you who have no money come, buy and eat. Come, buy wine and milk without money and without cost. Why do you spend money for what is not bread, and your wages for what does not satisfy? Listen carefully to me, and eat what is good, and delight yourself in abundance. Incline your ear and come to Me. Listen, that you may live.

I love that line, "Why do you spend money for what is not bread, and your wages for what does not satisfy?" Doesn't that describe America? Have you ever just stood in the malls and watched the people looking, desiring, and buying? Sometimes I stand there and I think, "Lord, how many of these people really know You?" Oh, if only we would lay aside our stereo headphones and turn off the noise of the television and the radio . . . if we would leave the malls, get out of the stadiums and go be alone and be quiet. If we would just come to Him, then we would find that satisfaction we so long for. " 'I, the LORD, am your God, who brought you up from the land of Egypt; open your mouth wide and I will fill it" (Psalms 81:10).

Finally, Beloved, if you want to increase your hunger and thirst for righteousness, receive what He gives you. I've already shown you this in Matthew 13:12, but it bears repeating. " 'For whoever has, to him shall more be given. . . .' " What has God told you to do? What has He shown you from His Word that you are to obey and you have said no? Know this, that a continual no will diminish your appetite, your hunger for righteousness.

Are you hungering and thirsting for righteousness? I leave you with a promise uttered from the very throne of God: "you will be satisfied."

# 9 - How Can I Be Merciful ... Pure?

## DAY 1

He clutched his blanket tighter about him. His arms hugged his drawn-up knees, not so much to stop the trembling, but rather to put flesh next to flesh. Curled up like a ball, he sat in the corner of his damp, frigid cell. He'd been so preoccupied with the cold that he hadn't heard the approaching footsteps. Startled, he watched the form of a bleeding, beaten human being tossed in the opposite corner like a filthy rag. His new cell-mate was naked from the waist up. Sobbing, he stayed in his corner, head down. As the man surveyed the condition of his new cell-mate he thought, *He'll never make it through the night. He'll be dead by morning.* Then came that still, small familiar voice.

"Give him your blanket."

"But, Lord, if I give him my blanket I'll not survive the night."

"I know. But you will be with Me. Give him your blanket."

The human ball slowly stretched out, the stature of a man. The blanket slipped from his bent shoulders. He walked across the cell and handed the man his blanket.

"Here. The Lord Jesus Christ told me to give you my blanket." For the first time he saw the man's face. It was incredulous with hope.

Another corn of wheat had fallen into the ground! The giver of the blanket died; the recipient lived. He told the story over and over of how he had life through the loving mercy of another, and how he came to know God and His Son, Jesus Christ.

"Blessed are the merciful, for they shall receive mercy" (Matthew 5:7).

As we come to this fifth beatitude, you will notice that the remaining beatitudes take on a manward aspect. How do those who are poor in spirit respond to others? The answer is: with mercy, because God has been merciful to them. As Jesus set forth this beatitude before His disciples, He was not teaching them a new concept or a new condition for receiving mercy. The prophet had said long before, "With the merciful Thou wilt shew thyself merciful ..." 2 Samuel 22:26.

Several different Hebrew words in the Old Testament are translated "mercy" and "merciful." One of them depicts a heartfelt response by someone who has something to give to one who has a need. How well this is illustrated in the true story which I just told you. Another word, sometimes translated "mercy" in the King James Version, is rendered "kindness," "lovingkindness," "love," "unfailing love," or "loyalty," in other versions. Although there has been some debate among scholars about how it is to be translated, still it is apparent that love, mercy, and kindness are intertwined and cannot be separated from one another.

The New Testament word for merciful means "not simply possessed of pity but actively compassionate."[13] Mercy then is "an outward manifestation of pity; it assumes need on the part of him who receives it, and the resources adequate to meet the need on the part of him who shows it."[14]

To a degree, in and of ourselves we can act in mercy. And yet that mercy will always be limited by our humanity until we come to know Jesus Christ.

True mercy has its origin in God. When we studied the character of God we saw that one of His attributes was His mercy. In the light of this, I want to share something that is important and yet may seem a little heavy. If you can understand it, it will help you tremendously to fully understand how mercy behaves.

Do you remember the tabernacle that Moses built under God's direction? Behind the veil, in the Holy of Holies, was the Ark of the Covenant, a box made of acacia wood and covered with gold. (See the drawing of the tabernacle on the next page.)

On top of that box was a lid called "the Mercy Seat." Inside the Ark were the tables of stone which bore the Ten Commandments, Aaron's rod which had budded, and a pot of manna. When God looked down and saw those Ten Commandments which man had broken, it called forth His just judgment. Man was condemned because he had transgressed the Law. However, God, because of His love, made provision for a Mercy Seat which covered the Ark of the Covenant.

Annually, on the Day of Atonement, the high priest would enter the Holy of Holies, once for his own sins, and once again for the sins of the people. He would sprinkle the blood of a bull and a goat on the Mercy Seat to make an atonement (or a covering) for their sins. All of this was

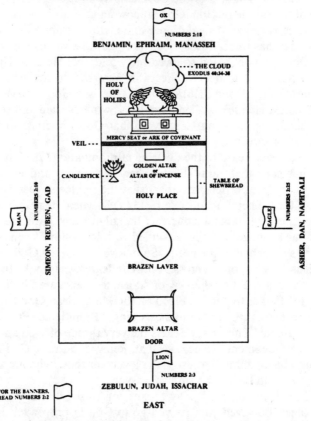

OX

NUMBERS 2:18

BENJAMIN, EPHRAIM, MANASSEH

···· THE CLOUD
EXODUS 40:34-38

HOLY
OF
HOLIES

MERCY SEAT or ARK OF COVENANT

VEIL ···

CANDLESTICK ··

GOLDEN ALTAR
or
ALTAR OF INCENSE

TABLE OF
SHEWBREAD

HOLY PLACE

MAN

NUMBERS 2:10

SIMEON, REUBEN, GAD

EAGLE

NUMBERS 2:25

ASHER, DAN, NAPHTALI

BRAZEN LAVER

BRAZEN ALTAR

DOOR

LION

NUMBERS 2:3

ZEBULUN, JUDAH, ISSACHAR

FOR THE BANNERS,
READ NUMBERS 2:2

EAST

a picture, pointing to something that was to come. It was a foreshadowing of Jesus' sacrifice at Calvary.

Read Hebrews 10:1–4. This is the sacrifice I was just explaining to you. The blood of bulls and goats was a shadow or a picture of Jesus' blood which would take away our sin (Hebrews 10:12).

Look at Hebrews 8:2–5. From that passage, how many tabernacles are there and where is each? Write it below.

We need to see that mercy has its origin in God. The earthly tabernacle that Moses pitched was patterned after the real or the true tabernacle in heaven. The Ark of the Covenant with the Mercy Seat was a picture of the throne of God. God is showing us that the very essence of His being is mercy. A God of love and mercy sits upon that throne. Because man has transgressed God's holy Law, he stands condemned before God. And yet "God so loved the world, that He gave His only begotten Son, that whoever believes in Him should not perish, but have eternal life" (John 3:16). Because God is a God of love and a God of mercy, He took pity on man. He saw man's need and sent His Son to shed His blood on Calvary so that God's holiness might be propitiated or satisfied.

Have you ever heard of the doctrine of propitiation? In simple language, it means that Jesus' blood, shed at Calvary and applied to God's Mercy Seat, propitiates or satisfies the righteous, just, holy demands of God. Therefore in Luke 18:13 (KJV), when the man cries out, "God be merciful to me a sinner," it literally means "God, be propitious to me a sinner." Mercy is bonded with love—love's compassion which acts on behalf of the needy. So in love and mercy God sent His Son, Jesus, to die upon the cross. After His death, Jesus took His blood and, as the priest did on the Day of Atonement, appeared in the presence of the Father to put His blood on the Mercy Seat. God looked at that blood and all the heavenly hosts sang, "Propitiated! Propitiated! God is satisfied!" The Mercy Seat is the very throne of God and it triumphs over judgment. Remember that, Beloved, because God is calling you to be merciful; not just to the lovely, or those who are kind to you, but even to those who sin against you.

We'll see it tomorrow. Today I want you to see that it was out of mercy that God saved you. As you go to God in prayer ask Him to open the eyes of your understanding so you will walk in mercy and thus receive mercy.


## DAY 2


Jesus' life was a continuous manifestation of the mercy of God. The Pharisees wanted to stone the woman who was caught in adultery, but Jesus, in mercy, pardoned her. When He saw the multitudes "He felt compassion for them because they were like sheep without a shepherd" (Mark 6:34). Compassion moved Him to heal them, to feed them, and to teach them, for He knew that man does not live by bread alone but by every word that proceeds out of the mouth of God. His mercy caused Him to call His disciples to beseech the Lord of the harvest to send out workers into His harvest. His life was one constant manifestation of the Godhead. If you had seen Him you had seen the Father. And God always acts in mercy because He is merciful. Thus, even when Jesus hung on the cross listening to the taunts of those who had sought His death, in mercy He cried out, " 'Father, forgive them . . .' " (Luke 23:34).

Mercy meets the need of forgiveness. How vital it is that you see this because you will not receive mercy unless you are merciful. And if you are going to be merciful, you must forgive others. Mercy and forgiveness are like Siamese twins with one heart. They can't be separated!

Matthew 18:21–35 makes this very clear. Take a few minutes to read those verses and, as you do, mark every use of the words *mercy, compassion, forgive,* and *forgave.* Then answer the questions below.

1. What particular situation prompted Jesus to tell this story?

2. What did the slave of the king see?

3. What did his fellow slave owe him?

4. What did the king do to the slave who owed him so much money?

5. What did the slave do to his fellow slave who owed him so little in comparison?

6. Why was the king upset with the man he had forgiven? What did he do as a result?

7. What is the point of the story according to Jesus? (verse 35)

This is a difficult passage, isn't it? Especially if there is someone we are not willing to really and truly forgive? It's hard because God is telling us that if we are not willing to forgive others then God is not going to forgive us. We see the same thing in Matthew 6:15 which says, " 'But if you do not forgive men, then your Father will not forgive your transgressions.' "

I have seen people argue this point, saying that this makes God's mercy conditional! But look at it. What does it say? Put it with Matthew 5:7: "Blessed are the merciful, for they shall receive mercy.' " What does that imply? It implies that if you are not merciful toward others, you are not going to receive mercy yourself. That has to be true or otherwise it means nothing to be blessed. If I can get mercy without being merciful, then why bother to be merciful? Mercy is not for the worthy; it's for the needy. And forgiveness is not based on worthiness.

Perhaps you're saying, "But you don't know how badly they have hurt me. You don't know how unjustly I have been treated!" I understand. I know it's hard. But let me take you back to God's throne. What is on it? A Mercy Seat. And that is where your sins were forgiven. When Jesus told the story in Matthew 18, He wanted to make a very vivid point. The slave owed the king ten million dollars and the king forgave it all. Are you sure you can't forgive? Are you sure you have had too much pain to be forgiving? O Beloved, have you never seen what your sin did to the heart of perfect Holiness? And yet what came from His Throne? Was it not love and mercy? As you have obtained mercy, will you be merciful? Don't read any further until you settle this with God.

Now let me share with you four ways that you can show mercy. To neglect any one of them is to fail to be merciful.

1. When you see a person in need and you can meet their need, do so (James 2:15, 16).

2. Fully forgive anyone who is indebted to you in his behavior or attitude (Colossians 3:12–15).

3. If you are going to be merciful then you need to give understanding rather than judgment. Ask yourself, "Have I sat where they are living?" (*See* Ezekiel 3:15).

4. Be merciful toward the character of others. We all have different personalities, different temperament types. Therefore, you need to be merciful and respond to others in the light of their personality need. Some people need assurance—give them assurance. Some people are insecure—confirm them. Some people are weak—support them (1 Thessalonians 5:14, 15).

"Grace, mercy, and peace be unto you." Grace is that unearned favor which saves us. Mercy is that undeserved favor which forgives us. And peace is that unsought favor which reconciles us.

O Beloved, there is a whole world of needy people out there. Many of them are rude, crude, obnoxious, and self-centered. They're lost people, destitute and desperate. They are people who don't deserve mercy, but who need it—who need forgiveness. Won't you tell God that you want to be merciful even as He is merciful? Mercy, remember, is not for the worthy but the needy.

### DAY 3

Do you want to see God, see Him as He really is? To know Him intimately? Do you want to behold Him face to face someday? Then you must be pure in heart. "Blessed are the pure in heart, for they shall see God" (Matthew 5:8). Purity of heart must precede the seeing. The mood of the Greek verb (indicative) for *see* means a certainty or a reality. You are going to be seeing God and God is going to be seeing you. God promises it is going to happen.

If only the pure in heart are going to see God, then we need to know what it means to be pure. And we need to know what God means when He talks about the heart. The word *pure* does not mean naturally pure; it means "pure as being cleansed." In other words, God is not saying that if I want to see Him I have to have a heart that has never been dirty or tainted. Rather, it is a purity that comes from having been cleansed. Aren't you thankful! I am! Otherwise, I would never see God! I've been too dirty!

The heart can refer to several things. However, in this instance, it refers to the seat of grief or joy, desires or affections, perceptions or thoughts, understanding or reasoning, imagination or conscience, intentions or purpose, will or faith.[15] It is used in all these various ways in the New Testament. Therefore, when we speak of purity of heart, it is purity of actions, purity of thoughts, purity of desires and motivations, purity of proper reasoning. If I am going to have a pure heart, I am going to have to think properly and reason properly. This goes along with the Scripture: "as (a man) thinketh in his heart, so is he" (Proverbs 23:7 KJV). That is why you have to "watch over your heart with all diligence, for from it flow the springs of life" (Proverbs 4:23). If you and I are going to see God continuously, then we must keep our hearts cleansed. The question is, how?

First, let's look at the initial cleansing of our hearts that comes at salvation. According to the New Covenant of grace, God's Law is written in our hearts and we receive a new heart (Jeremiah 31:33 and Ezekiel 36:26). 2 Corinthians 5:17 says, ". . . if any man is in Christ, he is a new creature; the old things passed away; behold, new things have come." You have a new heart, you're a new creature; yet, how do you live? Do you live in the light of the truth that your sins have been forgiven and God remembers them no more? Do you remember that your old man is dead and because of that you have been freed from sin's power (Romans 6:6, 7)? Discovering who you are in Christ Jesus and all that He has wrought for you can radically transform your walk.

Turn in your Bible to Hebrews 10:19–22. These verses talk about us walking through the veil into the Holy Place, or the Holy of Holies. In this passage we see that we enter the Holy of Holies by the blood of Jesus. If the high priest tried to enter without a blood sacrifice, God would kill him. Remember also how we saw that the tabernacle on earth is a picture, a type, or a shadow of the true tabernacle in heaven? Well, the veil of the Hebrew tabernacle was a picture to us of the flesh of Jesus Christ. It stood between man and God. God was showing us the truth of John 14:6: Jesus said, "I am the way, and the truth, and the life; no one comes to the Father, but through Me." He was also showing us the truth of 1 Timothy 2:5, that there is one God and one mediator between God and man—the Man, Christ Jesus. The only way that we can go into the presence of God is through Jesus. No man can come to the Father but by Him. Jesus is the way to God and is, therefore, our High Priest.

The author of Hebrews is telling us that we can have confidence or boldness to enter into the presence of God and stand before the throne of mercy because the blood of Jesus Christ has been put on that Mercy Seat. Therefore, since we have that confidence, we can draw near to God with a sincere heart in full assurance of faith.

You might say, "Oh, no, Kay, I couldn't do that. I'm too filthy. My heart is too deceitful and desperately wicked." And I would have to say, "Beloved, if you're a Christian, that's not true. According to Hebrews 10:22 your heart has been sprinkled clean from an evil conscience and your body has been washed with pure water. You've been purified, sanctified."

Look at Hebrews 10:14: "For by one offering He (Jesus) has perfected for all time those who are sanctified." Where does a pure heart begin so that you can continuously keep on seeing and beholding God? It begins with salvation. It begins with the sacrifice of the blood of the Lamb—the Lamb without spot or blemish (1 Peter 1:19).

Isn't that beautiful? Isn't it exciting to know that God has cleansed your heart so that you might see Him! Why don't you spend time today worshiping God, thanking Him for His Mercy Seat and for the rent veil of His flesh that allowed you to come to Him with a heart sprinkled clean from an evil conscience.

Do you know what I do sometimes, Beloved? I worship God by mentally walking through the tabernacle. Let me show you how.

First, I start at the altar of bronze which is a picture of the Cross of Jesus Christ. There I thank God for the Cross and all that it means to me—the love of God who gave His only begotten Son, the willingness of Jesus to die for me. Then I move behind the altar to the laver and thank God for the daily cleansing that I have through His pure Word. I thank Him that He has kept His Word pure and that it is a mirror showing me my spots and blemishes so that I might be made clean through the washing of the water of the Word.

Then I enter into the holy place and stop at the table of shewbread on the righthand side. I praise God for Jesus who is the Bread of Life, telling God that I want to feast on Him daily. I thank Him for His body which was broken for me. Then I cross to the left side to the menorah, the seven-branched candlestick, thanking Jesus that He is the Light of the world and that I don't have to walk in darkness if I walk as He walked. I thank Him for taking me out of darkness and into His marvelous light. I tell Him that I want to be filled with the oil of His Spirit so that I might burn brightly for Him. Then I walk to the altar of incense. I thank God that I have a great High Priest who ever lives to make intercession for me. I praise Him that He is a high priest who really feels my own infirmities, who was in every way tempted as I am, yet without sin.

Then, looking at the veil, I think of His flesh torn in two, the sacrifice of the New Covenant, and I thank Him for the new and living way whereby I can enter into the very presence of God. Standing before the Ark of the Covenant, I praise God for His throne and for the character of the One who sits upon the throne. I join the cherubim and the seraphim and the twenty-four elders as they "... do not cease to say, 'HOLY, HOLY, HOLY, is THE LORD GOD, THE ALMIGHTY, who was and who is and who is to come ... Worthy art Thou, our Lord and our God, to receive glory and honor and power; for Thou didst create all things, and because of Thy will they existed, and were created' " (Revelation 4:8, 11).

Walk through the tabernacle and praise Him!

## DAY 4

Having been cleansed by the blood of Jesus Christ from an evil conscience, how do you keep your heart pure? The first thing I want you to see is that you keep your heart cleansed through the Word of God. When the Word cleanses us, it cleanses from wrong thinking, wrong doctrine, and wrong behavior.

1. Look up Ephesians 5:26 and write it out below.

2. Look up John 17:17 and write it out below.


The word *sanctify* has the same basic root as the word *holy* and it means either holy or set apart.

3. According to these two verses, how are you made holy? How are you kept clean?


4. How often do you think that this cleansing is necessary? How much do you think it takes to make or keep you clean?


I have heard some people say, "Just spend three minutes a day alone with God." In a sense I understand what they mean. After all, three minutes with God is better than none. But the question is: "Are we selling God short? Are we selling God's Word short?" Is Deuteronomy 8:3 true when it says that ". . . man does not live by bread alone, but man lives by everything that proceeds out of the mouth of the LORD"? Was Paul a fool for laying down his life in order to declare to others the whole counsel of God? Is the Word of God truly ". . . profitable for teaching, for reproof, for correction, for training in righteousness, that the man of God may be adequate, equipped for every good work" (2 Timothy 3:16, 17)? In three minutes a day can I really present myself "approved to God as a workman who does not need to be ashamed, handling accurately the word of truth" (2 Timothy 2:15)?

You know, Beloved, why so many are so messed up, don't you? I believe it is because we have not esteemed God's Word more precious than our necessary food. We have not known His Word so that it has become a light to our feet and a lamp to our paths. Therefore, we have walked in darkness and have stumbled. I am absolutely amazed and appalled and grieved at the number of people who come to me after I have spoken and say, "But, Kay, I don't know these things. I didn't know that that's what God's Word said. I didn't realize that I was going against the will of God."

So many have been conformed to the world instead of being transformed by the renewing of their minds. That's why lives, homes, and relationships are in such disarray. Oh, do you see why I am so thankful for people like you; why I treasure you; why we at Precept Ministries devote our energies to establishing you in God's Word? It's vital if you're going to have a pure heart. Settle this with God. Talk to Him about it. But before you do, let me give you one more insight.

Your heart is also kept cleansed through confession. In 1 John 1:9 God says, "If we confess our sins, He is faithful and righteous to forgive us our sins and to cleanse us from all unrighteousness." *Confess* means to say the same thing or to speak the same word. Therefore, to confess our sins is to agree with God that what we have done is sin. To do that we name it as sin. We say, "God, I have permitted _____ to rule me and that is sin. I confess it as sin right now and I want to turn from that sin."

When we do this, we have a marvelous promise. Because God is faithful and because He is righteous, He forgives our sin. He looks at that blood of Jesus on the Mercy Seat, the blood that cleanses us from sin.

He also cleanses us from all unrighteousness. Have you ever wondered where you would stand with God if you couldn't confess some sin because you couldn't remember it? 1 John 1:9 promises you that when you confess every known sin then God cleanses you from *all* unrighteousness.

Isn't it wonderful to be pure? The reason so many people can't really see God and don't have an intimate relationship with Him is that their hearts are so defiled. They are so filled with the filth of this world—and I mean filth—that they have no spiritual sensitivity. That is why it is vital that you spend time being made clean every single day. Stand in the holy shower of God's Word and scrub yourself from head to toe. Get rid of the stench of this world. I promise you; it will transform you and your life will be such a sweet fragrance in the nostrils of God. Think about these things, Beloved. Talk to God about them. Do business with Him. If you have neglected His Word, then you need to confess that and then get into the habit of going through God's Word consistently. Study guides like this or Precept can help you, but you must also make sure that you read through God's Word consistently.

I love you. We'll talk more tomorrow.

# DAY 5

Confession helps you keep your heart pure before God. But if you want your heart to be totally cleansed so nothing stands between you and God, or you and others, then restitution may be necessary.

Does your heart sometimes condemn you? Are there things that you've done to others in the past that were wrong and that weigh heavily on your conscience? If your answer is yes, then it's very probable that you need to make restitution. If that absolutely panics you, please don't let it. I promise you that it's one of the most freeing actions that you could ever take.

Let me take you to Ezekiel 33:14–16:

> But when I say to the wicked, "You will surely die," and he turns ①from his sin and practices justice and righteousness, if a wicked man restores a pledge, pays back what he has taken by robbery, walks by the statutes which ensure life without committing iniquity, he will surely live; he shall not die. None of his sins that he has committed will be remembered against him. He has practiced justice and righteousness; he will surely live.

When you read the Scriptures, you should continuously ask yourself the Five W's and H, *Who? What? When? Where? Why?* and *How?* Let me show you by asking you some of them; write out the answers as you refer to Ezekiel 33:14–16:

1. To whom is God speaking?


2. What is going to happen to this man?



3. How can it be prevented?

(Before you answer, look again at the text. There is a list of things here that if this wicked man does he will live and not die. Not only will he live, but none of his sins will be remembered against him because to do these things is to practice "justice and righteousness.")

Observation is the most valuable and essential part of Bible study and yet it is the most neglected, because people don't know how to do it. Part of observing Scripture is looking for lists in the text. Let me show you one in the Ezekiel passage.

God gives a list of things that this man should do if he wants to live. The first one is to turn from his sin. So, above "turns from his sin," write a little 1 and circle it. (Look, I did it for you!) Secondly he is to practice justice, so put a 2 above "practices justice." Thirdly, he is to practice righteousness, so put a 3 above "practices righteousness." Fourthly, he is to restore a pledge. Put a 4 above "restore a pledge." Fifthly, he is to pay back what he has taken by robbery, so put a 5 above that. And sixthly, he is to walk by the statutes which ensure life. In other words, he is to walk in obedience to God's Word and not sin. Put your 6 above "walks by the statutes." Now, back to the question. How is this man going to keep from dying? He is going to keep from dying by doing these things you have marked.

Two things in this list deal with restitution. The first is restoring a pledge. Suppose I wanted to buy a piece of property from you, but didn't have the money. So, I said to you, "Look, I don't have the money, but I want to buy it. Let me give you a hundred dollars as a pledge that I'm going to buy this property." Well, three weeks later I come back and say, "There's no way I can buy it. I just can't get the money together and I'm in desperate straits." What are you to do? Are you to say, "Ah-ha! You kept me from selling my property so the hundred dollars is mine!" No, that's what the world would do. The world would take advantage of this situation. But we are not to be like the world. We are to *restore* a pledge.

The second means of restitution referred to in this passage is paying back what has been taken by robbery. Many people who have sat under this teaching have told me that they have been convicted by the Lord because they had not been honest in their dealings with others. Some have actually stolen things. Others have cheated on exams in school, or bought things that they knew were stolen. Because these people went to God seeking a pure heart, God reminded them of these unrighteous dealings. What about you, Beloved? Do you need to make restitution? (If you want to understand more about restitution, read Leviticus 6:1–5.)

Now let me anticipate a question. "But if I ask God to forgive me, isn't that enough?" It is if you have sinned only against God. But it is not enough if you have stolen something, or extorted funds, or not returned what was borrowed, or cheated on your income tax. Confession is not enough. Those people whom you have sinned against don't know that you have asked God to forgive you. And even if they did they would say, "What difference does that make to me? I'm still out what you stole from me." O Beloved, if you want to have a pure heart, then you must make restitution. And when you do, God will not mention your sins to you anymore because you have done what is just and right. If they are being mentioned to you, then you can know that it is the devil reminding you rather than God, because you have done what is right in the eyes of God.

Now, the next main point. If you're going to have a pure heart, you need to keep your heart cleansed by carefully watching what you think about. Every thought needs to meet the qualifications of Philippians 4:8.

Look at Philippians 4:8 and then list below what kind of things you are to think upon.




The things that you imagine can also get you into trouble. When you entertain wrong thoughts, eventually they can become strongholds. Read 2 Corinthians 10:5 and then, in your own words, put down God's instructions to you from this verse.




Not only do you need to carefully watch what you think, but you also need to watch the company you keep. Earlier we looked at 1

Corinthians 15:33: "Do not be deceived: 'Bad company corrupts good morals.'" God clearly warns us not to walk in the counsel of the wicked, nor stand in the path of sinners, nor sit in the seat of scoffers (*see* Psalm 1). When we do, we become like them and our hearts become contaminated. One bad apple is not made good by a bushel of good apples! Instead, the one bad apple will eventually ruin the whole bunch.

Finally, if you are going to have a pure heart and see God, according to James 4:8 you need to purify your heart and not be double-minded. (We will look at this again later in the Sermon on the Mount.) How do you purify your heart? Colossians 3:2 says, "Set your mind on the things above, not on the things that are on earth."

There is a very sobering verse in the New Testament and I leave it with you to meditate upon. Look up Hebrews 12:14 and write it out below. Isn't it awesome that God tells us that we are to pursue holiness because without it no one will see the Lord? What are you pursuing, Beloved? Will you see God?

# 10 - Peacemakers . . . But Persecuted. How Do You Handle It?

### DAY 1

You have heard it said over and over by desperate men in hard situations . . . by people on the street . . . even by school children stopped in their play. When asked what they want more than anything else, unanimously they say, peace. They don't ask for wealth or fame. Their only request is peace.

We were not born for conflict, were we? "All I want is peace!" It has been shouted, sobbed, screamed through clenched teeth: "All I want is peace." Maybe you have said it. I remember times when I have said it. I said it in an unhappy marriage, but I didn't know Jesus then. In a typical mother's anger I have said it to my sons. There have been times in these past eighteen years of ministry that I have said it. And I bet, if you were honest, you have said it, too.

How would you like to have not only peace, but happiness as well? It's all wrapped up in the seventh beatitude: " 'Blessed are the peacemakers, for they shall be called sons of God' " (Matthew 5:9). Did you see the beatitude that follows it? "Blessed are those who are persecuted"? It doesn't seem to fit, does it? Peacemakers—but persecuted? That is what it says and that is what we are going to look at in our prayer and study time together this week. How do peacemakers live? What are they, anyway? And why are they called "sons of God"? Then we are going to look at being persecuted and see how the two go together.

Peace is a very important word. It appears in every New Testament book except 1 John. According to John MacArthur, there are four hundred references to peace in the Bible. Can you see how important this word is in the Word of God?

The Greek word for peace signifies a harmonious relationship. This is important because it shows that peace is not merely the absence of war: peace is harmony. It is not a cold war. It is not two parties sitting back to back with arms folded, thinking that just because there is no yelling or fighting there is peace. No, peace would be a willingness to turn around and embrace one another in spite of differences of opinion. That is harmony. And, oh, how man needs harmony! How he needs peace! We were not born for conflict. It takes a terrible toll on our minds and on our bodies.

Today, as usual, there is a lot of talk about peace. The problem is with our motives. We are seeking peace, but we want it for ourselves, on our own terms. We want peace horizontally—with mankind. But we cannot have peace because we do not have it vertically. There will be no true peace among men until there is true peace with God. It's impossible! Do you know why? Let's examine a few verses that might give the answer.

1. Read Genesis 8:21 and write out below the part of this verse that would explain the reason for the problem.

2. Now look up Jeremiah 17:9 and write it out.

It is hard to have peace when you have a heart like that, isn't it? Yet, stop and look at the Beatitudes again.

3. What beatitude precedes peacemakers? Write it out.

Do you know where true peace originates? By now you should know that the answer is Jesus. You say, "Yes, but I thought He was to bring peace on earth. Isn't that what the angels said—'Peace on earth . . .'? What happened? Where's the peace?" These are good questions. Let's do a little bit of research.

4. Isaiah 9:6 is a prophecy about the Lord Jesus Christ. Read it and then write out which of Jesus's titles pertains to our lesson.

5. Read Luke 2:13, 14 in the New American Standard Bible (it is more accurate): "And suddenly there appeared with the angel a multitude of the heavenly host praising God, and saying, 'Glory to God in the highest, and on earth peace among men with whom He is pleased.' " Does this verse say that Jesus is going to bring peace on earth, or does it say that He is going to bring peace among men with whom He is well pleased? Underline which you think is correct.

6. Now look at Luke 12:51–53 and in your own words write out what Jesus is saying regarding peace.

7. One last verse to look up: John 14:27. Write in your own words what you learn about peace from this verse.

Jesus did come to bring peace, but it is a different kind of peace than what the world is thinking about. When the United Nations was instituted in 1945, its motto was "To have succeeding generations free from the scourge of war." But there has not been a day of peace since 1945. Peace on earth? It will not happen until Jesus returns to reign as King of kings. Even then, it will be an enforced peace, for Jesus will rule with a rod of iron. Why? Because even at that time, all men's hearts will not be right toward God. At the end of Jesus' thousand-year reign, Satan will be loosed from the bottomless pit to gather out of Jesus' kingdom all those who still resist the lordship of Jesus Christ. There will be a battle—the battle of Gog and Magog. Then God will destroy this earth by fire and there will be a brand new heaven and a brand new earth. Then and only then will there be true peace.

"But do I have to wait that long?" No, Beloved. Jesus came that you might have peace now—no matter what your circumstances are. Today think about the things that you have learned. Talk to God about them in prayer. Ask Him questions; He will give you answers.

## DAY 2

"Blessed are the peacemakers, for they shall be called sons of God" (Matthew 5:9).

What makes me a peacemaker? First, if I'm going to be a peacemaker, I must be at peace with God. Sinners are at enmity with God. Enmity is a state of disharmony, the feeling that enemies have for one another. It is hatred, hostility, or animosity. Therefore, reconciliation is necessary. To reconcile means "to take two who were separated from one another because of enmity and to bring them back into oneness or harmony." Man separated himself from God. It is God who has sought to reconcile man to Himself. When man moved away from

God because of his sin, God, because of His love, moved toward man to bring man back to Himself. How did He do it?

Read Colossians 1:20–22. Note the words *peace* and *reconcile* and answer the following questions:

1. Who did the reconciling?


2. What was the state of man when he was being reconciled?


3. How were the reconciliation and peace made possible?


Now read Romans 5:10, 11 and answer the questions that follow:

1. What were we when God reconciled us to Himself?


2. How were we reconciled to God?


3. Through whom did we receive the reconciliation?


Now, what have you seen? If you are going to be a peacemaker, you must first have peace with God. Jesus is the Prince of Peace, the child that was born to die so that you, an enemy of God, might be reconciled through the death of His Son. Jesus is God's Peace Child.

Have you read Don Richardson's book, *Peace Child?* It is a gripping story. Don Richardson and his wife were missionaries among the Sawi people, head-hunting cannibals of Netherlands New Guinea who pillowed their heads on the skulls of their victims. With them, treachery was more than a way of life. It was an ideal. They revelled in treachery! Because of this they lived in constant conflict; Sawi villages constantly fought among themselves. Peace seemed impossible. Finally unable to bear all their wars and deaths, Don Richardson, known as Tuan, approached the people to whom he had been ministering and told them that if they did not make peace he would leave them. The people were panic-stricken. How could Tuan leave them? In desperation the men met, and then approached Don. They promised: "Tuan, tomorrow we are going to make peace!"

Peace! How could people make peace when treachery was their ideal! Little did he realize that the next day he would witness a ceremony that would be God's means of unlocking the chains that held the Sawi bound in darkness, prisoners of Satan. Don Richardson didn't realize it, but according to their tribal laws, there would never be peace until a "peace child" was given to the enemy. You must read the book! The story will tear at your heart as you see a mother screaming, struggling to break free of those restraining her, crying, "No! No! He's our only son." Her husband, clutching their son in his arms, continued to walk resolutely into the camp of the enemy. Peace had to be made, no matter the cost.

Kaiyo's chest was heaving with emotion as he reached the edge of Haenam. The leading men of the village were massed in front of him now, expectantly eyeing the child Kaiyo held in his hands. Kaiyo scanned the row of enemy faces before him. . . . Then he saw the man he had chosen and called his name. "Mahor!" he cried.

"Mahor! Kaiyo challenged. "Will you plead the words of Kamur among your people?"

"Yes!" Mahor responded, "I will plead the words of Kamur among my people!"

"Then I give you my son and with him my name!"

Mahor shouted, "Eehaa! It is enough! I will surely plead for peace between us! . . ."

Suddenly Mahaen reappeared in the forefront of the crowd. Facing Kaiyo, Mahaen held aloft one of his other baby sons and cried, "Kaiyo! Will you plead the words of Haenam among your people?"

"Yes!" cried Kaiyo, holding out his hands toward Mahaen.

"Then I will give you my son and with him my name!"

They had exchanged sons and they had exchanged names. Richardson did not understand.

"Why is this necessary?" [he] asked.

"Tuan, you've been urging us to make peace—don't you know it's impossible to have peace without a peace child?"[16]

Oh, Beloved, don't you know that it's impossible for you to have peace without a peace child? God left heaven and came into the enemy's camp. He brought you His only Son and said, "Peace among those with whom God is well-pleased." God is well-pleased with those who come to him in poverty of spirit, confessing that they are sinners and accepting God's Peace Child. Oh, Beloved, do you have God's Peace Child? Without Him, you'll never be a son of God. Without Him, you'll never be a peacemaker.

## DAY 3

What makes you a peacemaker? First, it is having peace with God. Secondly, it's having peace with the body of Jesus Christ. Ephesians 4:1–3 tells us very clearly that if we are to walk "in a manner worthy of the calling with which you have been called," we must be "diligent to preserve the unity of the Spirit in the bond of peace."

Read 1 Thessalonians 5:13 and then note below what it says about peace.

Read Matthew 5:22–24 and answer the following questions.

1. When it says "be reconciled to your brother," do you think that He is talking about a literal blood-brother? Explain your answer.

2. Who is to go to whom? Why?

3. How do you think this agrees with 1 Thessalonians 5:13?

What is God telling us in these verses? Is He not saying that if we are going to be obedient to Him, then we have a responsibility to live in peace with one another? If we know that a brother in Christ has something against us, are we not then, as peacemakers, responsible to go to that brother and make peace? Blessed—spiritually prosperous—are the peacemakers. Are you blessed of God because you are making and keeping peace in the body?

A third thing that makes you a peacemaker is having the ministry of reconciliation. Not only do you have to have peace with God in order to be a peacemaker; not only are you to make peace within the body; you are also responsible to bring the gospel of peace to other people so that they in turn might have peace with God. You and I are not only to make peace among ourselves, but we are to make peace with those who are outside Christ. There is really only one way to do that—introduce them to the Prince of Peace.

Read 2 Corinthians 5:14–21 and then answer the following questions.

1. According to verses 14 and 15, for whom did Jesus die?

2. Because He died for us, for whom are we to live?

3. To whom has God given a ministry? And what kind of ministry is it?

Ambassadors for Christ—that is what you and I are to be! The question is—are we? If not, then are we really peacemakers? God has given every child of God the ministry of reconciliation. He has committed to you the word of reconciliation, the gospel of Jesus Christ. Isaiah 52:7 says "How lovely on the mountains are the feet of him who brings good news, who announces peace and brings good news of happiness, who announces salvation. . . ." The glad tidings of good things is the gospel of Jesus Christ which brings forgiveness of sins.

Look at your feet. Are they lovely in the eyes of God? Jesus' feet were nailed to a cross so that your feet might someday walk streets of gold. Are you going to walk them alone? Or will others walk beside you because you have shared the good news with them that they, too, could have peace with God?

"But it's hard! I don't know what to say! I get so embarrassed!" I know that it's hard, that sometimes you just don't know what to say. But those are not adequate excuses. Jesus said, " 'Go . . . and lo, I am with you always' " (Matthew 28:19, 20). Give Him your mouth and He will give you His words. Be willing to be made a fool for Christ's sake and He will make you an ambassador for the world's sake. I have found myself in all sorts of situations—situations I would have gladly retreated from except for one fact: How are men going to believe in someone of whom they have never heard? And how are they going to hear except someone tells them (see Romans 10:14)? You and I are not to be "ashamed of the gospel, for it is the power of God for salvation to every one who believes, to the Jew first and also to the Greek (Romans 1:16).

A number of years ago, I found myself staying in the same hotel where John Wayne was staying. "The Duke" has always been one of my favorite actors and so when one day I happened to be on the elevator with him and several other people, I was absolutely speechless. Later, as he walked through the hotel lobby with that famous stride of his, people gawked; others wanted his autograph. As I watched, God spoke to my heart and I knew that I was to share the gospel with him. I thought my heart was literally going to bounce out of my chest and roll around on that marble lobby floor. Although I was as weak as a kitten, I managed to get out of the hotel door. He was waiting for a cab. I was nervous, but I remember saying to him that everybody was always wanting something from him and asking for his autograph. All I wanted to do was share Someone with him, Someone who had changed my life drastically. With that I gave him a tract which he politely accepted. My attempt was not polished, to say the least. I felt dumb before man, but I had been obedient to God.

You know, Beloved, when I heard that The Duke had died I was so thankful that I had been obedient. I knew that John Wayne's blood would never be upon my hands. Paul wrote, "Therefore I testify to you this day, that I am innocent of the blood of all men. For I did not shrink from declaring to you the whole purpose of God" (Acts 20:26, 27).

Are you a peacemaker? Do you have peace with God? Do you seek to keep the unity of the Spirit in the bond of peace? Are you sharing the gospel of peace with others? If so, you will be called a son of God. Like Father, like son! Isn't it wonderful!

## DAY 4

Peacemakers, but persecuted! To those who do not understand spiritual things the two don't seem to fit. Yet those who are familiar with Jesus' sojourn here on earth know that it describes the life of the Prince of Peace. For "He came to His own, and those who were His own did not receive Him" (John 1:11). Instead they plotted against Him to take His life. They would not have this man to rule over them! He was light in the midst of darkness, but men preferred darkness rather than light because their deeds were evil. So they sought to put out the Light. He was of the truth but they were of their father, the devil. And they wanted to do the desires of their father, the father of lies. So they crucified Truth.

Jesus warned His disciples. " 'Remember the word that I said to you, "A slave is not greater than his master." If they persecuted Me, they will also persecute you; if they kept My word, they will keep yours also. But all these things they will do to you for My name's sake, because they do not know the One who sent Me' " (John 15:20, 21).

Because of what Jesus was, they persecuted Him. Because of what Jesus makes you, they will persecute you also. In this last beatitude, "Blessed are those who have been persecuted for the sake of righteousness . . . ," we clearly see the conflict that results from the character of those first seven beatitudes. Remember our outline of the Sermon on the Mount:

Matthew 5:3–9
    The Character of Those Who Belong to the Kingdom of Heaven

Matthew 5:10–12

The Conflict of Those Who Belong to the Kingdom of Heaven

Matthew 5:13–7:27

The Conduct of Those Who Belong to the Kingdom of Heaven

As we have seen, the Sermon on the Mount shows us the righteous life-style of those who belong to the kingdom of heaven. Such a life-style will inevitably bring persecution, because it makes us radically different from the rest of this world, those who walk the broad path that leads to destruction (Matthew 7:13).

I believe that a great time of persecution is coming to the United States, and my heart's burden and question for you is: Are you prepared to handle it? How I pray that the taste that I give you will whet your appetite for more and that you will want to learn how to dig into God's Word for yourself.

You need to know some things regarding persecution and suffering. But first, look at Matthew 5:10–12. There are two "blesseds" here and yet I do not believe that there are two separate beatitudes. Both of them refer to a blessedness for those suffering persecution. Verse 10 says, "Blessed are those who have been persecuted for the sake of righteousness." "Have been persecuted" is in the perfect tense and the passive voice. The perfect tense denotes past, completed action with a continuous or ongoing result. The passive voice means that the subject is receiving the action of the verb. In other words, these people have already undergone persecution.

To whom is Jesus referring? Are they different from those He speaks of in verse 11: "Blessed are you when men revile you, and persecute you, and say all kinds of evil against you falsely, on account of Me"? I believe that Jesus had two different audiences in mind. When he said, "Blessed are those who have been persecuted," He could have been referring to those like John the Baptist who were already undergoing persecution because of their righteous stand and life-style. Those in verse 11, I believe, are referring to His immediate audience, but the application is to you and me. In referring to both, He is simply uniting those who *have already been and are being* persecuted, and those who *will be* persecuted.

Remember that the Sermon on the Mount was delivered in the early days of Jesus' ministry. Persecution was not yet in full bloom. Jesus is saying that whenever a man is persecuted for the sake of righteousness, to whatever degree, he can rejoice. The word for "rejoice and be glad" means to be exceedingly happy. Why? Because: 1) His reward in heaven is great (and the word means exceedingly great!); 2) He is in the company of the prophets who were persecuted before him. (He has joined the ranks of godly men and women who counted it a privilege to lay down their lives for their God.)

For the sake of review I think we should do a little assignment on these three verses: Read Matthew 5:10–12 and then answer these questions.

1. Why are they being persecuted?

2. According to these verses, what form does that persecution take?

Now let's look at some things you need to know regarding persecution and suffering. First: suffering is a certainty for every Christian. It is a certainty because suffering is a sign of your salvation. Read Philippians 1:27–30 and then answer these questions.

1. According to verse 29, two things have been granted you for Christ's sake. What are they? List them.

2. According to this passage, how are we to conduct ourselves?

3. What are we to do when we are opposed? How are we to respond to our opponents?

4. What does this type of response show our opponents?

5. What does this kind of response show us?

Through the apostle Paul, God is telling us that with the gift of faith in Christ Jesus also comes the gift of suffering. The two go together. Therefore, when you stand before your opponents and you are not alarmed, it becomes a sign of salvation for you. You realize that you have a home in heaven. So, if God permits them to take your life He is simply saying, "But, my child, you're coming home!" That kind of an attitude alarms your opponents! When they see you standing firm before them without being alarmed, it "is a sign of destruction for them" because they know that if they were in your shoes they would absolutely panic! And to you, it becomes a testimony of the reality of your faith!

What insight does this give you into presenting the gospel to others, or in discipling brand-new Christians? The book of 1 Thessalonians helps answer that question. The first three chapters of 1 Thessalonians give us a view of what happened when Paul, Silvanus, and Timothy went to Thessalonica to deliver the gospel. In 1 Thessalonians 3:3, 4 we discover what Paul taught his new converts. Among other things, he dealt with suffering and told them not to be disturbed by the afflictions that they were facing. "For you yourselves know that we have been destined for this. For indeed when we were with you, we kept telling you in advance that we were going to suffer affliction; and so it came to pass, as you know." Paul had taught them, and very wisely so, that suffering and persecution go with salvation. Do we do this? Is this part of the gospel we deliver—of the discipling we do?

Isn't this what we see in the Sermon on the Mount? What is the blessedness of those who are persecuted? It's the same as the blessedness of those who are poor in spirit: "theirs is the kingdom of heaven." It is a present-tense possession. The Beatitudes begin and end with the promise, "theirs is the kingdom of heaven." Therefore, everything in between is all inclusive. It's a package deal. These beatitudes become the attributes or character of the child of God, a character that results in conflict. But that conflict becomes the very surety of our salvation!

Because I don't want to overwhelm you—because I want you to keep wanting more—let me list a few more Scriptures on suffering for you to look up at your own convenience: 1 Peter 4:1, 2; 12–16; John 15:18; 16:33; 2 Timothy 3:12.

As you go to the Lord in prayer, remember that there are degrees of persecution. First Peter 4:13 points this out: "But to the degree that you share the sufferings of Christ, keep on rejoicing." I think God is saying this: the greater the obedience, the greater the righteousness; the greater the righteousness, the greater the suffering; the greater the suffering, the greater the rejoicing. O Beloved, are you suffering at all for the gospel of Jesus Christ? Do men revile you or say things against you falsely? If not, do you suppose then that it is because you are not all that you ought to be for Christ? Could it be that you have compromised His standard of righteousness? Are you so like the world that your life does not expose their sin and, therefore, they feel very comfortable with you? Or are you so isolated and insulated in your own little Christian atmosphere that you are too comfortable to step out into the world to be a peacemaker? Have you forgotten that you are an ambassador for Jesus Christ? Have you forgotten that He commissioned you to witness to the lost? Or have you refused to go where Jesus said to go because you did not want to endure hardness or suffer persecution? You need to examine yourself now, before your life is gone and you don't have any more days to live for Him who lived and died for you.

## DAY 5

Yesterday we saw that suffering is a certainty for the child of God. It is a sign of our salvation. Today we want to look at several other things that we need to know regarding persecution and suffering.

We need to know that suffering prepares us for glory. This helps, doesn't it? If you and I can realize that our suffering has an eternal purpose, or a purpose at all, then it is worthwhile. Romans 8:16, 17 makes this point. "The Spirit Himself bears witness with our spirit that we are children of God, and if children, heirs also, heirs of God and fellow heirs with Christ, if indeed we suffer with Him in order that we may also be glorified with Him."

When it says, "if indeed we suffer with Him," the "if" means *since* "we suffer with Him." In other words, we see that we know we are heirs of Christ and children of God because we suffer. But we also see another truth—suffering is necessary in order that we may be glorified with Him.

How does suffering prepare us for glory? Suffering gets rid of the dross in our lives; it is God's crucible of purification. In this light, read 1 Peter 1:6, 7. What do I mean by "God's crucible of purification"? We can understand this from the example of silver, which when mined from the earth, is full of many impurities. It is purified in a crucible over a hot flame. Usually, some seven different fires—each heated to a greater degree of intensity—are needed before the metal releases all of its impurities.

After the silversmith leaves the silver in the fire a while, he will scrape off the impurities that float at the top of the liquid silver. As he does, he looks into the molten silver to see what kind of an image he gets of himself. At first the image is very dim; he knows that the silver is still filled with many impurities. So, he builds another fire of greater intensity. As he again puts the crucible into the fire, he never leaves it unattended, but hovers beside it, watching it closely. As the impurities rise to the surface, he scrapes them off. He repeats the process over and over until, finally, when he can see a clear and perfect image of himself—when the silver becomes a mirror—he knows it is pure.

This, Beloved, is how suffering and persecution prepare us for glory. It is a fire that God uses to consume the dross of our lives so that we finally reflect a clear and perfect image of Him—so when we see Him, we will not be ashamed.

Haralan Popov in his outstanding book, *Tortured for His Faith,* tells what happened to the church as a result of the Communists' horrendous persecution.

> As the fires of persecution grew, they burned away the chaff and stubble and left only the golden wheat. The suffering purified the church and united the believers in a wonderful spirit of brotherly love such as must have existed in the early church. Petty differences were put aside. Brethren loved and cared for one another and carried one another's burdens. There were no nominal or "lukewarm" believers. It made no sense to be a halfhearted Christian when the price for faith was so great. There came a great spiritual depth and richness in Christ I had never seen in the times before when we were free. Every man,

woman, and youth was forced to "count the cost" and decide if serving Christ was worth the suffering. And to the Communists' great regret, this was the healthiest thing they could have done for the church, for the insincere gave up but the true Christians became aware of what Christ meant to them and became more dedicated than ever before.[17]

Even the Old Testament saints recognized that suffering prepared them for glory. Hebrews 11:35 says, ". . . and others were tortured, not accepting their release, in order that they might obtain a better resurrection." O Beloved, do not run away from suffering. You can know with certainty that it is to prepare you for glory and for a better resurrection.

Since suffering is certain, it is vital that we know how to respond in suffering. As we have already seen in Matthew 5:12 and 1 Peter 1:6, we are to rejoice. But in the midst of our suffering, how do we respond to those causing our persecution? This is answered for us in 1 Peter, which has much to say about suffering and glory. Read 1 Peter 2:18-25 and then answer the questions that follow.

1. What kind of suffering finds favor with God? In other words, which type of suffering is a just suffering?

2. Who is our example in suffering?

3. Note below the specific things that Jesus did when He was suffering. Be brief but explicit in your answer.

Jesus was an example; we are to follow in His steps. This Greek word for *example—Hypogrammos—*means "an outline, a drawing, or a copybook of letters to be used by the pupil." It is used only here in the New Testament. What we see in 1 Peter 2:21–25 is a pattern for us to follow when we suffer.

First, when Jesus suffered, He did not sin. Many times when we suffer we are tempted to react in a very fleshly way and to walk independently of God. So, in the midst of suffering we need to cry out to God and cast ourselves upon Him so that we hold ourselves in check and do not sin.

Second, we see that Jesus kept His mouth shut. He uttered no threats. No deceit was found in His mouth. He didn't revile when they reviled Him. He didn't say, "You're going to get yours later!" In the midst of persecution it is a temptation to retaliate with our mouths, isn't it?

Third, Jesus prayed. He stayed in communion with God. He "kept entrusting Himself to Him who judges righteously" (1 Peter 2:23).

Fourth, not only did He pray; He trusted God. O Beloved, one of the benefits of persecution is intimate communion with the Father and the Son. They know, they understand. Your Father is the God of all comfort, but He can comfort only those who stay in communion with Him. His arms are always opened wide, but you must run into them.

Last of all, Jesus took the persecution. He bore our sins in His body. As we saw, the verb in Matthew 5:10 "have been persecuted" is in the passive voice; those referred to received the persecution. They did not flee from it. They were willing to endure.

You are not to fear. God is sovereign. He is in control. It is all being filtered through His fingers of love. Therefore, you can bear it and in the bearing of it, you will give testimony to the reality of your faith in Jesus Christ. You, like Christ, might bring others into His kingdom through your suffering.

Finally, you must know your responsibility to those who are suffering. Hebrews 13:3 says, "Remember the prisoners, as though in prison with them, and those who are ill-treated, since you yourselves also are in the body."[18]

We are to suffer with those who suffer. We are not to stand on the sidelines and allow others to suffer alone. We are not to be ashamed of the testimony of our Lord, or of His prisoners, but we are to "join [with them] in suffering for the gospel according to the power of God" (2 Timothy 1:8).

Yes, they were peacemakers ... but persecuted. The two really do go together. May the longing of your heart be to "know Him, and the

power of His resurrection and the fellowship of His sufferings ..."
(Philippians 3:10). And may we never forget Jesus' words of warning,
" 'Woe to you when all men speak well of you, for in the same way
their fathers used to treat the false prophets' " (Luke 6:26).

# 11 - Salt and Light—and You

## DAY 1

It was December, almost Christmas. The airport was jammed. Our
flight had been delayed, and there was no place to sit down. I stood at
the window, watching the bright lights decorate the darkness of night.
Blue, red, yellow. My heart was full. I was on my way to Augusta to
speak, and it was all because of Him. My eyes went from the lights on
the runway to the heavens above, as in my heart I communed with my
Father. I was awed by His love. I thought of Jesus, born to die that I
who was dead might have life—a life I longed for but never really
knew existed. Oh, how He had changed me.

Suddenly my thoughts were interrupted by a voice behind me. "Oh
Christ! That's not the way it was. . . ."

An arrow pierced my heart! Where did that come from? I turned. He
was easy to identify because he continued to use the Lord's name in
vain. There he stood, a handsome man, about in his late thirties, well
dressed, in all probability an executive or a salesman. I turned back to
the window. I didn't want to hear what he was saying. It hurt.

But I could hear nothing else. The pressure within me continued to
mount. I knew that God wanted me to speak to the man. But how?
What would I say? How should I approach him? I stalled for time and
for composure. My heart was thumping rapidly and when it does that,
and I have to talk, my voice gets high and trembly.

Finally I walked over, smiled and said, "Excuse me. I couldn't help
overhearing your conversation. I know this is presumptuous, but may I
ask you a question? Are you going to celebrate Christmas this year?"

"Yes. . . ."

"Do you know what Christmas is all about?"

From there I shared Christ and the gravity of taking God's name in vain. His response was interesting. He wanted to talk, to apologize, and to listen.

Salt and light, that's what we are supposed to be—and if we're not, what then? Jesus said, "You are the salt of the earth; but if the salt has become tasteless, how will it be made salty again? It is good for nothing anymore, except to be thrown out and trampled under foot by men. You are the light of the world" (Matthew 5:13, 14). Salt and light—two metaphors—following a series of "blesseds." Their purpose is highly significant. Suddenly we see our reason for being. We have worth. We are needed. Our lives can count. The amount of salt makes a difference, doesn't it? We know because we measure it when we use it. Therefore, each one of us makes a difference to our world.

Others aren't enough—you're needed! It's the same with light. One more lighted candle decreases the darkness. You are significant!

In Roman times, soldiers were paid in salt; hence the question, "Are you worth your salt?" This is God's question to you this week. Are you what you ought to be?

Today I want you to compare Matthew 5:13 with two other cross references on salt. Under each reference list everything that you learn about salt from that passage.

**Matthew 5:13**                    **Mark 9:50**                    **Luke 14:33–35**

It may seem premature to you, but write in your own words what you think Jesus is saying in Matthew 5:13. How would you explain this passage to another person in the light of what you have learned from Mark 9:50 and Luke 14:33–35?

# DAY 2

We must never forget that although the Word of God is a timeless book and speaks to men of all generations, still it is a book that has its own particular setting in time, culture, and history. It must always be considered within the framework of these contexts.

The salt of biblical times was not like our pure, refined salt. Instead, it was found in varying degrees of purity; thus its uses were quite varied. In Leviticus, God instructs His people to use salt in their sacrifices. A covenant of salt is referred to in the Old Testament. Lot's wife was turned into a pillar of salt.

Practically speaking, salt was used to season food, to make it more palatable. Thus Paul says: "Let your speech always be with grace, seasoned, as it were, with salt, so that you may know how you should respond to each person" (Colossians 4:6).

Salt was used then, as it still is, as a preservative, to stop the spread of corruption, and as an antiseptic to kill germs. Inferior sorts of salt were used to decompose the soil or as a fertilizer. However, too much salt would result in sterility so that nothing could grow. A conquering nation might sow a city with salt, demonstrating the city's irretrievable ruin (*see* Judges 9:45). Finally, when salt had no savor at all and was simply a crystal of some sort, it was cast out on the ground or used to make paths for men to tread upon.

In light of the historical context, it becomes easier to understand the passages from the Gospels that you studied yesterday, doesn't it? Luke 14:35 summarizes part of what we have seen: " 'It is useless either for the soil or for the manure pile; it is thrown out.' "

Apparently the salt that Jesus referred to was of a different composition than our salt. It could lose its savor altogether and become totally useless.

Jesus is talking about the character of a Christian. The Christian's life is to have a distinctive flavor; if it loses this character it is worthless. If you and I are not what we ought to be, then we really have no worth as far as this earth is concerned.

It's the same way with the metaphor, " 'You are the light of the world.' " Light has an obvious character. It is to be seen of men. The purpose of a lamp or a candle is to give light. If it doesn't give light, it is not good for anything else.

When I think of salt and light I cannot help but think also of the vine and branches mentioned in John 15:1–6. A branch is only good for one thing—bearing fruit. If a branch does not bear fruit, it is thrown away and dries up. Then men gather them and cast them into the fire and they are burned. Why? Because a branch only has one function. Salt only has one function. Light only has one function. That is why we are to have salt in ourselves (Mark 9:50). Savorless salt has no function!

In essence, Paul is saying the same thing in 1 Corinthians 9:27: "But I buffet my body and make it my slave, lest possibly, after I have preached to others, I myself should be disqualified." If my body is going to dominate me rather than God's Spirit, then God is going to have to disqualify me. Why? Because I am not what I ought to be as a child of God. In each of these instances, the message is one: the Christian life is not just a matter of doing; it's a matter of being. And if you aren't going to be what God has ordained you to be, then you have no value to the kingdom of God. You are good for nothing.

That's kind of hard, isn't it? Kind of stringent, narrow! Yes, it is. And a lot of people don't like that. They won't buy it. They want an easy believism, a gospel that makes no demands, that does not call for a wholehearted commitment. They want to short-circuit the radical implications of a life of discipleship. They want their own brand of Christianity. But you see, Beloved, we are not the ones who are calling the shots! God is. And that is why the Sermon on the Mount, in statement after statement, shows us just how small that gate is and how narrow the way is that leads to life. Is it any wonder that few find it?

Are you salty salt? Does your presence in the world cause others to thirst after the Fountain of Living Water? Is your life such that it serves to stop the spread of corruption in your society, in your city, in your schools? Why don't you spend some time with God in prayer, and in honest objectivity ask Him to show you how salty you are?

## DAY 3

The first mention of salt in the Bible is found in Genesis 19:26. God rained fire and brimstone on Sodom and Gomorrah, but before He could do that He had to get Lot and his family out of Sodom. As they left Sodom, Lot's wife looked back and, as a result, became a pillar of salt. In essence, Lot lost his salt in Sodom!

Lot had a problem. His focus was wrong. When you follow his story in Genesis 13 through 19, you see that he made self-centered choices. We see this in Genesis 13. Because of the strife between the herdsmen of Lot and those of Abraham, Abraham offers Lot the choice of a land that God had given to Abraham. "And Lot lifted up his eyes and saw all the valley of the Jordan, that it was well watered everywhere—this was before the LORD destroyed Sodom and Gomorrah—like the garden of the LORD, like the land of Egypt as you go to Zoar. So Lot chose for himself all the valley of the Jordan" (Genesis 13:10, 11). Without consideration for his uncle, Lot chose the best for himself.

Next we find him pitching his tents toward Sodom, a city where "the men ... were wicked exceedingly and sinners against the LORD" (Genesis 13:13). In Genesis 14:12, Lot is living in Sodom, and then in Genesis 19:1, we find him sitting in the gate of Sodom where men of prominence in the city usually sat.

Stop now and read Genesis 19:1–17; then answer the following questions.

1. What did the men of Sodom want to do to the two angels who came as men to Lot's house?

2. When Lot rebuked the men, how did they respond to him (Genesis 19:7)? What does this tell you about his apparent relationship with them?

3. According to verse 14, what kind of influence did Lot have upon his sons-in-law?

Before we summarize, it is important for you to read 2 Peter 2:4–9. Answer the following questions and then we will put it all together.

1. Why did God condemn the cities of Sodom and Gomorrah?


2. How does God refer to Noah in this passage?


3. How does He refer to Lot?


4. Was Lot comfortable living in Sodom? As you answer this question make sure you use a verse from 2 Peter 2:4–9 to support your answer.


From 2 Peter 2 we see that Lot was a man who believed God and was apparently considered righteous by God, for God could not destroy Sodom until Lot left the city. He was righteous, but it seems that he had lost his salt. Lot lived in Sodom, but he was not a partaker of their evil deeds. Yet, what kind of an impact did he have upon Sodom? Why was he living there? How had he obtained a position of respectability? Apparently by compromising and keeping his mouth shut! His life did not have a righteous impact upon those with whom he lived! His term "brother" seems to denote a tolerance and acceptance of these evil men. From Genesis 19:9 it seems that until this time Lot had not opposed his neighbors or called them to accountability for their actions. From Lot's relationship to his sons-in-law it is evident that his words carried very little impact; "he appeared to his sons-in-law to be jesting."

God tells us in Ephesians 5:11, "And do not participate in the unfruitful deeds of darkness, but instead even expose them." Not only had Lot failed to be "salty salt"; he also had hidden God's light of truth under a bushel. Although he did not participate in the unfruitful deeds of darkness, he apparently did not expose them. How can you sit at the gate and be a popular man when you expose the sins of those with whom you live? The two cannot possibly go together.

Lot was saved, but he had no witness among those with whom he lived, no effect upon his society. He lost his salt and so his life did not create a thirst in others for God.

Why is there so much corruption around us? Is it because we have failed to be the salt of the earth? Let me give you just one last illustration. Do you realize that in 1983 fifteen million American Christians were not registered to vote? Is that being salty salt?

When vile movies or places of obscene entertainment come to your town, do you sit in apathy in your salt shaker? Or do you get out into the world to stop the spread of corruption? Do you, as Ephesians 5 says, expose the unfruitful deeds of darkness? Do you stand firm against all the attacks of the enemy, Satan, or are you ignorant of his methods and devices? Do you keep abreast of current legislation and how to oppose bills that are in direct opposition to the principles and precepts of God's Word? Or do you sit in your salt shaker, criticizing those who are the salt of the earth? How I pray that God will speak to you in a very clear way so that your life will not be worthless, cast out and trodden under foot of men in mockery. George Truett once said, "You are either being corrupted by the world or you are salting it." There is no middle ground.


## DAY 4


"Unbelievers are often kept from evil deeds," says *The Wycliffe Bible Commentary*, "because of a moral consciousness traceable to Christian influence." If this is true, and I believe it is, what does it tell you about the Christian influence in the United States of America now?

In our last two days of study this week we want to look at Jesus' statement, " 'You are the light of the world.' " As we said before, light has one purpose: to dispel darkness. In Matthew 5:16 Jesus' admonition is very clear. We are to let our light shine before men so that they may see our good works and glorify our Father in heaven.

Our good works cause the light to shine. But those good works are to be done in such a way that they do not glorify us, but our Father. If they do not point men beyond us to the Father, then something is wrong with the way we are letting our lights shine. I am not saying that it's wrong for people to love you and appreciate you. This is obviously going to happen if you are used of God in a significant way in somebody's life. However, that love and appreciation should never stop with you, but it should focus on the true Light—the Source of all light—Jesus. The lampstand is not significant, but the light that comes from the lampstand is. The lampstand is merely a vessel to give light to those who are in its presence. Just as the moon reflects the sun's light, so we are to reflect the Son's light!

Let's look at some Scriptures that will give us insight into the Light of the world and how we relate to that Light. Read John 1:1–9 very carefully.

1. John 1:1 talks about the Word. John 1:14–17 tells us who the Word is. Who is it? What is His name?

2. According to John 1:4, what relationship did this One have to light? (Before you answer this, check John 1:9.)

3. What was John's relationship to the Light?

4. What do you think John 1:5 is saying?

5. Read John 8:12, a verse that clearly tells us that Jesus is the Light of the world. What do you learn from this verse about those who follow Him?

6. Look at John 9:5 and write out what it says.

7. According to this verse, Jesus is no longer in the world. Is there any light in the world now that Jesus has left?

8. From what you have seen so far, who is the Light of the world?

9. Read John 12:46. (I love it!) According to this verse what happens to those who really believe in Jesus?

Now let's summarize some of the things that we have seen. Before He came into the world, Jesus was the Word of God, He was with God, and He was God. He always has been God and He always will be God. In John 1:4 we saw that Jesus was the Source of light and He became the Light of men, which according to John 12:46, took men out of darkness.

As John was a witness of the Light, so that people might believe through Him, so you and I are to be witnesses of the Light. Jesus, the Light of the world, has returned to the Father. Yet He has not left the world in darkness, because we, His people, remain here. As Matthew 5 says, you and I are the light of the world. But did He leave us on earth to hide our lights under a peck-measure? Of course not! The purpose of light is to be seen. "A city on a hill cannot be hidden." If you are a child of God, you are a part of that Holy City, the new Jerusalem, which will someday come down out of heaven from God. That city will have no need of the sun or moon to shine upon it for the glory of God will illumine it. Its lamp will be the Lamb, and the nations will walk by His light (Revelation 21:2, 23, 24). Until the new heaven, the new earth, and the new Jerusalem come down out of heaven, you and I, who are citizens of heaven, are to be like a city set on a hill that cannot be hidden. We are to let men know where light is.

This is why John is so adamant in his first epistle.

And this is the message we have heard from Him and announce to you, that God is light, and in Him there is no darkness at all. If we say that we have fellowship with Him and yet walk in the darkness, we lie and do not practice the truth; but if we walk in the light as He Himself is in the light, we have fellowship with one another, and the blood of Jesus His Son cleanses us from all sin.

*1 John 1:5–7*

You cannot walk in darkness and say that you are sharing in common the life of Jesus Christ. Fellowship is sharing something in common. If you say you have fellowship with Jesus and you are walking in darkness, you can know that you are lying, because in Jesus there is no darkness. John tells us, "the one who says he abides in Him ought himself to walk in the same manner as He walked" (1 John 2:6). Do you realize how many people say that they know God, that they belong to Him, and yet walk in darkness? Their very deeds, their lifestyles deny the reality of the light of God. Light dispels darkness; it does not contribute to it! The two are totally incompatible.

John also goes on to tell us, "The one who says he is in the light and yet hates his brother is in the darkness until now. The one who loves his brother abides in the light and there is no cause for stumbling in him. But the one who hates his brother is in the darkness and walks in the darkness, and does not know where he is going because the darkness has blinded his eyes" (1 John 2:9–11). Those who truly have the life of God within them, who truly walk in the light, cannot walk in hatred. They must walk in love. Why? Because God is not only light, but also love (1 John 4:8).

Take time today, Beloved, to go to the Lord in prayer and ask Him if you are walking in the light. Ask Him to show you how your good works are glorifying His name so that you might be encouraged. Ask Him also to show you what good works you might do in order to glorify Him even more. Write down your insights.

# DAY 5

If you are going to let your light shine before men so they may see your good works and glorify your Father in heaven, how are you going to walk? Ephesians 5:1–16 has some very good insights for us regarding this matter. Take a few minutes and read that passage. Then I will give you some exercises to help you see more clearly what it says.

1. One of the key words in this passage is *walk*. From Ephesians 5:1–16, make a list of everything that you learn about how we are to walk.

2. Now read through the verses again and note everything we are to do if we walk as children of the light.

3. What is the most significant thing you have learned today? How has God spoken to you this week? What steps are you going to take in order to apply to your own life what He has said?

Not long ago, Jim Bird, our director of operations, was approached by Barry, one of his Precept students, who had recently come to know Jesus Christ. Barry's life was being transformed through his diligent study of God's Word, but he was troubled.

Before he became a Christian, Barry had bought some stolen railroad ties. They had been taken from one railroad company and from a woman who owned a landscaping business. He knew when he purchased them that they were stolen, but it was such a good deal! Or so he thought at the time! Now, the Lord kept bringing them to mind! The more Barry studied the Sermon on the Mount, the more it troubled him. His homework on mourning over sin brought before him the issue of restitution. Finally, he went to Jim for counsel.

Jim led Barry through the Scriptures for his answer. Barry walked in obedience. First, he went to the railroad, hoping to confess his wrong to a clerk. But no clerk was there—only the "big boss"—so Barry told him. And he said that he wanted to make restitution. Did they want the ties back? What could he do?

Barry's light was shining! The "big boss" saw it. The landscape lady saw it. Jim told my husband and me, so we saw it. Now you, too, have seen Barry's light. How our Father is glorified! Barry was formerly walking in darkness, but now he is walking as a child of light, dispelling the darkness.

Remember, Beloved, you are the salt of the earth, the light of the world. If your salt is not salty and your light is not shining, then your life is meaningless as far as God is concerned. It has no value to this world because it is not what it is supposed to be.

Let's walk with Barry and light up this whole dark world!

# 12 - How to Have a New Heart— and Be Set Free from Sin!

## DAY 1

Have you ever stopped to wonder why man cannot achieve peace on earth? Our world is filled with brilliant men and women. We have achieved unbelievable and really awesome feats in medicine, technology, and science. The world is in touch with the world. Man has communicated with man. We have organized projects of mercy and rehabilitation; we have sat at the peace tables. The United Nations has gathered us together to make us accountable to one another. Yet, despite all these things, man has not changed.

Is it possible for man to straighten out man? Will we ever be able to bring peace on earth, to live in good will toward one another? We have an historical account of man's affairs for the past six thousand years, but peace has yet to be a reality. The question is, will we ever see it?

Is it any wonder that the Sermon on the Mount leads men to resurrect from the grave of history their hope of peace? Scales are removed from the eyes of visionaries, and the hearts of leaders once again are aflame with a passion to lead man to greatness. The Sermon on the Mount calls for a life-style that brings all that man is longing for—a kingdom of righteousness upon the earth. The only problem is that men think they can instill the ethics of the Sermon into the hearts of men without installing Jesus as their King.

Thinking that the Sermon on the Mount is the solution to the ills of the world, leaders of the social gospel movement have taken the Sermon as their Magna Carta. They thought that peace could be attained by understanding and applying its principles to culture.

Believing that our youngest son, David, has the gift of leadership, Jack and I took him to see *Gandhi*. We sought to use Gandhi's life as a teaching tool and compare it with biblical principles of leadership.

As a natural man, Gandhi was much to be admired. A man of convictions, he practiced turning the other cheek, and taught that peace could be achieved apart from violence. He was a man of devotion, of prayer, of self-denial; a visionary, a great leader, and multitudes followed him. There was only one problem. He could change men's direction, but he could not change their hearts. The life-style to which he called them was thus impossible.

Whereas Gandhi's followers could take the blows of the British—turning the other cheek, being dragged away bloody and battered—they could not live among themselves without destroying one another after achieving their independence. They could handle external wars, but not internal ones. Why? Because the natural man's heart is deceitful and desperately wicked. Gandhi never learned the secret of transforming men's hearts. When I flinched in surprise and horror at the assassin's bullet, I realized that Gandhi had just stepped into a Christless eternity. Gandhi had appreciated Jesus Christ. He had sought to follow some of His teachings, but the kingdom of heaven was not his because he did not do the will of the Father who is in heaven. He did not believe that Jesus Christ was God incarnate—Lord and Master—the Way, the Truth, and the Life—the only means of salvation.

Some look at the Sermon and say, "It's an impossible life-style. It serves no purpose except to show men their sin." Others cry, "No, it's another interpretation of the Law. It does not belong to the age of grace. It stands in opposition to Christ's atoning work. Grace would not demand such a life-style."

Albert Schweitzer, a brilliant, self-sacrificing man, said that the Sermon on the Mount was merely "interim-ethics" which make one suitable for the kingdom of God. In other words, if we could live it in our own strength, it would hold us until the kingdom of heaven was realized. Ultradispensationalists have said it is not for today, but belongs to the kingdom age when Jesus rules on earth for a thousand years. (A dispensation is an era of time when man is tested with respect to a specific revelation of God's will. Thus, an ultradispensationalist is one who rigidly adheres to God's working during a specific time with specific people.)

The Sermon on the Mount tells us who will inherit the kingdom of heaven.

The kingdom is the present-tense possession of the poor in spirit and the persecuted. It belongs to those whose righteousness exceeds that of the scribes and Pharisees; it is for those who do the will of the Father. This rules out Schweitzer's "interim-ethics." It also shows that the seemingly impossible demands of the Sermon are possible. They are possible to those who come to God in poverty of spirit—who take the narrow way, the small gate—who hear and act upon the words of God. To those who say that the Sermon on the Mount is for the kingdom age, I would answer that when Jesus Christ comes, I will no longer be persecuted for righteousness' sake, nor will I have to turn the other cheek. I won't have to allow men to sue me, or force me to go one mile, for during the Millennium we will rule and reign with Jesus Christ.

Is the Sermon on the Mount an impossible life-style? No. It is the life-style of Jesus Christ, the manifestation of the righteousness of God. It is being perfect as our heavenly Father is perfect. *It is possible,* because in the New Covenant, the covenant of grace, God gives us a new heart. He puts His Spirit within us, causing us to walk in His statutes and keep His commandments (Ezekiel 36:26, 27).

It is true. We cannot straighten out ourselves, but God can! The world can only conform us, but God can transform us. O Beloved, how important it is that you realize this as you study the Sermon on the Mount. It is not merely a code of ethics or a life-style to which you must try to conform. It is, rather, the outworking of the transforming work of God. Think upon these things and talk to God about them. Tomorrow we'll see how God transforms us.


## DAY 2


The *Chicago Tribune* carried an article quoting Will Durant, the well-known historian, saying:

> In any generation there may be eight or ten persons who will be alive in the sense of continuing influence three hundred years after. For instance, Plato still lives and Socrates still lives, but in all of western civilization, the person who stands out above all others is Christ. He undoubtedly was the most permanent influence on our thoughts but not on our actions and that's an important modification. Our actions are very seldom Christian but our theology often is. We wish we could behave like Christ.

That's quite a statement, isn't it? Apparently Will Durant respected the teachings of Jesus. He must have felt, however, that they were impossible to put into action. He couldn't make them work. What Will Durant did not know is that theology can never work apart from God's presence within a man. Christianity is a matter of the heart.

I know that you have looked at these Scriptures before, in an earlier lesson. However, it will be good review for you to look at them again.

1. Look up Genesis 8:21 and write down what you learn about man's heart.



2. Look up Jeremiah 17:9 and write down what it says about man's heart.



Now read Romans 7:14–24 very carefully.

14 For we know that the Law is spiritual; but I am of flesh, sold into bondage to sin.

15 For that which I am doing, I do not understand; for I am not practicing what I would like to do, but I am doing the very thing I hate.

16 But if I do the very thing I do not wish to do, I agree with the Law, confessing that it is good.

17 So now, no longer am I the one doing it, but sin which indwells me.

18 For I know that nothing good dwells in me, that is, in my flesh; for the wishing is present in me, but the doing of the good is not.

19 For the good that I wish, I do not do; but I practice the very evil that I do not wish.

20 But if I am doing the very thing I do not wish, I am no longer the one doing it, but sin which dwells in me.

21 I find then the principle that evil is present in me, the one who wishes to do good.

22 For I joyfully concur with the law of God in the inner man,

23 but I see a different law in the members of my body, waging war against the law of my mind, and making me a prisoner of the law of sin which is in my members.

24 Wretched man that I am! Who will set me free from the body of this death?

Underline the words *doing* and *practicing*. Both of these words are present-tense verbs in Greek; they speak of continuous or habitual action. Using some sort of symbol, possibly a cloud like this ⬭ mark the phrase "sin which indwells me." In verse 23 is the phrase, "the law of sin which is in my members." Mark it in the same way. Now note and mark in some distinctive way every use of the word *law* as it refers to the Law of God. (This means that you would not mark "the law of sin," verse 23.)

1. In your own words, describe the state of this person. What is frustrating him and why? What does he want to do that he can't do?

What is he doing that he doesn't want to do? Put it all down in your own words.

2. Considering all the Scriptures that you have looked up, do you think that it's possible for a person like the one in Romans 7 to live according to the Sermon on the Mount? Think on it and then we'll talk about it more tomorrow.

Once again I just have to take a moment to tell you how much I love you and appreciate you. I am so thankful for people who take their Christianity seriously. Thank you for wanting to go on to greater maturity. I know that it requires a lot of discipline and a lot of saying no to other things. I realize that it's a battle, for the enemy would seek to keep you from the Word of God. After all, the Word is your shield and your sword, your defensive and offensive weapon against him. So thank you for persevering, for enduring hardness as a good soldier of Jesus Christ, for keeping your priorities straight. May God bless you exceeding abundantly above all that you can ask or think. I love you.

## DAY 3

In your study yesterday you saw several things. You saw that man's natural heart is deceitful and desperately wicked and that the intent of his heart is wicked even from his youth up.

You saw that the Law is spiritual; the Law is good. Matthew 5:17 says that Jesus did not come to abolish the Law, but to fulfill it. The next verse tells us that "not the smallest letter or stroke will pass away from the Law, until all is accomplished." The Law gives us God's standard of righteousness. There is nothing wrong with the Law; the problem is us!

Man cannot keep the Law because of the condition of his heart and of his flesh. You saw in Romans 7 that sin dwells in man; even though man may desire to do what the Law says, he is unable to do it because sin dwells in him. As it says in Romans 7:14, we are "of flesh, sold into bondage to sin." The dilemma that we saw in our study yesterday was this: some men desire to walk in obedience to the Law but cannot do it because of the power of sin in them.

Now you may want to ask, "Can unsaved men desire to be holy—to want to keep God's Law?" Of course. For years John Wesley sought to serve God. He went through all sorts of religious disciplines and yet it was many years later that he saw that salvation is by grace. Then he entered into the New Covenant. His own writings tell us this.

The scribes, the Pharisees, the religious Jews of Jesus' day also sought to keep the Law. They realized that it is spiritual, that it is good. The problem was, they had uncircumcised hearts. Their hearts had never been circumcised by the Spirit of God. (Romans 2:29 says ". . . circumcision is that which is of the heart, by the Spirit, not by the letter.") The scribes and Pharisees were trying to deal with their old, sinful hearts by living according to the letter of the Law. They were blind to the teaching of Ezekiel and the New Covenant which promised a new heart.

For the sake of clarity, let's summarize man's problem and then we will see God's solution. In and of himself, man cannot live according to the Sermon on the Mount. He looks at the Sermon and drools over its holiness; yet he does not know how to achieve it. He has a problem. He has a deceitful and wicked heart; sin dwells in him, making him a prisoner to sin. Try as he may, he cannot keep the Law. Finally he cries out, "Wretched man that I am! Who will set me free from the body of this death?" (Romans 7:24). Who will set him free from his heart that is deceitful and desperately wicked? Who will set him free from this principle of sin and death that reigns in his body? The answer is found in Romans 8:2: "For the law of the Spirit of life in Christ Jesus has set you free from the law of sin and death."

What is God saying? Well, the word *law* in Romans 8:2 refers not to the Ten Commandments but to a principle. For instance, we speak of a law or a principle of gravity. Here Paul talks about two principles: the principle of the Spirit of life in Christ Jesus versus the principle of sin and death which rules in unsaved men. Romans 8:2, then, tells us that this principle of the Spirit of life in Christ Jesus is the principle that sets us free from the law or principle of sin and death which kept us from being righteous.

In Romans 8:3 God explains how He sets us free from this principle of sin and death. "For what the Law could not do, weak as it was through the flesh, God did: sending His own Son in the likeness of sinful flesh and as an offering for sin, He condemned sin in the flesh."

Let's analyze what God is saying. The Law (the Ten Commandments, the Old Covenant) could not change us. It could not make us righteous. It could not set us free from the principle of death indwelling our bodies. Why? Because the flesh would not cooperate; it couldn't because it was weak, due to the power of indwelling sin. Therefore, since the Law could not set us free from our flesh and indwelling sin, *God set us free.*

Are you saying, "WOW!"? I hope so! I hope that the veil is going to come off your eyes and that you're going to see that you are no longer a slave to sin. That is because God, through the Spirit of life, has set you free from this slavery to sin, the principle of sin and of death.

But how did God set us free? Romans 8:3 gives us the answer. God's Son took on our humanity and came in the likeness of sinful flesh as an offering for sin. When Jesus hung on the cross, God condemned sin in the flesh. That verb *condemned* is an aorist active indicative verb. I know that sounds complicated, but I want you to grow so let me stretch you! The aorist tense means "at one point in time." The active voice means that the subject performed the action of the verb. The indicative mood is the mood of reality. Therefore, God is saying that at one point in time He, all by Himself, condemned sin in your flesh. In other words, He deposed sin of its dominion or power to rule over you.

Do you see what this means? If you are really a Christian, you are no longer enslaved to sin. You have been set free from sin's dominion over you! Let me show this to you in two separate passages.

Read John 8:34–36 and then answer the questions that follow:

1. According to Jesus, what makes us a slave of sin?


2. According to Jesus, how can you be set free from that slavery to sin?

This passage is talking about being set free from sin's power by believing on the Lord Jesus Christ. Until a man comes to salvation he may desire to be good, and please God, but because of the power of indwelling sin he is unable to live the way he even desires to live. First he must be set free from his slavery to sin. Only Jesus can set man free. This is brought out very clearly in the next passage that we want to consider.

Read through Romans 6:1–7, printed below, very carefully and then do the assignment that follows. But first, let me encourage you to stop right now. Ask God to open the eyes of your understanding to the truths of Romans 6. They are absolutely liberating, as you will see.

### Romans 6:1–7

1 What shall we say then? Are we to continue in sin that grace might increase?

2 May it never be! How shall we who died to sin still live in it?

3 Or do you not know that all of us who have been baptized into Christ Jesus have been baptized into His death?

4 Therefore we have been buried with Him through baptism into death, in order that as Christ was raised from the dead through the glory of the Father, so we too might walk in newness of life.

5 For if we have become united with Him in the likeness of His death, certainly we shall be also in the likeness of His resurrection,

6 knowing this, that our old self was crucified with Him, that our body of sin might be done away with, that we should no longer be slaves to sin;

7 For he who has died is freed from sin.

Mark every use of the word *sin* by underlining. Then write out here everything that you learn about sin from these seven verses.

1. Now put a [          ] around each use of the word *died* or *death*. What do you learn about those who died with Jesus? Write it out.

Read Romans 6:6. Do you see the word *that* used two times in this verse? Those are called purpose clauses; they tell you the purpose of something, or the reason for something. Let me help you to see what Paul is saying in this passage.

2. What happened to the old self or old man?

3. Looking at *that* as a purpose clause, what was the purpose of this happening to the old self?

4. What happened to the body of sin according to verse 6?

5. According to Romans 6:6, what was the purpose for doing this to the body of sin?

6. According to verse 7, who is freed from sin?

In this passage God is saying that those who are in Christ Jesus have died to sin. Verse 3 tells us that those who have been baptized into Christ Jesus have been baptized into His death. The word *baptize* does not always refer to water. There is a baptism of fire, a baptism of the Holy Spirit, a baptism of water. As a matter of fact, Hebrews 6:1 talks about the doctrine of baptisms. *Baptize* simply means "to be identified with or united with." Therefore, Romans 6:3 is saying that those who have been united with Christ Jesus have been united into His death. I have drawn you a simple diagram to show what God is saying.

Since we have been united into His death, we will be united with Him in His burial. And according to Romans 6:5, we will also be united with Him in the likeness of His resurrection. Therefore, God is teaching us that we died with Christ, we were buried with Christ, and we are raised with Christ. Romans 6:4 says that we are raised so that "we too might walk in newness of life." In other words, after we are saved we are going to have a whole new life. This reminds me of 2 Corinthians 5:17: "Therefore if any man is in Christ, he is a new creature; the old things passed away; behold, new things have come."

What makes things new? What causes old things to pass away? How can this happen? Romans 6:6 has the answer. Our old self, or old man, was crucified with Jesus so that our body of sin might be done away with, so that we should no longer be slaves to sin.

What is God saying to us in this passage? The term *old man* or *old self* appears only three places in the New Testament: here, Ephesians 4:22, and Colossians 3:9. In Ephesians and Colossians the Word says that the old man or old self has been laid aside and the new man, the new self has been put on. This means that everything that you were before you were saved has been crucified with Jesus Christ. It is dead. It has been laid aside. You are now a new creature and are able to walk in newness of life because the death of the old man set you free. You are no longer a slave to sin.

Remember John 8:36? "If therefore the Son shall make you free, you shall be free indeed." In John 8 we saw that we are set free from being a slave to sin. And that's exactly what Romans 6 is about. The old man was crucified in order that your body, which was a slave to sin, might be set free from that slavery. Romans 6:14 summarizes it. "For sin shall not be master over you, for you are not under law, but under grace." When you receive Jesus Christ as your Savior you become a participant in the New Covenant, the covenant of grace. You are no longer under the Law. And because you are no longer under the Law, sin cannot be master over you. The word *master* in the Greek means "to rule over, to lord over, or to have dominion over." Romans

6:18 says, "having been freed from sin, you became slaves of righteousness."

Now let me take you back to Romans 8 and wrap it up for today. Remember we saw in Romans 8 that it is the law or the principle of the Spirit of life in Christ Jesus that has set us free from the law (the principle) of sin and death. Who is it that sets us free from being a slave to sin? It is the Holy Spirit, the Spirit of life in Christ Jesus. Let me repeat it again. How did God set you free? Romans 8:3 tells us. God did it by "sending His own Son in the likeness of sinful flesh and as an offering for sin." God, through Jesus, condemned sin in the flesh. That means He deposed it from its dominion. He took away sin's power to reign in your mortal body.

Why did He do it? So that you might fulfill the requirement of the Law. Look at Romans 8:4. "In order that the requirement of the Law might be fulfilled in us, who do not walk according to the flesh, but according to the Spirit." In Romans 8 there is a contrast between two things—those who are in the flesh or walk according to the flesh and those who are in the Spirit or walk according to the Spirit. Those who are in the flesh are people who do not have the Spirit of God dwelling in them. Romans 8:8, 9 tells us, "those who are in the flesh cannot please God. However, you are not in the flesh but in the Spirit, if indeed the Spirit of God dwells in you. But if anyone does not have the Spirit of Christ, he does not belong to Him." If the Holy Spirit is not in you, then you do not belong to God; you are not a Christian.

Because you are now in Christ "you have not received a spirit of slavery." You are no longer a slave. Remember John 8:35, 36 says that "the slave does not remain in the house forever; the son does remain forever. If therefore the Son shall make you free, you shall be free indeed." When Jesus came to live inside of you, He cast out the slave. He set you free from slavery to sin so that you need not fear. God adopted you as a son of God. Thus, Romans 8:15 says, "For you have not received a spirit of slavery leading to fear again, but you have received a spirit of adoption as sons by which we cry out, 'Abba! Father!' "

Now let's go back to our questions about the Sermon on the Mount. Man cannot straighten out man, but God can. By ourselves we cannot live the Sermon on the Mount, but indwelt by the Holy Spirit we can! Why? Because the Holy Spirit sets us free from our slavery to sin and enables us to walk in newness of life.

Your next question may be, "But what about my sinful and deceitful heart? What am I going to do with it?" God took care of it under the New Covenant. We'll see that tomorrow, Beloved. Until then, meditate on these truths. They are so rich, so liberating, and they will open your eyes to what true Christianity is.

## DAY 4

The question before us: "Is the Sermon on the Mount an impossible life-style?" The answer is no. The Sermon on the Mount was the life-style of Jesus, and it is the life-style that He lives out to one degree or another in every single believer.

We saw yesterday that we can be set free from sin's indwelling power over us—through the work of Jesus Christ in His death, burial, and resurrection. We saw that if the Son sets us free from the slavery of sin, we will be free indeed. When we are saved, we have newness of life, because our old man (self) was crucified so that our body, as an instrument of sin, might be rendered inoperative and we will no longer be slaves to sin. It is the Spirit that sets us free from the law of sin and death, and it is the Holy Spirit that enables us to fulfill the just requirement of the Law (Romans 8:4) and thereby have a righteousness that exceeds the righteousness of the scribes and Pharisees.

Today we want to look at how the New Covenant of Grace takes care of the problem of our deceitful, desperately wicked heart. Until John the Baptist came announcing the New Covenant, the Law and the Prophets were proclaimed. The Law was a schoolmaster to shut us up to obedience until faith in Jesus Christ should come. However, the Law was never given to make a man righteous. Instead, the Law was given to show men their sin so that they might come to God in poverty of spirit and receive the righteousness that comes by faith through the death of Jesus Christ. Jesus was made sin for us that you and I might be made the righteousness of God in Him (2 Corinthians 5:21).

Turn in your Bible to Hebrews 10 and read verses 1, 9, 10, 14–18. In Hebrews 10:1 we see that the Law could not make men perfect. Year after year the Jews kept offering the same sacrifices for sin, and yet they were never changed. Hebrews 10:4 says, "For it is impossible for the blood of bulls and goats to take away sins." Therefore, God sent His Son Jesus into the world. When He came He said, " 'Behold, I have come to do Thy Will.' He takes away the first [the Old Covenant of the Law] in order to establish the second [the New Covenant of Grace]" (Hebrews 10:9). According to this verse, by this New Covenant we are sanctified once for all through the offering of the body of Jesus Christ. The Law could not sanctify us or make us perfect, but the death of Jesus Christ can. Why? You saw it yesterday. Because the death of Jesus Christ sets us free from sin's power and dominion.

Now let's look at Hebrews 10:14–16.

> For by one offering He has perfected for all time those who are sanctified. And the Holy Spirit also bears witness to us . . . saying, "This is the covenant that I will make with them after those days, says the LORD: I will put My laws upon their heart, and upon their mind I will write them."

Here is a very definite reference to the New Covenant. The author of Hebrews is quoting a promise that was given to the Old Testament prophet Jeremiah. His quote continues: " 'And their sins and their lawless deeds I will remember no more.' " Look at this New Covenant and see how it takes care of our sin problem as well as the problem of our deceitful and desperately wicked heart that leads us into sin. I want you to see how the New Covenant enables you to fulfill the Law so you can have a righteousness surpassing that of the scribes and Pharisees.

Turn to Jeremiah 31:31–34, and note especially verses 31 and 32. Jeremiah is talking about God making a new covenant with the houses of Israel and of Judah. It will be a different covenant than He made with their fathers when He took them out of Egypt. That covenant was the Law, given at Mt. Sinai. The Ten Commandments or Law is the covenant which they broke.

Now look at Jeremiah 31:33. In this verse God tells us what this New Covenant will do for man. First, He says, " 'I will put My law within them, and on their heart I will write it.' " In the Old Covenant, the Law was written on tables of stone. In the New Covenant, the Law will be written on hearts of flesh; it will not be an external thing but an internal thing.

Take a minute and read 2 Corinthians 3:2–9. The ministry of death was the Law, the ministry of the Spirit, the New Covenant of grace.

Second, He says, " 'I will be their God and they shall be my people.' " The New Covenant brings a new relationship with God. It's a relationship of possession, of ownership. God becomes yours; you become His.

In Jeremiah 31:34 God tells us a third thing about the New Covenant. " 'They shall not teach again, each man his neighbor and each man his brother, saying, "Know the Lord," for they shall all know Me, from the least of them to the greatest of them.' " I believe that God is showing us that there will be an inward knowing of Him, a witness of God's Spirit within teaching us about Him. What you learn from the Lord will not come merely from what man tells you about Him; God within you will be your Teacher. It's like 1 John 2:27: "And as for you, the anointing which you received from Him abides in you, and you have no need for any one to teach you; but as His anointing teaches you about all things. . . ." In other words, you will have a resident Teacher.

Fourth, God says He will forgive your iniquity and your sin He will remember no more. This is what we saw quoted by the author of Hebrews when he told us about the New Covenant that Jesus brought. O Beloved, if you ever get hold of this, it will open up your understanding of the Christian life in a whole new way!

Let's look at one last passage in Jeremiah that deals with the New Covenant. Read Jeremiah 32:38–40. Verse 38 gives us a reiteration of God's promise in Jeremiah 31—" 'They shall be My people, and I will be their God.' " In verse 39, He gives you even more insight into this New Covenant. He tells you that He will give you one heart and one way so that you will fear Him always—for your good and for the good of your children who will come after you. In other words, your life will be an example to your children as they see your reverence for God.

In Jeremiah 32:40 God tells you that this is an everlasting covenant. It will never end! God promises you that He will never turn away from you. He will not stop doing you good. This is a wonderful promise! It reminds me of Hebrews 13:5 where God promises that He will never leave us or forsake us.

Have you ever been afraid that you might walk away from God, that you might turn away from Him? I understand. I had this fear also until I read Jeremiah 32:40 and saw God's wonderful keeping power. In the New Covenant, God promises us that He will put the fear of Him in our hearts so that we will not turn away! Praise the Lord! This reminds me of Paul's words in 2 Timothy 1:12 when he said that he was convinced that God is able to guard what Paul had entrusted to Him until that day. Also, it supports 1 John 2:19.

One thing you have seen about your heart is that God writes His laws there; He puts them within. Isn't that wonderful? Then there comes an inward knowing of what pleases God and what displeases Him.

I do pray that you are growing, Precious One, and that I am explaining this to you in a very clear way. Your faces are ever before me. I so long to be one who accurately handles the Word of God, for I know my great accountability before God, as a teacher of His Word.

## DAY 5

Finally we are going to find out how God takes care of that deceitful and desperately wicked heart! I want to begin by looking at Ezekiel 36:26, 27—two very significant verses. Here is God's promise of a new heart. " 'Moreover, I will give you a new heart and put a new spirit within you; and I will remove the heart of stone from your flesh and give you a heart of flesh.' "

Ezekiel calls it "a new heart," "a heart of flesh," while in Romans 2:29 Paul calls it a "circumcised heart." Circumcision is a cutting away of the old in order to reveal the new. In Romans 2:29 we see that this circumcision is by the Spirit and not by the letter. In other words, God is saying that heart-circumcision comes through the New Covenant and not through keeping the Law. When you see Paul referring to "the letter" Paul is referring to the Law. In Ezekiel 36:26 you also see the promise of a new Spirit within. Do you remember that the Beatitudes begin with a poverty of spirit, a realization before God that you are utterly destitute, spiritually bankrupt? When you came to Him in your poverty of spirit (the deepest form of repentance), then God gave you the kingdom of heaven. In giving you the kingdom of heaven, He gives you the gift of His Holy Spirit.

This is what Ezekiel 36:27 says: " 'And I will put My Spirit within you and cause you to walk in My statutes, and you will be careful to observe My ordinances.' " Here is the promise of God's indwelling Holy Spirit, of the Enabler who will enable us to keep God's laws, and walk in obedience to His commandments. Here is the promise of the Spirit of life in Christ Jesus—the One who sets you free from the law of sin and death (Romans 8:2)—the One who gives you a new heart!

O Beloved, by now I'm sure that you have seen it. It is impossible for us to fulfill the Law apart from the Spirit of God dwelling within. That is why Gandhi and others could not live the whole Sermon on the Mount. Gandhi could turn the other cheek and go the extra mile. But he could not live it all because he did not walk under the lordship of Jesus Christ. Please don't think that I am judging. It's simply that Gandhi himself never claimed to think of Jesus as anything other than a great man. To Gandhi, as to others, the Sermon on the Mount was simply a code of ethics, an ideal to strive for. They just didn't see that it is an impossible life-style for those who do not have a new heart and God's Spirit living within. They all missed the first beatitude, which alone gives men the kingdom of heaven, and in the giving, the Holy Spirit of promise. This is what Ephesians 1:13 means when it says, "After listening to the message of truth, the gospel of your salvation— having also believed, you were sealed in Him with the Holy Spirit of promise."

Now let's put all that we have learned this week into the context of Matthew 5:17–20. In verse 17, Jesus says, " 'Do not think that I came to abolish the Law or the Prophets; I did not come to abolish, but to fulfill.' " It was important that the Jews understand Jesus' relationship to the Law and the Prophets. That term, "the Law and the Prophets," is a summation of all the Old Testament. Jesus was the fulfillment of the Old Testament. He was the seed of the woman, the seed of Abraham, the personification of the righteousness of the Law who would become the curse of the Law, for "cursed is every one who hangs on a tree" (Galatians 3:13). His dying on the very same day that the Passover lamb was sacrificed demonstrated to all who would believe, that He was the Lamb of God who would take away the sins of the world. He was the Child whom the virgin would bear as prophesied in Isaiah 7:14. His name would be called Immanuel, "God with us." He was the Child who was to be born, the Son who was to be given, the One whose name would be called Wonderful Counselor, Mighty God, Eternal Father, Prince of Peace (see Isaiah 9:6). He was the One whose bones would not be broken, who would cry out, "My God, my God, why hast Thou forsaken me?" (Psalms 22:1).

According to Zechariah 12:10, He would be the One whom the Jews would pierce and whom they would someday look upon and mourn because they did not know the day of their visitation. He was the Messenger of the covenant who would come suddenly to the temple (*see* Malachi 3:1). Jesus was the fulfillment of all that the Law and the Prophets pointed to. Not one jot or tittle would pass away from the Law until He had accomplished it all. "Forever, O LORD, Thy word is settled in heaven" (Psalms 119: 89).

This is why Jesus goes on to say, " 'Whoever then annuls one of the least of these commandments, and so teaches others, shall be called least in the kingdom of heaven; but whoever keeps and teaches them, he shall be called great in the kingdom of heaven' " (Matthew 5:19). God's word is not to be tampered with. The commandments are not to be annulled. Jesus came to fulfill the Law and that is what you and I are to do with it also.

"But, Kay," you say, "I thought that we were now under grace, no longer under the Law!" That's right, Beloved, but that grace does not make us lawless. Grace fulfills the Law. Grace calls us to a righteousness surpassing that of the scribes and Pharisees, a righteousness that is absolutely essential if we are to enter the kingdom of heaven (Matthew 5:20). According to Romans 8:4, this is why the Holy Spirit is given to us: "in order that the requirement of the Law might be fulfilled in us, who do not walk according to the flesh, but according to the Spirit."

In Matthew 5:19 we see that if we are to be great in the kingdom of heaven we must first keep and then teach God's commandments. Note which comes first—the keeping! And all of this is possible because God has given us His Holy Spirit.

Man cannot straighten out himself. But what is impossible with man is possible with God! Have you been trying to straighten out yourself? Have you been trying to shape up? Are you totally frustrated? Do you cry out with Paul, "Wretched man that I am! Who will set me free from the body of this death?" (Romans 7:24)? Come to God in your poverty of spirit and let Him straighten you out. He will put to death that old man and He will make a brand-new you, so that you can be freed from sin's dominion and walk in newness of life. Hallelujah! What a Savior!

# 13 - How Do You Handle Anger, Murder, Lust, and Adultery?

## DAY 1

Christianity is not keeping a set of rules, simply avoiding what is evil. It is, rather, hungering and thirsting for righteousness—a righteousness that is an inside-out reality—not merely an external righteousness of the letter, but an internal righteousness of the heart.

In Matthew 5:21–48 Jesus gives his hearers six examples of how their righteousness is to exceed the righteousness of the scribes and Pharisees. He deals with murder (21–26), adultery (27–32), divorce (31, 32), vows (33–37), and revenge (38–42).Then He talks about loving our enemies (43–48).

If you were to mark the key phrases in these passages, you would mark, "You have heard that . . ." and Jesus' response, "But I say to you. . . ." Obviously, Jesus is contrasting what they have heard from others with what He has to say.

As we study, it is important for us to realize that these are not conflicting contrasts between the Law of Moses and the teaching of Jesus Christ. They cannot be, because Jesus did not come to abolish the Law but to fulfill it. Neither is He giving another law, because to do so would be to annul the Law of God and teach others to do the same. In doing this Jesus would be going against His own words in Matthew 5:19, "Whoever then annuls one of the least of these commandments, and so teaches others, shall be called least in the kingdom of heaven; but whoever keeps and teaches them, he shall be called great in the kingdom of heaven."

Jesus is not in any way altering the Law or diminishing it; rather He is showing his hearers the true intent of the Law. Why? Because the scribes and Pharisees had seated themselves in the chair of Moses. In doing so they "required rigid observance of 365 prohibitions and 250 commandments," notes J. Dwight Pentecost in *The Sermon on the Mount*. In all their prohibitions and additional commandments, they had tied up heavy, unbearable loads, laid them on men's shoulders, and said, "This is the righteousness that God requires. Keep these laws and you will be pleasing to Him." It is true that this kind of righteousness only took care of the outward appearance and left the heart unchanged. Therefore, Jesus had to show them the true heart of the Law.

Was this a problem only of Jesus' day? One by one, look at the examples Jesus gave. Read Matthew 5:21–26, and then write your answers.

1. What had they heard?

2. Does Jesus contradict what they had heard? If so, how?

3. According to Matthew 5:22, man will be held accountable for three other things. These are denoted by the words "everyone" and "whoever." What are they?

4. What are Jesus' instructions in verses 23, 24?

5. What are Jesus' instructions in verses 25, 26?

Now let's take apart these six verses point by point. God's concern for the sanctity of life came long before Moses received the commandment, "You shall not murder" (Exodus 20:13). From the Garden of Eden man has been considered his brother's keeper. When an angry Cain rose up and killed Abel, God did not let his crime go unpunished. Life matters to God.

After the ark rested upon the mountains of Ararat, God made the sanctity of man's life very clear to Noah; He instituted capital punishment. "And surely I will require your lifeblood; from every beast I will require it. And from every man, from every man's brother I will require the life of man. Whoever sheds man's blood, by man his blood shall be shed, for in the image of God He made man' " (Genesis 9:5, 6). Murder is a hideous crime because it contradicts the value that God has placed upon man. Marred or not, man was made in the image of God. To murder a man is to destroy what God had created, and only God has the right of life and death.

At this point, you may say, "Kay, that's why I am against capital punishment. Who are we to play God and take another man's life?"

I would have to ask, "Who are we to break God's Law?" The King James Version translates Exodus 20:13, "Thou shalt not kill," but the Hebrew word literally means "to murder intentionally." Hence, the New American Standard Bible renders it, " 'You shall not murder.' " This is God's command. It is very plain. Murder is a sin. That sin must be punished. How? " 'Whoever sheds man's blood, by man his blood shall be shed' " (Genesis 9:6).

But what if someone did not intentionally kill a man? What if it were an accident? God made provision for this in Exodus 21:12–14.

> He who strikes a man so that he dies shall surely be put to death. But if he did not lie in wait for him, but God let him fall into his hand, then I will appoint you a place to which he may flee. If, however, a man acts presumptuously toward his neighbor, so as to kill him craftily, you are to take him even from My altar, that he may die.

God had the children of Israel establish three cities of refuge. When a man killed another man unintentionally, he could flee to one of the cities of refuge and live there (Deuteronomy 19:1–4). However, if a man had murdered another, and then run to a city of refuge, the elders of that city could take him out and deliver him to the avenger of blood that he might die. They were not to take pity upon him, but were to purge the blood of the innocent from Israel so that it might go well with the nation (Deuteronomy 19:11–13). I am giving you these extra Scriptures so that you might have a biblical view of capital punishment. I am also giving them to you so that you might understand what Jesus is saying about anger and the sanctity of life.

Look at Matthew 5:22. We have seen that murder was wrong and was to be judged in a court where the just penalty would be carried out. However, Jesus goes on to tell us that everyone who is angry with his brother should be guilty before the court. Anyone who calls his brother "Raca" should be guilty before the supreme court, the Sanhedrin. And everyone who would refer to a brother as a fool would be guilty enough to go to Gehenna, the lake of fire.

What is Jesus trying to show us? I think He wants us to see the value of a person. Murder, like all other sins, has its beginning in a man's heart. Matthew 15:19 says, " 'For out of the heart come evil thoughts, murders, adulteries, fornications, thefts, false witness, slanders. These are the things which defile the man.' " You can murder a man in your heart without ever killing him physically. Murder begins with anger.

There is a righteous anger and there is an unrighteous anger. We see righteous anger demonstrated in the life of Jesus Christ when He became angry and overturned the tables of the moneychangers in the temple. We see this righteous anger in God when He wanted Moses to get out of His way so that He could kill the children of Israel. Ephesians 4:26 says, "be angry and yet do not sin; Do not let the sun go down on your anger." The word *angry* in Ephesians 4:26 is the same word as used in Matthew 5:22. When it says "be angry, and do not sin," that type of anger, obviously, is not a sin in God's eyes. However, in Matthew 5:22, when Jesus says that everyone who is angry with his brother shall be guilty before the court, obviously this is wrong anger.

What makes it wrong? In the context of Scripture, we see that it is wrong because it is directed toward the sinner rather than the sin. It is an anger that, if unchecked, would lead to murder. Therefore, if you are going to be righteous before God, you cannot permit this kind of anger in your heart. It is not wrong for you to become indignant over sin, but it is wrong for you to have an anger within your heart that would destroy a man who is made in God's image. This is why saying "Raca" is so bad. "Raca" is an Aramaic word for empty-headed, or good for nothing. If I say to an other person, "You aren't worth anything," it's the same as if I said, "Raca." That person was made in God's image; he was made to glorify God. To call a man a fool is to disdain the fact that God has given him life. The word *fool* is *moros*. From the context of Matthew 5:22, we can see that the word *fool* is a degree worse than "Raca." W. E. Vine says, "The latter scorns a man's mind and calls him stupid; *moros* scorns his heart and character; hence the Lord's more severe condemnation." *Fool* means morally worthless. If Matthew 5:28 summarizes everything that precedes it, and we are to be perfect even as our heavenly Father is perfect, then we must view others in the same way that God does. We must value every person.

How far does this respect for life go? It goes so far that if you know that your brother has something against you, you are immediately to seek reconciliation. That is how important relationships are to God. Just before Jesus went to Calvary, He prayed to the Father that we might be one even as He and His Father are one (John 17:17). God does not want a schism in the body. Therefore, our gifts mean nothing to Him if we are not going to walk in peace with our brothers.

Can you see that it is not the *letter* of the law that God is interested in, but the *spirit* of the law? External conformity is not enough. Internal righteousness is what He requires. Remember the beatitude "blessed are the pure in heart"?

We have seen truth; now we must apply it. What is your heart's attitude toward your fellowman as you interact in the marketplace, as you move in the business world, as you sit behind the desk as a teacher, as you fulfill the role of a parent, as you live with your mate? How does your heart feel toward those with whom you come in contact? Do you respect them as created by God in His image, distorted as it may be? Do you value the sanctity of their lives or do you despise God's creation? What is in your heart?

Take a few minutes to take stock of your attitudes toward others. Ask God to search you and see if there is any wicked way in you. If so, ask God to reveal it to you that you might confess it, turn from it, and embrace a righteousness that is not of the letter but is of the spirit.

## DAY 2

After dealing with murder, Jesus turned to the issue of adultery. Why did He choose these two commandments? Is it not because they are primary areas of weakness: our relationship with our fellowman and to our sexuality? As with murder, Jesus wants to show that adultery is not just an external act, but is a matter of the heart!

Recently I spoke with a young man who was grieved over his mother's actions. My heart hurt as he told me the classic story that is repeated in so many homes. His mother had left his dad for another man. That man had left his wife and now the two were caught in a web of adultery. "Mom says I'm living under legalism when I tell her that she is not doing right. She says that she's under grace—not to worry about her." Does grace allow us to habitually commit adultery, either physically or mentally? Does adultery happen only when you actually have relations? No, not according to Jesus. Jesus says, "Every one who looks on a woman to lust for her has committed adultery with her already in his heart" (Matthew 5:28).

"You mean to tell me that if I just have a dirty thought come into my mind, a thought about sex, that I've committed adultery!!" No, that is not what Jesus is saying. The verb *look* is in the present tense in the Greek, thereby implying a continuous or habitual action. What Jesus is saying is, if you keep on looking on a woman or a man, to lust after that woman or man, you have committed adultery with that person in your heart. Remember what we saw yesterday in Matthew 15:19—"For out of the heart come . . . adulteries"! Adultery begins a long time before you ever get in bed. It begins with a look that is not brought under control. It begins with a thought that is not turned away but entertained.

Was Jesus' evaluation of adultery something new? Oh, no! Job understood it well. Turn to Job 31:1, 9–12; and I want you to see it in your Bible so that you can remember where it is. As a matter of fact, at the top of that page in your Bible you might write "a covenant with my eyes." Job well understood that men were turned on by sight. So he made a covenant with his eyes that he would not gaze at a virgin. According to verse 4, he knew that God saw his way and numbered all his steps.

Job was fully aware of the weaknesses of his flesh, of the ability of a man's heart to be enticed by a woman. So, he was determined to flee lust by making a covenant with his eyes; he would not permit them to gaze on what would entice him and consume his righteousness.

If my heart has been enticed by a woman,
Or I have lurked at my neighbor's doorway,
May my wife grind for another,
And let others kneel down over her.
For that would be a lustful crime;
moreover, it would be an iniquity punishable by judges.
For it would be a fire that consumes to Abaddon,
And would uproot all my increase.

*Job 31:9–12*

The young man's mother had been enticed by sin. She had lurked at her neighbor's doorway. She had committed a lustful crime that would consume her and uproot and destroy the blessing of life that God had intended for her.

She's counting on grace, but according to Jude she is an ungodly person who has turned the grace of our God to licentiousness. She has denied her Master and Lord, Jesus Christ (Jude 4). Is He her Master and Lord, or could that simply be what she has called Him? Remember, Beloved, the Sermon on the Mount ends with Jesus telling those who call Him "Lord, Lord" to depart from Him because they are practicing lawlessness: they are not doing the will of the Father.

How serious is adultery? It is so serious that it can take you to hell. In Galatians 5:19–21 Paul writes, "Now the deeds of the flesh are evident, which are: immorality, impurity, sensuality, idolatry, sorcery, enmities, strife, jealousy, outbursts of anger, disputes, dissensions, factions, envyings, drunkenness, carousings, and things like these, of which I forewarn you just as I have forewarned you that those who practice such things shall not inherit the kingdom of God." If a person practices adultery you can know that they will not inherit the kingdom of God. They will spend eternity in hell. As you read, pay close attention. I did not say a single act of adultery would keep a person from entering the kingdom of heaven. That is not what God is saying. He is saying that if adultery is the *practice* of your life, then you will not enter the kingdom of heaven. The verb that is translated "practice" in Galatians 5:21 is in the present tense; it is a habitual or continuous thing in a person's life.

How serious is this matter of adultery? America certainly needs to know, because we are a nation of adulterers. Immorality abounds on every hand. Sex permeates almost every aspect of our culture. Even the rough and tumble sport of football is not immune from it. Scantily-clothed cheerleaders parade their wares for all to see. Where are man's eyes safe? Or woman's? Adultery is awakened by what the eye sees or what the hand touches. Thus Jesus tells us "If your right eye makes you stumble, tear it out, and throw it from you ... if your right hand makes you stumble, cut it off, and throw it from you; for it is better for you that one of the parts of your body perish, than for your whole body to go into hell" (Matthew 5:29, 30).

What is God advocating? Is Jesus telling you to literally pull out your eye? To literally cut off your hand? No. Jesus is saying that adultery is a sin that can take you to hell. Therefore, get rid of anything that would cause you to commit adultery. Bring it under control. If you don't it will destroy you. "Do not be deceived; neither fornicators, nor idolators, nor adulterers, nor effeminate, nor homosexuals, nor thieves, nor the covetous, nor drunkards, nor revilers, nor swindlers, shall inherit the kingdom of God" (1 Corinthians 6:9, 10). If you are not going to inherit the kingdom of God, then your whole body will be thrown into hell: the lake of fire, where the worm dies not and the fire is not quenched. Therefore, whatever you have to do to keep yourself from committing adultery, do it. Do not put youself in a position of vulnerability. The spirit is willing but the flesh is weak.

Is it any wonder that teens are immoral? Look at their examples. I believe we are going to see more and more immorality, even among those who name the name of Jesus Christ. Why? Because we don't have an overriding passion that will control the passion of our flesh. What is that overriding passion? It is a passion to be holy, a passion to please God, to be perfect even as our heavenly Father is perfect.

Why don't we have that passion? Because we have been enticed by temporal things, temporal pleasures. Because we have not loved and esteemed His Word more precious than our necessary food.

My son, give attention to my words; incline your ear to my sayings. Do not let them depart from your sight; keep them in the midst of your heart. For they are life to those who find them, and health to all their whole body. Watch over your heart with all diligence, for from it flow the springs of life. Put away from you a deceitful mouth, and put devious lips far from you. Let your eyes look directly ahead, and let your gaze be fixed straight in front of you. Watch the path of your feet, and all your ways will be established. Do not turn to the right nor to the left; turn your foot from evil.

*Proverbs 4:20-27*

Drink water from your own cistern, and fresh water from your own well . . . Let your fountain be blessed, and rejoice in the wife of your youth. As a loving hind and a graceful doe, let her breasts satisfy you at all times; be exhilarated always with her love. For why should you, my son, be exhilarated with an adulteress, and embrace the bosom of a foreigner? For the ways of a man are before the eyes of the LORD, and He watches all his paths. His own iniquities will capture the wicked, and he will be held with the cords of his sin. He will die for lack of instruction, and in the greatness of his folly he will go astray.

*Proverbs 5:15, 18–23*

Think about it.

## DAY 3

The Jews knew that they could not commit adultery; it was against God's Law. So when they got tired of their wives, they simply wrote a bill of divorce, divorcing them for any reason whatever. They had taken Deuteronomy 24:1–3 and twisted it, perverting what God was saying. Instead of seeing Deuteronomy 24:1–3 as a protection for the woman who was abandoned by her husband, they used it as a proof text for their sin.

In the Sermon, Jesus next addressed the issue of divorce, quoting from Deuteronomy 24 and then saying, "But I say to you that every one who divorces his wife, except for the cause of unchastity, makes her commit adultery; and whoever marries a divorced woman commits adultery" (Matthew 5:32).

God hates divorce.* The sin of the Jews in divorcing their wives was not a New Testament problem. It was also a problem that God addressed in the book of Malachi. God was very upset with the priests. "You cover the altar of the LORD with tears, with weeping and with groaning, because He no longer regards the offering or accepts it with favor from your hand. Yet you say, 'For what reason?'" (Malachi 2:13, 14).

The priests were asking, "God, why aren't you accepting my offering? Why aren't you favoring me?" And they would weep and groan, but still God would be far from them because the Lord was "a witness

---

* For those who desire a comprehensive study on the subject of divorce in light of God's Word, the author recommends the Precept course, *Marriage Without Regrets*.

between them and the wives of their youth, against whom they had dealt treacherously, though she was their companion and wife by covenant" (Malachi 2:14). They dealt treacherously against their wives by divorcing them. This is why God goes on to say, "For I hate divorce, says the LORD, the God of Israel, and him who covers his garment with wrong" (Malachi 2:16). God hates divorce because it mars his earthly example of the heavenly union of Christ to His bride, the church—a bride He will not divorce!

How I pray that you will see that "the body is not for immorality, but for the Lord; and the Lord is for the body. Flee immorality. Every other sin that a man commits is outside the body, but the immoral man sins against his own body" (1 Corinthians 6:13, 18).

Sexual immorality leaves an awful scar: a scar that is ugly, that mars the beauty of God's creation, a scar I myself have borne. Is it any wonder that since I've come to know Jesus Christ that 1 Corinthians 6:19, 20 has meant so much to me? "Do you not know that your body is a temple of the Holy Spirit who is in you, whom you have from God, and that you are not your own? For you have been bought with a price: therefore glorify God in your body."

O Beloved, make a covenant with your eyes that you will not look upon another to lust after him in your heart and thereby commit adultery. Honor that marriage covenant; honor it out of obedience to God.

I want to stop here, but I can't because in my spirit I know that some who are reading this are caught in a lust, in a desire, in a dream! It's wrong and you know it. It's sin and you know it. The Bible puts it very clearly. "Fornicators and adulterers God will judge" (Hebrews 13:4). I know that you think that you can't bear to do without the one you want, that if you can't have that person, life is not worth living. You're wrong. You will survive. Life will not be worth living if you transgress God's holy commandments. If you are a Christian, the Holy Spirit is there. Walk by the Spirit and you will not fulfill the lust of the flesh. Make the phone call. Tell him or her that you are calling it quits, then go get on your knees and ask God to break your heart as you have broken His, so that you will abhor your sin and flee. Flee, Beloved, flee!

# DAY 4

It's Sunday afternoon as I write this. We have just finished our Teen Conference. This weekend, the Lord led me to teach the young people from the book of Ephesians. Our first three sessions were spent in seeing who we are in Christ Jesus. Our session today was looking at our walk in the light of our wealth. The message there is very clear. We are to walk as Christ Jesus walked, worthy of the calling with which He has called us. We dealt with Ephesians 4:17–5:18 until we ran out of time, which is quite typical of me. I never have quite enough time!

These verses in Ephesians deal with some hard-hitting issues that scratch teens right where they itch. One of the things we discussed was cheating, which is a common problem among teens today, even in Christian high schools. Among the kids who hung around after the conference to talk and to share and to pray was one very precious young lady.

"Kay," she said, "I don't do the other things you mentioned. I really walk pretty straight except for one thing: I cheat. Kay, what do I do? God says that we are to expose the deeds of darkness, but how can I expose them when I myself cheat? I'm going to stop cheating, but what do I say to my teachers? What do I say to the kids I've helped cheat?"

I cannot tell you the love that welled up in my heart for this young woman; I know that it was the love of the Lord. God loves integrity. Here was a young woman who wanted to be honest before God and man. I can't wait to get her letter to hear how it goes when she speaks to teacher after teacher, confesses her sin and says she is willing to take the penalty or make restitution. I can't wait to hear what happens as she stands before her classmates and asks their forgiveness for marring the image of Jesus Christ by cheating.

God is concerned with our integrity, with the honesty of the words of our mouths. Our yes are to be yes and our nos are to be no. What we say we are to mean. Our pledges are not to be broken. Our words are not to be couched in deceit.

Jesus took his hearers back to the Old Testament law on making vows, showing them how that law had become twisted and how they had missed its true intent. Let's look at it.

Begin by reading Matthew 5:33–37 and then answer the questions that follow:

1. According to Matthew 5:33, what did the Law say about making vows?

2. Matthew 5:34–36 lists four things by which they were not to swear. What are they?

_____          _____

_____          _____

Look at what the Old Testament taught about vows or oaths. Read the following Scriptures and next to each, write what you learn. Determine in each instance whether an oath or a vow was wrong.

1. Leviticus 19:11, 12

2. Numbers 30:1, 2

3. Genesis 24:2, 3

4. Deuteronomy 23:21–23

Now then, let's draw some conclusions.

1. Did the Old Testament forbid vows or oaths?

2. What was the purpose of vows? In other words, why were men permitted or allowed to make oaths?

3. Summarize, in general, what you have learned from these Scriptures about making oaths or vows.




These Scriptures show that men living under the Old Testament Law were permitted to make vows. A vow made an agreement binding. It was a man's means of saying, "I promise you that I am going to do what I said," whether he said it to God or to man. We see this in the incident of Abraham and his servant. When his servant put his hand under Abraham's thigh, he was pledging himself by all of his strength that he would fulfill the word of his master.

We could look at far more in the Old Testament on vows, but if we did, it would only confirm what we have already seen: oaths were in accordance with God's Law. They were a call or a pledge to integrity. A man who made a vow was saying, "I am sincere. I will be honest to carry out what I'm saying."

In the Sermon on the Mount, is Jesus altering God's law? Or is this a fulfillment? Think on it.

Are you a man—woman—of integrity or honesty? Is your Christian walk honest before God? Can others trust you, or do you cheat? Cheating can take all sorts of forms. It doesn't necessarily have to be in school when you take an exam. You can cheat the government. You can cheat on contracts. You can fail to tell the whole truth. You can pad the statistics for emphasis. You can advertise and exaggerate. You can tell little white lies. You can save your neck by getting around your words. You can do all these things but then, Beloved, where is your integrity?


## DAY 5


There is a great deal of similarity between the Sermon on the Mount and the book of James. In James 5:12 we read, "But above all, my brethren, do not swear, either by heaven or by earth or with any other oath; but let your yes be yes, and your no, no; so that you may not fall under judgment." Both Matthew and James remind us of the need for the integrity of our lips.

Dwight Pentecost, in his book *Sermon on the Mount,* summarizes so well what Jesus is saying:

> Let your character, your reputation for honesty, your word be so obviously true and undefiled and without duplicity, that no man would think it necessary to put you under an oath because he suspects you are of deception. . . . Some words can have a double meaning, and some words can be interpreted in two different ways. But there is only one possible way of interpreting yes. Yes does not mean no. There is only one way you can interpret no. You can never interpret that as meaning consent. When you say yes, it means yes; when you say no it means no. The Lord demanded that one's speech be so trustworthy that men would not have to debate what was meant and interpret what was said. They would know what was meant because he was an honest man.[19]

Recently in prayer the Lord showed me that I had to go to my video department, gather them as a group and ask them to forgive me because I had fallen under their judgment, and, of course, God's also. My yes had not been yes, and my no had not been no. There had been times when I had made agreements to cut certain things for the video department and they had arranged their schedule accordingly. Then, because of other various pressures that came upon me, I sought to alter the commitment that I had made. Their hearts' desire is to help me and to assist me in the ministry that God has called me to and I so appreciate the preciousness of their hearts and attitudes. Yet, you can imagine how frustrating it must be to have your schedule constantly changed. This week, when Debra from the video department was talking with me about scheduling, she said, "Kay, I just want our yes to be yes and our no to be no. So let's think very carefully before we rush into our scheduling." At the time I tried to justify myself and yet when I hung up the phone, God began to speak to me. Clearly I was wrong. It is still Sunday as I write today's lesson. Tomorrow when the offices open, I will make a date with video. You see, Beloved, above all else, I want to be a godly woman. And to be a godly woman, I must have integrity in every aspect of my life.

There are tears in my eyes as I share this; I mourn because I have hurt my God. I have failed to be perfect even as my heavenly Father is perfect. You see, His yes is yes and His no is no. It is so wonderful, isn't it? We can trust our Father because He stands by His word. He will not alter the word that has gone from His lips. I want to be like Him, don't you?

May I make a suggestion? Spend the rest of today's study time in prayer. Ask your Father to show you if you are failing in any way to let your yes be yes or your no, no. Do you keep your word to your children? Do you keep your word to your mate? Do you hedge? Are you like me, in that many times you promise things you have a desire to do and yet you are not absolutely sure that you can fulfill that promise? Sometimes it seems that my heart's desires go far beyond my abilities and a 24-hour day.

I am going to search my heart. Why don't you search yours? I'm going to tell God to remind me, over and over, to watch over the commitments I make with my mouth. "Set a guard, O LORD, over my mouth; keep watch over the door of my lips" (Psalms 141:3).

# 14 - What Do You Do When You Get Ripped Off?

## DAY 1

An eye for an eye? A tooth for a tooth? That seems pretty hard, doesn't it? Yet this was God's law.

Do you think our judicial system is better? Are we more effective in dealing with man's injustice to man?

Jesus said, "Do not resist him who is evil; but whoever slaps you on your right cheek, turn to him the other also. And if anyone wants to sue you, and take your shirt, let him have your coat also. And whoever shall force you to go one mile, go with him two. Give to him who asks of you, and do not turn away from him who wants to borrow from you (Matthew 5:39–42). Was Jesus changing the Law by saying this? No, He couldn't. Jesus came to *fulfill* the Law.

But if He wasn't altering the Law, what was He doing when He said we are not to resist him who is evil? Once again, Jesus is taking us to the heart of the matter. He is going to show us that righteous men are controlled by a much higher law.

In the next two days, I hope to cover this passage in a fairly comprehensive way. If it is hard to understand "an eye for an eye and a tooth for a tooth," it is even harder to turn the other cheek when someone slaps you. Also, if someone wants to sue you and take your shirt, why are you to let him have your coat also? If people keep asking of you and want to borrow from you, are you to give them everything you have? And when people force you to go one mile, why on earth should you go with them two? Isn't one enough?

These are all legitimate questions that need legitimate answers. I pray that in the next two days you'll have God's insight so that you can know how to live in the light of Matthew 5:38–42.

First, let's look at "an eye for an eye, and a tooth for a tooth." Where did it come from?

1. Look up Exodus 21:23–25 and summarize what these three verses are teaching.

2. Now look up Leviticus 24:17–22 and simply record any new insights you glean from this passage.

3. Finally, read Deuteronomy 19:15–21, summarizing what you learn there.

How does the judicial system that God set up then compare with ours today? The two seem to be opposites, don't they? In biblical days the innocent were protected, whereas today the guilty are. Often in our society, the guilty do not get "like" payment. Have you ever wondered what would happen if we started reinstituting capital punishment without exception, when one has clearly been proven to be a murderer?

Did you notice that under God's judicial system no man would ever be sentenced under the testimony of a single witness? The testimonies of two or three witnesses were required. God also called the judges to investigate the case thoroughly and to deal swift retribution to those who gave false witness. But in our society if someone comes against us and accuses us falsely, many times it costs thousands of dollars to defend ourselves; and even then the false accuser walks away, scot-free.

"Life for life, eye for eye, tooth for tooth, hand for hand, foot for foot" certainly would keep people from getting far more than the injury is worth. So many times today people go to court to get all they can. They want vengeance. And many are greedy! As you probably have already seen, God's way of justice did several things. First, it protected against unjust retribution, getting more or taking more than was fair. This is good, isn't it? Many times, because of a man's sinful nature, he is determined to make the guilty one pay through the teeth for what was done. Anger rises and takes control of his reasoning. He wants vengeance and more! Can't you see the benefit of the "eye for an eye" principle?

Even the heathen felt that "an eye for an eye, and a tooth for a tooth" was a just retribution. We see this in Judges 1:6, 7. Can you imagine how such a principle of law would benefit society? It would accomplish several things. First, because the punishment was already set, it would curb the indignation of a judge who might tend to get so involved in the case that he would bring an unjust retribution against the guilty party. Or it would keep the judge from showing partiality or from being bribed to give a lesser sentence.

Second, if I decided to take out your eye, I knew that if I ever got caught I would lose my eye, in turn. If I decided that I would take another man's life, I knew without doubt that if I were caught, my life would be taken. So the law would serve as a deterrent. It would cause a man to think twice before committing a crime.

Third, this law holds man accountable for his behavior, doesn't it?

Yet man doesn't want to be held accountable. If he can't get away with breaking the law, what does he want? He wants mercy, yet he was not merciful! Think about it and we will consider it more tomorrow.

## DAY 2

Why was the law—"an eye for an eye, a tooth for a tooth"—given? I gave you several reasons yesterday. Today I want to give you another. *It was a law to protect innocent people from ungodly, sinful men.* In order to understand why you are to turn the other cheek, go the second mile, or give away your coat when a man asks for your shirt, then you have to understand this principle: God is not making the Law void when He tells you to turn the other cheek. Rather, He is calling you to a higher law.

"But we know that the Law is good, if one uses it lawfully, realizing the fact that law is not made for a righteous man, but for those who are lawless and rebellious, for the ungodly and sinners, for the unholy and profane, for those who kill their fathers or mothers, for murderers and immoral men and homosexuals and kidnappers and liars and perjurers, and whatever else is contrary to sound teaching" (1 Timothy 1:8–10). The Law, then, is for ungodly men. Anytime a judicial system changes to the point where it protects the guilty and lets them go free, or allows them to pay a lesser punishment than the magnitude of their crime deserves, lawlessness is encouraged. That judicial system is no longer a protector of the innocent. Can't you see that this is where we have gone so wrong? This is why lawlessness abounds. By clinging to our own humanistic philosophies, we are destroying ourselves and our society.

Do you remember Galatians 3:23? "Before faith came, we were kept in custody under the Law." The word for "custody" was a military term that meant to guard as a garrison, or to block the way to escape. The law—an eye for an eye and a tooth for a tooth—was meant to deter red-hot anger that would strike out against the life or limb of a man. O, that Ecclesiastes 8:11 would be remembered in our courts of law: "Because the sentence against an evil deed is not executed quickly, therefore the hearts of the sons of men among them are given fully to do evil."

The law of retribution was good. It was a law from God, and it was not to be annulled. The only problem was that it had been perverted by the scribes and the Pharisees. "An eye for an eye, and a tooth for a tooth" had been put on an individual level; it was no longer something decided by the judges. The scribes and the Pharisees insisted on retribution.

So what is Jesus saying with regard to this law? He is not saying that it is bad. He is simply telling us that righteous men are controlled by a higher law: the law of love. Jesus is calling for love, not legalism. Love has always been the true intent of the Law. Let's look at some scriptures that show us this.

1. Read Mark 12:28–34 and then in your own words explain how these verses show that love is the basis of the Law.

2. Now read Romans 13:8–10 and summarize what is said in your own words.

3. Now look at 1 Corinthians 13. Read verses 1–8 and write down what verse 7 says about love.

In Romans 13:10 we saw that love is "the fulfillment of the Law." Since it is, love does not have to demand an eye for an eye, and a tooth for a tooth. It realizes that the major purpose of that Law was twofold: to protect a person against unjust retribution and cause a man to think twice before committing a crime. Therefore, the Law can still be fulfilled by love turning its cheek. This is showing the world, once again, the reality of God in us as He was in Christ: "Reconciling the world to

Himself, not counting their trespasses against them" (2 Corinthians 5:19).

O Beloved, do you see it? If we are to be perfect as our Father in heaven is perfect, we have to go beyond the legalism of the Law to the true intent of the Law, which is love.

We have to show those who would insult us, who would seek our possessions, who would abuse our privileges, that because Christ is in us, we are not going to act under the just letter of the Law, but we are going to respond in the grace of God. We are not going to count their trespasses against them, but we will turn the other cheek, give our coats, go the extra mile, and not turn away from the one who wants to borrow from us. This will show man the meekness of Jesus. This will show him the mercy of God. This will help him to see the goodness of God which leads him to repentance (Romans 2:4).

Matthew 5:38–42 is *not* teaching the doctrine of pacifism. It has nothing to do with going to war. We cannot take these verses to Congress and say, "If we would simply do this and respond this way to Russia and other aggressors who would seek to take control of our country, God would be with us." That would be national suicide. It would also be taking a message intended for an individual and making it apply to a nation. This verse belongs to Christians, not judicial systems or nations.

God is also saying that we are not to keep on turning the other cheek until we are battered to death. We are not to give away our possessions until we absolutely go broke. Whenever you turn the other cheek, or give away your coat—whenever you go the extra mile, or you give to him who wants to borrow from you—you must remember that you are doing it out of love. Love always desires another's highest good. Therefore, if an alcoholic asks for money because he is hungry, but you know he would use it to buy alcohol, offer him a meal! What God is telling us, in essence, is that love does not demand its rights; it does not ask for a just reward. Love is always merciful. It looks beyond the immediate to another's eternal good.

What have you learned, Beloved, for your life? How can you apply the things that you have learned these last two days to your daily walk? Summarize it in a sentence or two and then talk to God about it.

# DAY 3

As a new Christian I read an impressive little tract called, "Others May, You Cannot." The essence of its message was the higher calling of those who would follow Christ fully. It pointed out that some things are lawful for the Christian, things that maybe the Law did not touch on directly, or that the Bible does not speak to specifically, and therefore were not known as specific transgressions. It said further that if we are to live life on the highest plane, there are certain things that God will call us to leave alone. These are things that possibly others could do but we cannot. In Matthew 5:38–48, God is calling us to a very high plane of life. He is calling us to live beyond the letter of the Law. He is calling us to catch the spirit of the Law. He is taking us beyond a legalism that wants to know how far it can go, to a love that never considers itself at all.

Love does not seek personal justice. Therefore if anyone wants to sue you and take your shirt, love says, "Here, take my coat also." Love will give up its rights in order to demonstrate the character of God. Love lives on a higher plane. It's not easy up there, is it? It separates you from others and lets people take advantage of you. But then, don't men take advantage of God? Yes, they take advantage of Him, but it never alters His character. Our character is never to be altered by man's response to us.

Love does not hold on to its personal possessions. Therefore, love gives to him who asks and does not turn away the one who wants to borrow. Love expands itself. Love gives the ultimate and in its giving disarms the receiver. Love lives on a higher plane. Love even loves its enemies and in compassion prays for those who persecute it. Love cannot restrain its affection, not if it is God's love.

If you are going to turn the other cheek, give away your coat, go the second mile, give to him who asks, and love your enemies, then you cannot be occupied or concerned with self. Of course, as you already know, this is meekness personified. Meekness is not occupied with self at all. It does not consider retaliation in any form. It does not defend its body; but is willing to turn the other cheek. It does not defend its own personal rights, but is willing to go the second mile.

During the time of our Lord, Roman soldiers overran Israel. A Roman soldier could compel a civilian to carry his burden the distance of one mile, but no more. The law was designed to keep the soldier from taking advantage of the civilian. Since righteousness is to be practical, Jesus addressed the current situation of His day, and in doing so gave all men a practical illustration. Love goes the extra mile; it goes beyond what it is compelled to do. Love lives on a higher plane than the Law.

The Jews were told that they were to love their neighbors and hate their enemies (Matthew 5:44). Note that I said "told," for nowhere does the Word distinctly say this. This was the scribes and the Pharisees' interpretation of Leviticus 19:18: "You shall not take vengeance, nor bear any grudge against the sons of your people, but you shall love your neighbor as yourself; I am the LORD."

From that they deduced that they were to love only their neighbors and were allowed to hate their enemies. This is why Jesus had to tell them the parable of the good Samaritan, a parable prompted by a man who wished to justify himself by saying to Jesus, " 'And who is my neighbor?' " (Luke 10:29). Through the parable of the good Samaritan, Jesus taught him that a neighbor is anyone in need. Therefore, loving our neighbors as ourselves means that we are to love all men as we love ourselves. When God sent Jesus to die for us, He sent Jesus to die for the whole world: "God so loved the world, that He gave His only begotten Son . . ." (John 3:16). Jesus is "the propitiation for our sins; and not for ours only, but also for those of the whole world" (1 John 2:2). Love does not discriminate because God does not discriminate.

I have never forgotten a few lines from Shakespeare that I memorized:

> Let me not to the marriage of true minds
> Admit impediments. Love is not love
> which alters when it alteration finds,
> Or bends with the remover to remove:
> Oh, no! it is an ever-fixed mark,
> That looks on tempests and is never shaken. . . .

If you are going to be perfect as your heavenly Father is perfect, you must not alter when you alteration find. Your love must be perfected "in order that you may be sons of your Father who is in heaven; For He causes His sun to rise on the evil and the good, and sends rain on the righteous and the unrighteous. For if you love those who love you, what reward have you?" (Matthew 5:45, 46). You and I cannot live the way others live. We must live on love's highest plane. Our love does "more than others."

"Others may, you cannot."

O Beloved, do you see what God expects of you? Do you see how high your calling is? In Acts 1:8 when Jesus says, "You shall be my witnesses," the word *witnesses* in the Greek is similar to the English word *martyr,* one willing to lay down his life. That's what God is calling us to do in Matthew 5:38–48. God laid down His life in the person of His Son for all mankind. Some would believe and respond, others would trample on love. It did not matter. Love was willing to be trampled.

So what do you do? You:

"Bless those who persecute you; bless and curse not."
"Never pay back evil for evil to anyone."
"Never take your own revenge."
"If your enemy is hungry, feed him, and if he is thirsty, give him a drink."
"Overcome evil with good."
"Owe nothing to anyone except to love one another."
*Romans 12:14, 17, 19, 20, 21; 13:8.*

Will you live on the highest plane? Do you have a choice?

## DAY 4

Today we begin Matthew 6. I'm going to give you a different assignment, because as we study together, I want to keep giving you principles of Bible study so that you will not be in danger of being "children, tossed here and there by waves, and carried about by every wind of doctrine, by the trickery of men, by craftiness in deceitful scheming" (Ephesians 4:14).

I have an exercise for you that I think will be profitable. It will also be a change of pace. If you will look in the back of the book at the Sermon on the Mount printed there in full, you will notice some lines separating various verses in Matthew 6. Each of these lines marks a new paragraph. Your assignment for today is to read through Matthew 6, paragraph by paragraph. As you do, pick out one or two words that best describe what each paragraph is about; then write that word next to the line that divides it from the next paragraph. If you will look at Chapter 6, you will notice that I have done this on the first paragraph.

When you have finished, write down the truth that spoke to you the most. Then spend some time in prayer, asking God to show you any way that you are practicing your righteousness to be seen of men rather than for your Father alone.

It's convicting, isn't it? I understand. I've been so convicted, and yet, it is so cleansing, and that is so wonderful. The Sermon on the Mount has created within me such a hunger and such a thirst for a deeper righteousness. I pray, Beloved, that God is blessing you in the same way. I love you. Have a good day.

## DAY 5

As we move into Matthew 6, we see that Jesus begins a series of warnings.

6:1—Beware of hypocrisy
6:19—Do not lay up treasures
6:25—Do not be anxious
7:1—Do not judge
7:6—Do not give what is holy to dogs

We have a new heart, but we must never forget that until we die and Jesus changes our mortal bodies into immortal bodies, we will still live in a body of flesh; the flesh will always be the flesh. Don't ever let anyone tell you that as long as you are in covenant with God and are walking in the light of that covenant, you will stop having a problem with the flesh. That is not true. Such teaching makes the Scriptures say what they do not say. It goes against the clear teaching of Galatians 5, where Paul says, "But I say, walk by the Spirit, and you will not carry out the desire of the flesh. For the flesh sets its desire against the Spirit, and the Spirit against the flesh; for these are in opposition to one another, so that you may not do the things that you please" (Galatians 5:16, 17).

Obviously, Paul is speaking to a Christian. A non-Christian does not have the Spirit living within him. Those who have come to Christ under the New Covenant have put to death the flesh with its passions and desires. Therefore, when the flesh cries out for satisfaction and wants its way, remember that you have chosen the Cross and your habit of life is to be following Jesus. The Wycliffe Bible Commentary notes:

> Those who are truly Christ's must be like Him in that they participate in His cross. They have crucified the flesh. Ideally, this points to their identification with Christ in His death (Galatians 2:20). Practically, it emphasizes the need of carrying the cross principle into the redeemed life, since the flesh with its affections and desires is still an ever present reality (Galatians 5:16, 17). The same tension between divine provision and human appropriation is found regarding the Spirit. We live in the Spirit by God's arrangement, by means of the gift of the Spirit at conversion. But we walk in the Spirit as a matter of personal volition, taking each step in dependence upon Him. If one is walking thus, he will not be desirous of (vain glory)—ambitious for self and frustrated when unsuccessful.[20]

So do not fulfill the desires of your flesh. Notice, it does not say that our flesh does not desire anymore. Desire is there. You cannot attribute all of your temptations to the devil. This is why Paul writes to the Christians in Colossae, "Therefore consider the members of your earthly body as dead to immorality, impurity, passion, evil desire, and greed, which amounts to idolatry ... But now you also, put them all aside: anger, wrath, malice, slander, and abusive speech from your mouth" (Colossians 3:5, 8).

The flesh wants to be seen, it wants to be noticed. Jesus knows this. Therefore, He warns us in Matthew 6:1, "Beware of practicing your righteousness before men to be noticed by them." He knows the flesh can have a problem with covetousness and so He warns us not to lay up earthly treasures (verses 19–24). He knows the flesh can be occupied with itself, concerned with its appetite and appearance, so He tells us not to be anxious and not to pursue anything but His righteousness.

He knows the flesh can play the hypocrite and judge others without judging itself. So, He says, "Do not judge."

God wants His children to be aware of the flesh putting on a show in order to be seen by men. This is the way the hypocrites live and we're not to live that way.

The first act of righteousness that Jesus deals with in Matthew 6 is giving alms, which were deeds of charity done on behalf of the needy. The Old Testament economy portrays basically three types of giving—the tithes, free will offerings and gifts to the poor. The latter, almsgiving, is the type of giving that Jesus deals with in Matthew 6. It was a giving that promised rich blessing from God. Let's look at several passages so that you can understand the Jewish mentality toward giving and blessing, and the promises God has for you as you give alms to the poor.

1. Look up Deuteronomy 15:7–11 and state in your own words what you learn about almsgiving.

2. Look up Proverbs 11:24, 25 and follow the same procedure.

3. Blessings that came from giving to the poor were quite varied, as is evident in Psalms 41:1–3. Read these verses and then list the various things the Lord promises to do for those who consider the helpless (the poor).

In Matthew 23 Jesus tells us that the scribes and Pharisees loved the praise of men: "But they do all their deeds to be noticed by men; for they broaden their phylacteries, and lengthen the tassels of their garments (Matthew 23:5). (Phylacteries are small boxes which contain Scripture verses and are bound around a person's forehead or arm. They can still be seen today, worn by devout Jews.) Jesus said that they were broadening their phylacteries, that is, making them larger so that they couldn't be missed.

When He spoke about lengthening the tassels of their garments He was referring to the fact that the Jews wore a shawl-type scarf with ribbons (or bands) of blue to remind them that they were a holy people. In Israel today, orthodox Jews walk the streets dressed in black. Dangling from underneath their suit coats are long tassels from their prayer shawls. The scribes and Pharisees were lengthening these tassels so as to draw greater attention to their devotion to God. Remember, I told you that sometimes the flesh likes to appear to be holy. "They love the place of honor at banquets, and the chief seats in the synagogues, and respectful greetings in the market places, and being called by men, Rabbi" (Matthew 23:6, 7). The flesh wants to be noticed by others.

Almsgiving then became a means of their getting the attention that they wanted from men. So, the scribes and Pharisees made a big ceremony out of their giving. Apparently they sounded trumpets in the synagogues and streets. I imagine the sounding of the trumpets was excused as a call to the poor to come and receive what would be bestowed on their behalf. The flesh can always find some way to excuse its showiness. After all, if they didn't sound the trumpets, the poor couldn't come running!!!

What about you? When you give to people, or to a ministry with needs, do you do it only if you get your name on a plaque or printed in the bulletin? Do you love it when certain churches publish lists of those who have met their monthly giving quota? Do you make certain you give so that you will not be embarrassed by the absence of your name from the list? Will you only give if in some way your giving is going to be recognized? If that is so, then according to Matthew 6 you have your reward in full. There's no more reward coming. But if when you give alms, you "do not let your left hand know what your right hand is doing that your alms may be in secret" then "your Father who sees in secret will repay you." When do you want your reward, now or later?

Go to the Lord and talk to Him about all that you've read. Share with Him about your fears. He loves to communicate with you in truth. Also, Beloved, examine your motives for giving. Examine your giving. Do you give? Ask God to examine your heart and your pocketbook.

# 15 - Praying and Fasting God's Way

## DAY 1

Have you ever cried out, "Lord, teach me to pray"? I have. As a matter of fact I've written a book* by that title on the Lord's Prayer. The Lord's Prayer was Jesus' answer to His disciples' plea: "Lord, teach us to pray."

Before we study the Lord's Prayer, see what you can discover on your own. Turn to the Sermon on the Mount (Appendix A) and read Matthew 6:5–15. As you read, notice each use of the repeated phrase "when you pray" or "when you are praying." This is a key phrase through which we can discern Jesus' instructions regarding prayer. Record His instructions below in a concise list. However, do not go into detail on the Lord's Prayer, for we will cover that later.

Now let's see what you learned about prayer from simply reading the text. Once again, Jesus tells His listeners that they are not to pray

* For information about the author's book, *Lord, Teach Me to Pray,* see the address at the back of this volume.

as the hypocrites, to be seen by men. The hypocrites pray in public. After all, if you are going to be seen by men, you have to be where they are. Apparently, they were praying in public but not praying in private. Where do you pray the most—in public or in private? Jesus' instruction on private prayer is very clear. You need to be alone. This doesn't mean that public prayer is wrong for we see other instances in the Word of God where men do pray in public. So, Jesus' purpose is not to condemn public prayer, but to show us that true prayer is a communication between God and man. Therefore, private prayer is absolutely essential.

Dwight Pentecost, in his book on the Sermon on the Mount, puts it so well.

> Two who are in love require privacy to properly communicate. Little real communications is possible in public. Volumes can be communicated in moments when there is privacy. In the busyness of life, communication with the Father is impossible unless there is privacy. That's why the Lord said if we are to communicate with the Father we must go to our room and shut the door. One prying eye can spoil communication. As soon as we are conscious of one observer, the privacy necessary to intimately communicate is gone, and we become conscious of the observer rather than the Father with whom we are talking. Therefore, the Pharisees could not communicate with the Father when they gathered an audience to hear their prayers. Prayer is private communication.[21]

Does this then mean that because prayer is private communication we can never carry on this communication publicly with God? Oh no, Beloved. Public prayer can be private communication if our hearts are united, if we are aware that we have come into the presence of God and are actually praying as a body to Him, joining in with one another in worshiping the Father or beseeching Him to move in a certain way. When praying in public, our prayers must be to God and not to men.

Reuben A. Torrey, an outstanding Bible teacher in the wonderful days of D. L. Moody, wrote *The Power of Prayer,* in which he says:

> We should never utter one syllable of prayer, either in public or in private, until we are definitely conscious that we have come into the presence of God and are actually praying to him. ... I can remember when that thought transformed my

prayer life. I was brought up to pray. I was taught to pray so early in life that I have not the slightest recollection of who taught me to pray.... Nevertheless, prayer was largely a mere matter of form. There was little real thought of God, and no real approach to God. And even after I was converted, yes, even after I had entered the ministry, prayer was largely a matter of form. But the day came when I realized what real prayer meant, realized that prayer was having an audience with God, actually coming into the presence of God and asking and getting things from Him. And the realization of that fact transformed my prayer life. Before that prayer had been a mere duty, and sometimes a very irksome duty, but from that time on prayer has been not merely a duty but a privilege, one of the most highly esteemed privileges of life. Before that the thought that I had was, "How much time must I spend in prayer?" The thought that now possesses me is, "How much time may I spend in prayer without neglecting the other privileges and duties of life?"[22]

Isn't this what Jesus is saying to us in Matthew 5? Pray when you are conscious of God's presence, for the purpose of prayer is to communicate with God, not to be seen of men.

Prayer is the secret of life. It is your communication with your Father which sustains you from day to day, which gives you confidence as you face the questions and complexities of daily living. Prayer is the Christian's compass, giving direction for the course of his life. It is daily finding a secluded place where you can be shut up alone with your Father, focusing on Him and Him alone, being aware of His person, knowing who He is, knowing that you are in His presence and then committing every care of life to Him.

As you will see tomorrow, communication with God can follow a certain pattern; however, it is not to be the repetition of meaningless words. It is to be an honest, heartfelt communication with the Father. Saying a lot, or going through a magic formula does not cause God to hear us. We are talking to our Father, a Father who knows what we need before we ever ask Him, who delights to "give what is good to those who ask Him" (Matthew 7:11). The asking is essential. Many words are redundant.

These are precious insights, aren't they, Beloved? Just think what a difference it could make in your prayer life if you took time to become definitely conscious of His presence before you ever begin to pray. Are you like me? You don't like to talk to anyone if you don't think they are listening? Why don't you stop and put into practice this one principle. If necessary, get up from where you are reading this book and get alone. Shut the door and tell the Father that you want to be with Him. Sit beside Him or kneel before Him. Thank Him for His presence. Then talk to Him. Begin by focusing on who He is. Then, from there, see where He leads you. Your Father is waiting.

## DAY 2

As Luke 11 opens, Jesus had just finished praying. Whether He had been praying aloud or not we don't know. Perhaps it was because of the way Jesus prayed or because they observed that prayer was so vital between Father and Son that the disciples asked Jesus, "Lord, teach us to pray just as John also taught his disciples." Jesus responded by telling them that when they prayed they were to say: " 'Father, hallowed be Thy name. Thy kingdom come. Give us each day our daily bread. And forgive us our sins, for we ourselves also forgive everyone who is indebted to us. And lead us not into temptation' " (Luke 11:2–4).

In the days of our Lord, the Rabbis would give the people a collection of brief sentences, each of which suggested a subject for prayer. These were called "index sentences" and would be used to lead the disciple into topics that needed to be covered in communion with God. Scholars believe that the Lord's Prayer, therefore, was given to the disciples as a list of index sentences, each one in and of itself becoming a topic for prayer.

What I have learned about the Lord's Prayer as a pattern for prayer has absolutely liberated me in my prayer life. By using this pattern I have found that whether I have fifteen minutes or an hour or so for prayer in the morning, if I use this pattern, I feel that my prayer time has been complete, and that it has gone full cycle. Of course, more time gives me more depth and breadth in prayer. But whatever time I do have, whether short or long, I feel that my prayer has been comprehensive when I follow this pattern.

As I have said, each sentence touches on a topic that needs to be covered in prayer. In your study today, I would like you to look at the

Lord's Prayer sentence by sentence and write out as briefly as possible the topic you think each sentence covers. This will be a good exercise for you and it will help you appreciate the Lord's Prayer even more if you do it on your own.

### The Lord's Prayer

_____ 1. Our Father who art in heaven, hallowed be Thy name.

_____ 2. Thy Kingdom come.

_____ 3. Thy will be done, on earth as it is in heaven.

_____ 4. Give us this day our daily bread.

_____ 5. Forgive us our debts as we also have forgiven our debtors.

_____ 6. Do not lead us into temptation, but deliver us from evil.

_____ 7 For Thine is the kingdom, and the power, and the glory forever, Amen.

Samuel Zwemer in *Prayer* said that the Lord's Prayer contains, "Every possible desire of the praying heart. It contains a whole world of spiritual requirements, and combines in simple language every divine promise, every human sorrow and want in every Christian aspiration for the good of others."

James Boice writes in *The Sermon on the Mount,* "The greatest minds of the Christian church have always known this, and as a result the Lord's Prayer has been used throughout centuries as an outline for countless expositions of the nature of prayer and Christian doctrine."

Andrew Murray in *With Christ in the School of Prayer* said that the Lord's Prayer is "a form of prayer that becomes the model and inspiration for all other prayer, and yet always draws us back to itself as the deepest utterance of our souls before God."

As I read through the Lord's Prayer, I saw worship, allegiance, submission, petition, confession and forgiveness, and deliverance. But where was intercession? I knew that intercession was an absolute, vital part of prayer. Then I carefully observed again and I saw that intercession is an integral part of the whole pattern. It is there in every "our," "we," and "us." To pray through this prayer is not to pray for myself alone, for its thrust is not to *my* Father, for *my* daily bread, *my* forgiveness, and *my* deliverance from the evil one. No, to pray God's way is to pray in behalf of those who belong to the body of Jesus Christ.

"But wait," you may say, "where does intercession come in for those who are lost?" I'm so thankful that you asked because it shows that you know how vital prayer is in bringing men, women, and children into the kingdom of heaven. Intercession for the salvation of others is covered in one of the index sentences. I will point it out as we go through this prayer, topic by topic.

As we approach each index sentence, I pray you will realize that this is simply a cursory observation of truths that must be mined diligently from the whole counsel of God on prayer. These sentences are like rich coal mines that have enough coal to ignite your heart in triumphant worship and confident petition.

"Our Father who art in heaven, hallowed be Thy name." The first index sentence lays the foundation of everything that follows. It puts us into the context of prayer, for it calls us to worship the One alone who is worthy and the One alone who from His sovereign throne can meet the needs of man and satisfy the deepest longings of his heart. Worship is looking at God's Word in order to focus on who God is. The Word of God gives us the perfect revelation of who He is, and worship becomes the basis of all true prayer. "He who comes to God must believe that He is, and that He is a rewarder of those who seek Him" (Hebrews 11:6).

What is our relationship to this God whom we worship? It is nothing less than that of a child to his Father. "Father." Can you imagine calling Jehovah, the self-existing, sovereign God, "Father"? To call God "Father" was unthinkable. No Old Testament Jew addressed God as Father. Here was a whole new concept, a whole new realm of intimacy, an intimacy that most of Israel never ventured into. O Beloved, what manner of love has been bestowed upon us, that we should be called the children of God!

The word that Jesus uses for Father is "Abba," the term a small child used for his daddy. Filled with devotion, love, admiration, confidence, and security, "Abba" contains all the trust of a little child. Thus, in this first index sentence we see that prayer is the privilege of the child of God. Our birthright! "We know that God does not hear sinners; but if anyone is God-fearing, and does His will, He hears him" (John 9:31).

Worship is the key that unlocks the door to effective prayer. It is the foundation upon which every petition finds its support. In many churches and prayer closets, worship is the missing spark that would ignite hearts in flames of holy devotion.

Let me make one further suggestion. Read 2 Chronicles 20:1–13 and see what part worship plays in this situation. Then when you finish, go to the Lord and just spend time with our El Elyon who sits on His sovereign throne in heaven. Hallow, reverence His name. He is Elohim, your Creator; El Shaddai, your almighty, all-sufficient Father; your El Roi, the God who sees; Jehovah, the I AM who as Jehovah-jireh has provided all you need through His Lamb. Kneel beneath the banner of your Jehovah-nissi, giving Him your allegiance, submitting to your Adonai as Lord that you might walk in righteousness as the son of Jehovah-tsidkenu. Let Jehovah-rapha heal your hurts. Seek the guidance of your shepherd, Jehovah-raha and know that as Jehovah-shammah, He is always there. The throne of El Olam, the everlasting God, is never vacant. Jehovah Sabaoth, who rules over the hosts of heaven, awaits your worship.*

## DAY 3

The second index sentence in the Lord's Prayer, "Thy kingdom come," shows our allegiance to God and to His kingdom. Had Jesus not given us the third index sentence, "Thy will be done, on earth as it is in heaven," this sentence would cover the topic adequately. For after all, if I'm going to give my allegiance, then I'm going to be willing to submit to His will.

In the first index sentence, our focus is upon God. We see Him as the Sovereign One ruling from heaven. Through various Scriptures we catch a glimpse of how wonderful heaven must be, where His will is not questioned or thwarted in any way, but carried out with total obedi-

* For an in-depth study of the names of God, see *Lord, I Want to Know You*, by the author.

ence. Having seen God, having reverenced Him, is it not logical that we would bow the knee and say to Him, "Father, we want Thy kingdom to come"? Here is our opportunity to daily affirm our allegiance to His kingdom above all else. And here is our opportunity in prayer to expedite the coming of His literal kingdom to earth. The great Shepherd of the sheep cannot come until all of the sheep are inside the fold. This index sentence is then the call for us to intercede, to pray for those who are outside the kingdom of God, to pray that Jesus' lost sheep would hear His voice, come to Him and receive eternal life.

When I pray "Thy kingdom come," I often pray Acts 26:18, for those who are lost, asking God to "open their eyes so that they may turn from darkness to light and from the dominion of Satan to God, in order that they may receive forgiveness of sins and an inheritance among those who have been sanctified by faith in [Jesus]." O, if we would only realize how vital is prayer in preparing man's heart for the seed of God's Word.

"Thy will be done." Before you bring any petition before God's throne, before your prayers can ever be effective, you must submit to the will of God. This is the purpose of this third index sentence. John 9:31 tells us that God does not hear sinners, but if anyone is God-fearing and does His will then God hears him.

In the pattern of the Lord's Prayer, petition follows on the heels of submission; the order cannot be reversed. How can God grant us our desires when we refuse to submit to His will, whatever it is? Submission to the will of God is the key to the storehouse of answered prayer. "And this is the confidence which we have before Him, that, if we ask anything *according to His will,* He hears us. And if we know that He hears us in whatever we ask, we know that we have the requests which we have asked from Him" (1 John 5:14, 15 *italics added*). If you would know the will of God, you must understand the Word of God! The will of God and the Word of God go together. They cannot be separated, for through His Word we are sure of His will. John 15:7 puts it so succinctly, "If you abide in Me, and My words abide in you, ask whatever you wish, and it shall be done for you."

"Give us this day our daily bread" is an index sentence of petition. As a child you have come to your Father. As a child it is only right that your Father meet your needs. Yet, notice where this index sentence falls in our Lord's Prayer. Petition comes after we have worshiped our Father, given Him our allegiance, and submitted to His will. Then and only then are we spiritually ready to ask Him to supply our needs.

These first three index sentences put us into the context of petition, for the promises of God regarding asking and receiving are always qualified by asking in His name—or in accordance with His name. Our petitions then must coincide with who He is and with who we are as children of God. How vital it is that we understand this so that we don't just grab John 14:13 and run away with it and wonder why God doesn't do what He said He would do—"And whatever you ask in My name, that will I do, that the Father may be glorified in the Son."

Some have taken this verse as carte blanche to ask for whatever their hearts desire without stopping to realize that whatever we ask must be asked in His name. If I ask in His name then I ask according to His character. Remember the pattern of prayer? It begins with "hallowed be Thy name." Reverence for His name then is what governs our petitions. Petitions for what? For when? It's interesting to me that the petition is "give us this day our daily bread."

God keeps us coming to Him, day by day, doesn't He? This is not a petition for next week's bread. It is a petition for the daily needs of life. I believe Jesus uses the term *bread* because it was considered the staff of life. Bread symbolically covers all of our physical needs, those things that are necessary to sustain our lives. Oh, there is so much I could say here, Beloved, but we will just have to move on. I pray that God will use it to make you hungry for more and that you will want to study the book, *Lord, Teach Me to Pray.*

"Forgive us our debts, as we also have forgiven our debtors." Here is a cry to God for forgiveness in relation to our forgiveness of others. Why do I say that? Because of one little two-letter word—"as."

As we saw in our study of the beatitude of mercy, God withholds forgiveness from those who will not forgive others. To fail to forgive others is a sin, and if we are walking in sin, how can we expect God to hear our prayers? Failing to forgive others shows that we have no comprehension of what we are really asking for, or of the magnitude of our debt to a holy God compared to man's debts to an unholy, imperfect man. So many people want to skirt the truth of these verses. They just don't want to believe them or they attempt to explain them away. And yet, you cannot explain them away. Why do men resist this truth? Technically it's because they want to come to God on their own terms. But remember, we've already prayed, "Thy will be done, on earth as it is in heaven." If we have prayed that prayer, then we are ready to forgive our debtors, even as God forgives our debts. How can a holy God answer the prayers of a man who refuses to obey? This then brings us to the issue of confession.

Confession is the acknowledgment of our debt to God. Somewhere, somehow, we have failed to walk in righteousness. This must be acknowledged and forsaken. The book of 1 John teaches us that if we are truly children of God, our lives will no longer be lived in habitual sin (1 John 3:6–10). However, he does assure us that as a child of God, "if anyone sins, we have an Advocate with the Father, Jesus Christ the righteous; and He Himself is the propitiation for our sins" (1 John 2:1, 2).

The verb *sins* in 1 John 2:1 is in the aorist tense and it implies a singular act of sin done at a point in time. Therefore, while a Christian cannot live in habitual sin, still a Christian can sin. Realizing this, God has made a wonderful provision for forgiveness in 1 John 1:9: "if we confess our sins, He is faithful and righteous to forgive us our sins and to cleanse us from all unrighteousness."

Remember when I told you that I needed to go to the video department and ask them to forgive me? Well, I did that, and they were sweet and loving. It is such a privilege to work with them. And I know that my joy will increase now that I have confessed my sin to God and confessed it to those against whom I transgressed. It's a wonderful feeling, Beloved, to be right with God and right with man. How I urge you that if anything is between you and God, or you and your fellow man, to settle it right away.

You can see from the phrase regarding our *daily* bread that prayer is to be something consistently made before God. And as we come before Him, asking Him to supply our needs, we must remember that we are to examine our hearts daily to see if we owe any debt of righteousness to God. If so, we need to confess it immediately.

"And do not lead us into temptation, but deliver us from evil." This next index sentence is a whopper. It has thrown many people into a tailspin. How can we say to God, "Do not lead us into temptation"? Would God lead us into temptation? Let me tell you what I believe is the purpose of this sixth index sentence.

I call it preventative prayer, or prayer for deliverance. It is the heart's cry of a child of God who longs for righteousness, and yet who is fully aware of the ever-present weakness of his flesh.

To me, it is saying, "Lord, my spirit is willing, but I know and understand the weakness of my flesh and I'm crying to You to keep me from temptation and to deliver me from evil." It's a beautiful heart's cry, isn't it? To me it ties in perfectly with Matthew 26:40, 41. Jesus is in the Garden of Gethsemane crying out to the Father regarding the cross that awaits Him. "And He came to the disciples and found them sleeping, and said to Peter, 'So, you men could not keep watch with Me for one hour? Keep watching and praying, that you may not enter into temptation; the spirit is willing, but the flesh is weak.' " The sixth index sentence is a means of watching and praying so that you might not enter into temptation.

Finally, we come to that last index sentence: "For Thine is the kingdom and the power, and the glory, forever. Amen."

We have now been brought full circle in our prayer. We began with worship. We close with worship. The word *for* seems to me to be the very reason for all that has gone before, because His is the kingdom, His is the power, and His is the glory forever. And we say, Amen, so be it. "For from Him and through Him and to Him are all things. To Him be the glory forever. Amen" (Romans 11:36).

Do you want to know how to pray? Is your heart's cry, "Lord, teach me to pray"? Jesus says: "Pray, then, in this way."

## DAY 4

Today, we turn to that twice-repeated phrase in Matthew 6:16–18, "Whenever you fast." Jesus is implying that His children will fast and when we do, there's a way to do it. Once again, it is not the hypocritical way, fasting to be seen by men, but it is to be directed toward our Father. Therefore, when we fast, we will not draw attention to our appearance or our hunger because fasting is between an individual and his God.

Fasting implies abstinence. It's usually doing without food for a limited period of time. As we study what God's Word has to say about fasting, we see that abstinence from food can be to various degrees and will sometimes include going without water. So that you may be familiar with some of the passages on fasting, let me simply list the different types of fasting I have come across in the Word of God, along with a

Scripture reference. Then you can look up each reference and make any notes that you feel are pertinent.

## Types of Fasting

1. Partial: Daniel 10:2, 3
2. Total: Matthew 4:1, 2
3. Absolute (no food or water): Esther 4:16; Acts 9:9
4. Voluntary (purposely taking no food): Daniel 9:3
5. Involuntary (cannot eat) because:
    a. Too grieved, or no desire: Daniel 6:18
    b. No food available: Matthew 15:32; 2 Corinthians 6:5

Why do men fast? Why are they to fast? In Zechariah 7:5 God asks the question, " 'When you fasted and mourned in the fifth and seventh months these seventy years, was it actually for Me that you fasted?' " "Are you seeking Me," God asks, "or are you trying to manipulate Me?"

God deals with the issue of manipulation in Isaiah 58. Take a few minutes to read Isaiah 58:1–12; when you finish, answer the questions that follow.

1. According to verses 1–4, why were they fasting?

2. Were they walking in righteousness before God?

3. Verse 5 tells you what they were doing when they fasted. List some of them.

4. According to verses 6 and 7, what kind of fast had God chosen?

5. In verses 8–12 the words, *then* and *if* appear several times in a very significant way. These show the end result of a godly fast. Read these verses, specifically looking for the "then's" and "if's."

Fasting is usually born out of a need. Jesus brings this out in Matthew 9:14, 15 when the disciples of John questioned Jesus' disciples because they were not fasting. Jesus replied by reminding them that the bridegroom was still with them and that when He was taken away, then they would fast. In essence, Jesus was saying, "I'm here, supplying their needs. Therefore, they don't need to fast. But when I'm gone, they will." When men fast, generally it will be because of a need! The needs can be quite varied, as we will see.

Fasting calls us from the mundane into communion with our Lord. Isn't this why more of us don't fast—we're too busy, too self-sufficient. We'll work and get it ourselves. Or, we will get involved in planning, scheming, and manipulating in order to bring about what we need. If we are that busy, who has time for fasting? Fasting is for those who will put aside all else, including food, to seek God on some particular issue or need. The needs can be quite varied, as we will see.

When, Beloved, was the last time you sought God in prayer and fasting?

## DAY 5

When do men fast? The Scriptures give various illustrations. Once again, let me list various times when men fasted. Your assignment is to look up the Scripture and make notes for your own benefit.

### When Do Men Fast?

1. In sorrow: 2 Samuel 1:12, Psalms 35:13
2. When pleading, or beseeching God: 2 Samuel 12:16, 21–23
3. When needing help: Ezra 8:21–23
4. In fear of judgment, or in danger: Jonah 3, Joel 1:14–2:13; 1 Kings 21:27–29
5. When interceding: Ezra 10:6

6. When needing guidance: Acts 13:2, 3
7. When seeking revelation: Daniel 9:2, 3
8. When serving God: Luke 2:37; 2 Corinthians 6:5

How I pray that you have taken the time to look up these passages because I really believe that God can use them to show you when you need to fast. God has given you examples of eight reasons for fasting. "When you fast. . . ."

Aside from Isaiah 58 and Matthew 6, there is really not a great deal of instruction in the Word of God regarding fasting. Only as we study various incidents of when people fasted do we gain more insights into the occasions that provoke men to seek God through fasting. Yesterday I said that fasting is usually born out of a need to diligently seek God. Therefore, what I want us to do today is to look at the times people fasted. As we do, I pray God will touch a sensitive chord in your heart.

Sorrow is often an occasion for fasting. This is seen in Hannah's life when her husband's other wife provoked her because of her barren womb. Hannah longed for children, but the Lord had closed her womb. Year after year when they went to the temple to worship, the pain grew worse. Peninnah, Elkanah's second wife who had children, constantly provoked Hannah. Hannah's bitterness of soul was so great that she would not eat (1 Samuel 1:6–8). What a contrast to our thinking today. Instead of fasting for children, we abort them!

David and his men mourned and fasted until evening the day they heard of Saul and Jonathan's death (2 Samuel 1:12). Torn by the malicious attacks of his enemies, David humbled his soul through fasting when he heard that his enemies were sick, mourning as if they were members of his own family!

I have not fasted a lot, but when I have it has usually been on occasions when I have sought the Lord's wisdom or intervention. I remember one time when I was to speak to the women who were attending a Christian convention with their husbands. I was so distressed by the superficiality of the teaching coming from the main teaching sessions, that I drank only water for three days. How I longed for God to break through in His power. I ached for God and for His glory. Every longing for food became a stimulus to prayer. I never saw God move through the main sessions, but men were drawn to our seminars, and, along with their wives, asked for extra teaching sessions.

David fasted when his child by Bathsheba was sick unto death, pleading for his life. When the child died, David's fasting ended for the situation was resolved (2 Samuel 12:15–23). Paul and Barnabas fasted and prayed when they appointed elders for the churches (Acts 14:23). Ezra proclaimed a fast at the river Ahava, that those traveling with him might humble themselves before God to seek from Him a safe journey through enemy territory. Rather than seeking the king's protection, he sought the Lord's glory through fasting and prayer and God honored his faith (Ezra 8:21–23). Thus we see men fasting because they needed God's help and protection.

Times of God's judgment have also provoked even ungodly men to fast. This was the case in Nineveh when Jonah came pronouncing destruction because of the iniquity of Nineveh. From the king all the way down to the animals of Nineveh, none ate or drank. The whole nation was called to turn from their wickedness and to call upon God. Nineveh was not destroyed! O that our nation would turn from its sin, fast and pray! I am sure that God would hear.

In Joel, God calls to Israel, "Return to Me with all your heart, and with fasting, weeping, and mourning; and rend your heart and not your garments" (Joel 2:12, 13). O that we would take that call to our hearts, that we would—

> Blow a trumpet in Zion, consecrate a fast, proclaim a solemn assembly, gather the people, sanctify the congregation, assemble the elders, gather the children and the nursing infants. Let the bridegroom come out of his room and the bride out of her bridal chamber. Let the priests, the LORD's ministers, weep between the porch and the altar, and let them say, "Spare Thy people, O LORD, and do not make Thine inheritance a reproach, a byword among the nations. Why should they among the peoples say, 'Where is their God?' " Then the LORD will be zealous for His land, and will have pity on His people.
>
> *Joel 2:15–18*

The desire for understanding and revelation of God's will caused Daniel to fast (Daniel 9:2, 3). Ezra fasted out of mourning as he interceded because of the unfaithfulness of the exiles who had returned to Jerusalem. In many manuscripts, Mark 9:29 and Matthew 17:21 indicate that certain kinds of demons only come out by prayer and fasting.

Finally, just the desire to serve God can be a cause for prayer and fasting. This is so beautifully seen in the prophetess Anna who served God day and night in the temple with fastings and prayers (Luke 2:37).

Well Beloved, what about you? Would Jesus say to you, "When you fast ..."? When do you fast, or have you no need to fast?

# 16 - How Do You Handle the Desire for Things?

## DAY 1

Evangelical Christians spend more for cat and dog food than they do for missions. You've probably heard that statement before. It's alarming, isn't it? But what I'm about to tell you is, to me, more startling. People who make $50,000 or more annually give an average of 1–2 percent of their income to the church. People earning $10,000 or less per year give an average of 10–20 percent of their income to the church.

These statistics are like warning shots in my ear. It would appear that the more we are able to accumulate "things," the more vulnerable we become to having our hearts enticed away from a sacrificial love for our God. Once money becomes our intimate companion and we no longer have to scrimp and save, we seem to spend it with greater ease until finally we are caught in the habit of self-indulgence. And so we begin to lay up treasures on earth and soon our hearts are captivated with the seductiveness of things.

How wise Agur was to ask of God what he knew he needed:

Keep deception and lies far from me,
Give me neither poverty nor riches,
Feed me with the food that is my portion,

Lest I be full and deny thee and say, "Who is the LORD?"
Or lest I be in want and steal,
And profane the name of my God.

*Proverbs 30:8, 9*

In Matthew 6:19, Jesus begins a series of *do nots*. The first regards laying up treasures upon earth. The second is "do not be anxious for your life nor for your body." We will look at these *do nots* this week. Would you begin your study with me by asking God to reveal to you where your treasures are and why you are anxious? Would you be willing to tell Him that you will walk in obedience to what He shows you, even if it's difficult? Will you ask Him to help you evaluate the ways you expend your energies, to show you if you are being wise in redeeming the time and making it count for eternity? Would you ask Him to give you a glimpse of the treasures you can have in heaven?

I would not ask you to do this alone, Beloved. I will do it with you, because God would not honor my efforts if I were unwilling to have Him work the same way with me as He does with you. Will you ask Him?

Our Lord's instructions are very clear, aren't they? "Do not lay up for yourselves treasures upon earth, where moth and rust destroy, and where thieves break in and steal. But lay up for yourselves treasures in heaven, where neither moth nor rust destroys, and where thieves do not break in or steal; for where your treasure is, there will your heart be also (Matthew 6:19–21).

Whenever I hear this verse I cannot help but remember when Jack and I, as newlyweds, were headed to Mexico as missionaries. When we met and married, I was a widow with two children and a whole house full of furniture. Time and time again I had told the Lord, "Father, I hold all this in an open hand. I want to serve You. It's Yours and I am willing to walk out and leave it." Now He was testing me. Did I mean it? We ran an ad in the newspaper:

Going to Mexico as missionaries. Everything for sale.

People converged upon our home looking for bargains. And bargains they found. In the midst of people rummaging through my cupboards a friend said to me, "Don't sell it, Kay, put it in storage. Who knows, God may not let you stay in Mexico!" Leaving Mexico had not even entered my mind—neither had putting our things in storage. As I considered my friend's proposition, Matthew 6:21 flooded my heart. The earthly treasures had to go. I could not go to Mexico with my heart in storage.

You know, Beloved, as I look back on those days I have no regrets. My friend was right. God did not leave us in Mexico. The heart condition that confined me to bed was in our sovereign God's design to bring us home in order to establish Precept Ministries. I must admit that I thought my heart would break when we left Mexico for truly the strings of my heart were entwined about the work God had given us in Guadalajara. The possessions packed in that crude homemade trailer behind our station wagon meant very little to me compared to the treasure of the hearts of the precious ones who had come to the Lord during our three and a half years in Mexico. Had not Jesus said, "Truly I say to you, there is no one who has left house or brothers or sisters or mother or father or children or farms, for My sake and for the gospel's sake, but that he shall receive a hundred times as much now in the present age, houses and brothers and sisters and mothers and children and farms, along with persecutions; and in the world to come, eternal life" (Mark 10:29, 30).

We had not given in order to get and yet God was to give us back a hundredfold through generous friends who shared their homes, their condominiums, their food, their clothing and their possessions. So, as I write this at the age of fifty, I find myself really not wanting for anything. Yet I am reminded by the Scripture that this is a very precarious position to be in lest I be full and deny the Lord. As Jesus warned in the Sermon on the Mount, "Lest the light that is in you become darkness" (author's paraphrase). The very blessings of the Lord can seduce our affections away from the Giver to the gifts.

We have sung it over and over again: "God Bless America." And He has. I don't think that any other nation on the face of this earth is as blessed as America has been blessed. And yet, in our prosperity we have turned from God. We have forgotten that no one can serve two masters. Our affections cannot be divided. God knows it and that is why He says either we will hate the one and love the other or we will hold to the one and despise the other. We cannot serve God and riches. Is this why America for the most part has turned its back upon God? Is this why so many Americans who profess to know Him simply give Him lip service? Have our hearts become captivated with the seductiveness of things rather than with a fervent sacrificial love for our God and for the furtherance of His kingdom? What do you really treasure?

Get on your knees, Beloved. I mean literally get on your knees and read through Matthew 6:19–34. As you do, ask God to cleanse you through the washing of the water of His Word.

## DAY 2

How do you keep from laying up treasures on earth? Or to put it another way, how do you handle the seductiveness of things that would consume your energies and draw you away from undistracted devotion to your God?

I think that Jesus gives us the answer in Matthew 6:22, 23: "The lamp of the body is the eye; if therefore your eye is clear [healthy], your whole body will be full of light. But if your eye is bad, your whole body will be full of darkness. If therefore the light that is in you is darkness, how great is the darkness!"

Our problem is our eyes. We have had that problem ever since the Garden of Eden when Satan enticed Eve. Her downfall came when she took her focus off God and put it upon the fruit of the tree of the knowledge of good and evil. "When the woman saw that the tree was good for food, and that it was a delight to the eyes, and that the tree was desirable to make one wise, she took from its fruit and ate; and she gave also to her husband with her, and he ate" (Genesis 3:6). As you read this verse you can see a progression. First, Eve saw, and what she saw was desirable; so she took it, then ate, and then gave to her husband.

We see that same pattern in the book of Joshua. When God gave Jericho to the children of Israel He clearly warned them that the city was under ban and that all the possessions of that city belonged to the Lord. They were not allowed to take any spoils of war. God had said, "But as for you, only keep yourselves from the things under the ban, lest you covet them and take some of the things under the ban, so you would make the camp of Israel accursed and bring trouble on it" (Joshua 6:18). Achan did not heed God's warning and as a result, trouble did come to Israel. As a matter of fact, they could not even conquer the small town of Ai. God was not with them because there was sin in the camp. When finally it was discovered that Achan was the cause, he told the story of his downfall, "When I saw among the spoil a beautiful mantle from Shinar and two hundred shekels of silver and a bar of gold fifty shekels in weight, then I coveted them and took them; and behold, they are concealed in the earth inside my tent with the silver underneath it" (Joshua 7:21). Once again you see a pattern similar to Eve's. Achan saw the spoil, he coveted it or desired it, and then he took it. His downfall began with the focus of his eyes.

We see the same problem in David's life in 2 Samuel 11—a progression. He sees a beautiful woman bathing and David desires her. He sends a messenger to inquire about her and, finally, he takes her. In all three incidences we have a pattern that moves from seeing, to desiring, to taking. Is it any wonder that Jesus tells us that the lamp of the body is the eye. Close your eyes for a moment. What do you see? Darkness. Nothing. Our eyes are the windows that let light into our bodies. Clean windows let in more light. Dirty windows obscure the light. Therefore, our eyes determine the amount of light that comes into our bodies.

My dear grandma Elsie who is ninety-two has unhealthy eyes. She has glaucoma and because of this her eyes don't adjust well to changes in lighting. She cannot distinguish colors well and as her vision grows more dim, she has to be very careful where she walks. It's easy to stumble. What is physically true of Grandma Elsie is spiritually true of many Christians. Their eyes are not healthy. Their focus is on the wrong things. Because of that their whole body is full of darkness and they stumble through life, groping, feeling things out because they cannot see clearly.

In John's first epistle he warned us about the lust of our eyes. "For all that is in the world, the lust of the flesh and the lust of the eyes and the boastful pride of life, is not from the Father, but is from the world" (1 John 2:16). Because our eyes can be an instrument of lust—because they can lead us into the sin of covetousness—it is absolutely vital that we keep our eyes healthy. But how?

It is a matter of our focus. We live in a world filled with all sorts of alluring things. Beautiful. Enticing. But distracting! Books, magazines, television, movies, and billboards are just some of the things that constantly display treasures belonging to this life and this life only. How then can a child of God keep his vision clear? Well, as I have said before, it is a matter of focus. As the author of Hebrews says, we need to fix our eyes on Jesus, the author and perfecter of our faith. Or as Paul says in 2 Corinthians 4:18, we need to look "not at the things which are seen, but at the things which are not seen, for the things which are seen are temporal, but the things which are not seen are eternal." We need to do as Moses did who turned his back on all of Egypt and its treasures, "choosing rather to endure ill-treatment with the people of God, than to enjoy the passing pleasures of sin; considering the reproach of Christ greater riches than the treasures of Egypt; for he was looking to the reward. By faith he left Egypt, not fearing the wrath of the king; for he endured, as seeing Him who is unseen" (Hebrews 11:25–27).

It's all a matter of perspective, Beloved. Eternal perspective. Where is your focus? Is it upon the things of this world? The treasures of this life that can be destroyed by moth and rust and stolen by thieves? Or is it upon heavenly treasures that have eternal value? We often forget, don't we, that we are strangers and pilgrims upon this earth. "Our citizenship is in heaven, from which also we eagerly wait for a Savior, the Lord Jesus Christ" (Philippians 3:20).

Someday everything on earth is going to be burned up, destroyed with an intense heat. All the records of the accomplishments of mankind, every monument, everything that can be made with human hands will be dissolved by fire (2 Peter 3:10–12). Only that which was done by the Spirit of God, through channels of human flesh, will abide. These will become our treasures in heaven—the things that we have done by the Spirit in accordance with the Word and for God's glory.

O that we would see this, Beloved. O that the eyes of our understanding would be open so that we would not give our time and energies to those things which would only bring us earthly treasures. What is your focus? What is your heart set upon? Where are your treasures?

## DAY 3

When we do not fix our eyes upon Jesus and things of eternity, we eventually will find ourselves no longer serving God, but serving mammon. To that you may say, "Oh, no, not me. I have them both in proper perspective." I remember a time when a friend of mine happened into a small, fast-service store. The magazines on the rack in that store were so perverted and distressing, my friend felt compelled to speak to the store owner. As she did she confessed Jesus Christ as her Savior to which the man replied, "I'm a Christian also, ma'am, but God is God and business is business." Is that true? Can God be kept in a Sunday box, served and worshiped one or two days out of the week while we devote the other days to "business"? Can we serve two masters? Jesus says no. "No one can serve two masters; for either he will hate the one and love the other, or he will hold to one and despise the other. You cannot serve God and mammon" (Matthew 6:24).

When He says that we cannot serve God and mammon, what did Jesus mean by the word *mammon?* James Boice, in his book, *The Sermon on the Mount*, explains it well:

> Mammon was a word for material possessions, but it had come into Hebrew from a root word meaning "to entrust," or "to place in someone's keeping." Mammon therefore meant the wealth that one entrusted to another for sake keeping. At this time the word did not have any bad connotations at all and a rabbi could say, "Let the mammon of thy neighbor be as dear to thee as thine own." As time passed, however, the sense of the word mammon shifted away from the passive sense of "that which is entrusted" to the active sense of "that in which a man trusts." In this case, of course, the meaning was entirely bad, and the word mammon which was originally spelled with a small "m" came to be spelled with a capital "M" as designating a god. This linguistic development repeats itself in the life of anyone who does not have his eyes fixed on spiritual treasures. Is that true of you? Have things become your God? Don't forget that these things are written to Christians, and that they are therefore meant to make you ask whether the Lord God Almighty occupies the central place in your life or whether things obscure him.[23]

Dwight Pentecost says:
Mammon is the personalization of God's chief rival—money or material things. Our Lord viewed the acquisition of wealth as a goal that brings a man into the most abject slavery, that prevents him from discharging his responsibilities as one enslaved to Jesus Christ. He becomes enslaved instead to money and can serve no one else, least of all God. When a man is consumed by a passion to accumulate material things, there is room for no other love. The Lord did not

condemn possession of wealth. He did condemn being possessed by that wealth. He viewed the love of money as gross idolatry.[24]

What is God's chief rival? I believe it's things. I don't want to use just the word riches because you may say, "I'm not rich. I just want enough to get by on. All I want are the necessities of life. That can't be wrong, can it?" Yes it can. That's why in the very next verse in Matthew 6 Jesus goes on to talk about anxiety over the necessities of life.

Are you serving God or are you serving things? You cannot serve both. Paul knew this and that's why he said, "I count all things to be loss in view of the surpassing value of knowing Christ Jesus my Lord, for whom I have suffered the loss of all things, and count them but rubbish in order that I may gain Christ" (Philippians 3:8). Paul's eyes were fixed on the prize of the upward call of God in Christ Jesus. He served One and One alone, his Lord Jesus Christ. Therefore, he learned to be content in whatever circumstances he found himself. He learned to get along with humble means and how to live in prosperity. In any and every circumstance of life he learned the secret of being filled and of going hungry, of having abundance and suffering need (Philippians 4:11, 12). Nothing mattered except that which had eternal value.

O Beloved, what about you? Where are you? To what are you giving yourself, your energies? Whom are you serving? What do you desire above all else and more than anything else in this life? What is your heart fixed upon? Is it God or the temporal things of unrighteous mammon? What possesses you? Is it a passion for God or a passion for the things of this life? Ponder these questions. Let them search your heart. Give God time to speak.

## DAY 4

"All I want are the necessities of life!!! I'm not interested in being rich, I just want to survive!!! Is there anything wrong with that?"

It all depends on how you intend to survive. If surviving means that you do not have time to seek God's kingdom and God's righteousness, then you are not serving God, but mammon. And God says that is wrong. Have you forgotten, Beloved, that you do have a heavenly Father and that it is the Father's responsibility to take care of His children? Fathers are expected to give their children the basics of life, to provide them with food and clothing. Since you are a child of God it is God's reponsibility as your Father to take care of the necessities of life. It is your responsibility as a child of God to seek first His kingdom and His righteousness.

Let me tell you a story, Beloved, that vividly illustrates the truth of Matthew 6:25–33. God has burdened me to pray for the body of Jesus Christ living behind the Iron Curtain. Several publications from different organizations give me plenty of fuel for prayer, one of which is called *A Bible for Russia*. In the December 1983 issue was a story entitled "Christmas Eve in Romania." When I finished reading it all I could do was weep and worship my God.

> Christmas was not to be the same this year. Isolated from the rest of the outside world, it was difficult with the seven children to celebrate the birth of Jesus, when their stomachs were empty. There were no decorations, no brightly lit candles, no Christmas tree, no cookies, and no beautiful wrapped gifts to exchange. The children were just as hungry today as any other day. Soon, dad will be telling the children about the Messiah, born in a manger, much like the little hut they lived in.
>
> This father, mother, and their seven children all under 14 years of age, were banished into exile in the far reaches of an uninhabited part of the country. The communist authorities hated the father because of his convicting preaching. He was nick-named by the believers, "The Golden Word," because of his eloquence. They were forced to move to a little village, inaccessible by car or train. What food they were given was flown in by helicopter. They lived in a tiny hut with a straw roof, under the constant surveillance of the prison guards.
>
> The village was established for those "undesirables" of society, which includes "religious fanatics." The stinging chill was made worse by the wind whipping snow across the flat barren land, unbroken by hills, and whistling its song through every crack and crevice in the small hut. For two days now, the guards had not bothered to bring them any food. They were too

busy preparing their own celebration with wine and pork. The children listened intently to their father telling them the story of Jesus, huddled together around the dim light of the gas lantern on the table. They were so intent, they forgot about their hunger. But when the story was over, one after the other began to cry. Before going to bed that Christmas Eve, the whole family knelt down on the dirt floor and prayed as never before: "Our Father, which art in Heaven ... Give us this day our daily bread...."

After they finished their prayer and said, "Amen," the children asked their mother and father many questions.

"Do you think God heard our prayer?"

"Of course He did."

"But what if He didn't hear it?"

"That isn't possible," the father replied.

"Do you think He will send us bread?" they asked.

"Yes, I'm sure He will," said the father.

"But when?" they cried.

The parents, heartbroken to see their children crying from hunger, could not answer. The children continued;

"Who will He send to bring us bread?"

"He will find someone," said the father reassuringly.

"But what if He doesn't find anyone?"

"Well then" ... the father paused ... "He Himself will bring it with His own hand. Now close your eyes and go to sleep."

The father blew out the little lantern as darkness descended on them, and the wind whistled to them in their sleep. Suddenly, the still darkness was shattered, a knock on the door!

The father got out of bed, and opened the door just a crack to keep the cold from blowing inside. A hand holding a large loaf of bread was stretched toward him. His heart pounding, the father reached out to take the bread, and at the same time opened the door widely to say thank you. But at that very moment, in the twinkling of an eye, the hand was gone, there was no one there. Bewildered, the father closed the door and turned around. All seven children leaped out of bed and surrounded him.

"Who was it, Dad? Who gave you the bread?"

"Children," he said with a tremble in his voice, "The Lord

did not find anyone to send to us with bread, so He Himself came and gave it to us with His own Hand."

Nobody could sleep anymore that Christmas Eve. The children couldn't stop singing about Jesus, and about how the Lord had spread a table for them in the wilderness.[25]

O Beloved, we can serve God and in serving God we need not be anxious about our lives or our bodies. Why? Because we are God's children and He promises to supply all of our needs according to His riches in glory through Christ Jesus our Lord (Philippians 4:19). Your responsibility is simply to seek first His kingdom and His righteousness and know that in doing so all these things shall be added unto you.

## DAY 5

Does seeking the kingdom of God and His righteousness liberate a man or a woman from all responsibility as far as earning a living goes? Is Matthew 6:33 a license for laziness or an undisciplined life? Does it mean that all I need to do is sit, pray, study, and meditate—and expect God to feed and clothe me?

Some think so, but their thinking is wrong. It is not according to the whole counsel of God. Every now and then we have people who come through Precept Ministries, "moving according to the Spirit's leading." They do not have jobs; they do not have money. They simply go "wherever the Spirit leads them." And yet, whose food do they eat? Someone not only had to buy it, but also someone had to cook it. Who paid the electricity bill so the room they sleep in would be warm? Who paid the water bill so they would have water to bathe—although bathing was not always the concern. And why were the sheets on the bed clean? It was because someone washed them. What are these people doing? They are seeking God's kingdom and His righteousness, or so they say. But what does God say? Is Matthew 6:33 a license for an undisciplined life? Does it set us free from the responsibility of earning a living? These are questions we must answer so that we don't go off on seemingly spiritual but unbiblical tangents.

Read 2 Thessalonians 3:6–15 and then answer the following questions:

1. According to this passage, what is an undisciplined manner of life? When you answer this, don't forget to note what verse 8 says.

2. What example did Paul and his companions set before others?

3. What was Paul's order or command in verse ten?

4. Now according to what you have seen in 2 Thessalonians 3, does Matthew 6:33 say that we do not have to work to earn a living?

I think it's obvious from the text that Matthew 6:33 is not a license for an undisciplined life. Rather, it is a combination of a command and a promise. The command is that we are to habitually seek first God's kingdom and His righteousness. I say habitually because the verb *seek* is in the present tense in the Greek. However, the word I really want you to notice is the word *first*. In all things God is to have the preeminence. The priority of our lives is to be His righteousness. God is not saying that you and I cannot do anything else. He knows that we live in a world and in this world we have responsibilities. Men are responsible to provide for their households. If they do not, according to God they are worse than infidels. A woman is to be a keeper of her home. The home is her responsibility. If she fails in keeping a proper home then she has failed in what God has ordained for her to do. Providing for a family, keeping a home, taking care of children all take time and energy. These things cannot be neglected nor does God expect us to neglect them for His Kingdom. However, He does expect us to keep them in proper perspective to the kingdom. Our love for Him is to supersede every other love and when it does we have the blessed promise: "All these things shall be added to you." Let me repeat it once more. There is a command: seek first His kingdom and His righteousness; there is a promise: all these things shall be added to you.

What then, Beloved, is the bottom line of it all? It's this: do not be anxious for tomorrow. How I love that statement "for tomorrow." Why doesn't it say don't be anxious for today? Because today, you are all right. It's not today that we normally worry about. Today you have something to put on your body. Today you have something, however meager it may be, to put in your mouth. But you may say, "What about tomorrow?" God says tomorrow will care for itself. Why? Because God is not only a God of today, but a God of tomorrow. Each day has enough trouble of its own. We are to live one day at a time. That's why Jesus taught us to pray, "Give us this day our daily bread." If He took care of you today, will He not take care of you tomorrow? Look at those little birds out there. Aren't you worth more than they? Of course you are. Your heavenly Father feeds them and He'll feed you also.

> And why are you anxious about clothing? Observe how the lilies of the field grow; they do not toil nor do they spin, yet I say to you that even Solomon in all his glory did not clothe himself like one of these. But if God so arrays the grass of the field, which is alive today and tomorrow is thrown into the furnace, will he not much more do so for you, O men of little faith?
> *Matthew 6:28–30*

Beloved, what kind of Father do you have? Is He faithless or faithful? Can He lie? Of course He cannot lie. He is faithful. "If we are faithless, He remains faithful; for He cannot deny Himself" (2 Timothy 2:13). You can trust Him, so quit being anxious. It is a sin. It is an accusation against God's faithfulness.

Are you poor? Then listen to God's word. "Godliness actually is a means of great gain, when accompanied by contentment. For we have brought nothing into the world, so we cannot take anything out of it either. And if we have food and covering, with these we shall be content" (1 Timothy 6:6–8).

Are you rich? Then listen to God's instructions. "Instruct those who are rich in the present world not to be conceited or to fix their hope on the uncertainty of riches, but on God, who richly supplies us with all things to enjoy. Instruct them to do good, to be rich in good works, to be generous and ready to share, storing up for themselves the treasure of a good foundation for the future, so that they may take hold of that which is life indeed" (1 Timothy 6:17–19).

Rich or poor? Set your affection on things above (Colossians 3:1). Seek first His kingdom and His righteousness and all these things will be added to you.

# 17 - To Judge or Not to Judge— That Is the Confusion!

## DAY 1

How many times have you heard, "Judge not, lest ye be judged" (KJV)? How many times have you called sinful behavior "sinful" and have been told, "Judge not, lest ye be judged"? Or have you ever mentioned to another that you were concerned about a person's salvation only to hear—"Who are you to judge? Don't you know the Bible says, 'Judge not'?"

In one form or another, we've all heard debate over this famous Scripture. Does the Bible say, "Judge not, lest ye be judged?" Yes, it does; in good old King James English, that is exactly what it says in Matthew 7:1.

The only problem is, that many who quote Matthew 7:1 have taken it out of its context. They forget the four verses which follow and explain what Jesus meant.

Is all judging wrong? That is what we want to study this week, so that you will know exactly what this verse means and how to apply it to your life.

Remember, in the Sermon on the Mount we are in a succession of *do nots*. Jesus has said, "Do not lay up for yourselves treasures," "Do not be anxious for your life; nor for your body," and "Do not be anxious for tomorrow." Three more *do nots* follow: "Do not judge," "Do not give what is holy to dogs," and "Do not throw your pearls before swine." If you stop and think about it, the last three seem incongruous. One says not to judge and the other two say not to give what is holy to dogs or throw pearls before swine. If you do not judge, how are you going to know who are dogs and who are swine? In the same chapter God tells us that we will know false prophets by their fruits. If I am not allowed to judge, then how am I going to inspect their fruit so I'll know who are false prophets?

Do all these questions create problems? Well, as we study judging in the context of the Word of God, I think that this will all become clear.

First, read Matthew 7:1–5, and then answer the questions that follow:

1. According to this passage, there's a problem with your brother's eye and your own eye. Note below what is in your brother's eye and what's in your eye.

2. Does this passage forbid you to take the speck or the mote out of your brother's eye?

3. Under what conditions?

4. What is Jesus' warning in verse 2? Put it in your own words.

5. What does Jesus call the person who tries to take the speck out of his brother's eye without taking care of his own eye first? Why do you think He calls him that?

6. Do you think this passage forbids judging or just a certain kind of judging? Explain your answer.

The word for *judge* is *krino* and it means to assume the office of a judge, to condemn, to give sentence, to undergo the process of a trial, or to execute judgment upon. To understand what God is saying to us in this passage, we need to look at three *whats* on judging. "What is the context and the content of this passage?" "What makes this judging wrong?" "What am I to judge, if anything?" We'll take these three *whats* and look at them thoroughly in the next few days.

What is the context of Matthew 7:1–5? It is situated in the midst of a series of commands that Jesus has given to those who belong to the kingdom of heaven. How do we know this? The word *you* is a key word in Matthew 5, 6, and 7. If you were to mark every instance of the word *you* and list all that you learn from each reference, you would find that those *you*s definitely refer to those who belong to the kingdom of heaven. Although the Sermon on the Mount was delivered to a group of people two thousand years ago, it was for everybody who would ever be a disciple of Jesus Christ. Scripture teaches that discipleship and salvation are synonymous. So here is God's Word to every child of God. "Do not judge" is a command. The question is: "Is all judging wrong?" To answer that we must see what makes the judging in Matthew 7 wrong. Does the passage refer to all judging or to a certain type of judging?

For today, read through the Sermon on the Mount one more time. This time, draw a little stick figure like this ⚧ and put it over every reference of *you, your, us,* or *our.* Then if you have time, list everything that you learned about *you, your, us,* or *our* in the context of Matthew 5, 6, and 7. It will be quite enlightening, I promise you.

Do you realize that we have only two more weeks together in our study of this Sermon? Sharing with you has meant so much to me. I cannot thank you enough for being one of those who truly hunger and thirst after righteousness. Thanks for being willing to study to show yourself approved unto God. Oftentimes when I read a book I wonder, "When was the author writing this, how long ago was he or she going through that, what was going on in their world at that time?" As I write this it is December 1983. Syria has just shot down two American planes—a bomb has exploded in an Israeli bus killing four and injuring fifty-two—countless fishermen on the Oregon and Washington coasts are wondering how they are ever going to survive beause of a strange, warm water current that has invaded their fishing waters and diminished their catch. An unusual frigid front has dipped deep into the South. America is faced with the coldest temperaures in half a century.

We are living in critical times, Beloved, and God is trying to speak to us in numerous and various ways. But are we listening? Jesus said that the day of His coming will be like the days of Noah and the days of Lot when they were eating and drinking and giving in marriage. They knew not that judgment was coming—they did not understand until it was too late. I want you to understand. I want you to know. I want you to be prepared. You must know God's Word. You must be convinced that it is true. You must know how to appropriate the promises of God which are always true. You must know how to live. You must be convinced that it is right to seek first His kingdom and His righteousness. You must know that all you need is yours for the asking, for the seeking, and for the knocking. You must never forget that the way is narrow and that the gate is small and few find it. You must be fully aware that false prophets will come to you in sheep's clothing but inwardly are ravenous wolves. You must know that heaven awaits only those who hear God's words and act upon them. You must know so that you can build your house upon the Rock so that when the rain descends and the floods come and the winds blow and burst against your house it will stand, for it's been founded upon the Rock. Persevere, Beloved, persevere. You're building on the Rock.

## DAY 2

On our refrigerator is a little sticker that says, "Christians aren't perfect, just forgiven." When you're a teenager in a family where your father is the president of a Christian organization, and your mother a Bible teacher and conference speaker, that's a good thing to remember. It's also good to remember that grace is available when the public expects a certain standard of behavior because of who his parents are. So we keep the little sticker on the refrigerator, not only for David's benefit but also for ours!

The message of the sticker is not an excuse for unrighteous behavior, but is a reminder that none of us has yet attained perfection. Is it any wonder that people have loved the little button that reads *PBPGINFWMY*? Please Be Patient, God Is Not Finished With Me Yet! That's what we want, isn't it—patience for our imperfection? Yet, is that what we give?

What makes the judgment in Matthew 7:1–5 wrong? We know that it's wrong because Jesus refers to those who judge this way as hypocrites. They are hypocrites because they have a beam in their own eye. They are not perfect and yet they are expecting others to be perfect. They have a judgmental attitude. Did you notice the contrast between the beam and the mote, the log and the speck? Quite a contrast, isn't it? What it shows is that those who judge are expecting the minutest in proper behavior from others when they have great big problems of their own. An attitude or expectation like this is not a loving concern of one brother for another, but rather a judgmental, condemning attitude.

Any person with a public ministry is especially subject to criticism. Our blunders in this day and age are often recorded on cassette tapes, reproduced quickly and projected across the country. The world of video and television has not only left us open to criticism for what we say, but also for the way we look, dress, or act. Every peculiar mannerism is recorded for the world to see. Obviously, anyone in this position leaves himself quite vulnerable, open to various types of criticism. Notice I said "various," for there is a place for constructive criticism; all criticism is not judgmental. Many times I have received precious letters born out of hearts of loving concern for the work of the Lord and for me. When I read a letter like that, I realize that my friends have been careful to remove the log out of their own eye. It is obvious that they are seeing clearly, for their surgery is done with extreme gentleness and the utmost of care. I know that they are not after my whole eye, just the bit of dust. I know that they love me because they have assured me of that love. They have not written me off as worthless because they have exhorted me, commending me for what is right. I realize that they know the problem is with my eye and not with my heart, and that means so much to me. You see, it's one thing to point out a brother's error; it's another thing to condemn his heart.

About two years ago I received a letter from a woman who has regularly taken part in our Precept Bible Study week after week. She has listened to me teach so she should know my heart. Yet her letter was very censorious. She didn't like it because I said that I had been prostrate on my face before the Lord in prayer, beseeching Him to give me His message, to speak through me. She thought it was prideful for me to talk about seeking the Lord in prayer, about weeping before Him, about longing for His message. She had missed my heart. She didn't understand the total impotence, the utter poverty of spirit that I feel as one who is accountable for the way I handle God's Word. Since then, she has criticized me about other matters. She has a reputation for criticizing teachers. She has a log in her own eye and because of it cannot see how to take the speck out of her brother's eye. We often project our own problem upon others. The problem is, of course, that we don't know that we have a problem!

This is well illustrated in Romans. In Romans 1, Paul gives a clear picture of the degradation to which unsaved Gentiles can descend. However, as he writes his letter to those in Rome, he knows that his audience is made up not only of Gentiles, but also of Jews. At that point, he can just see the Jews nodding their heads, "That's right, Paul. Those Gentiles are really depraved! Such immorality! Such greed! Such murder! Such malice! I tell you, it's horrible!" Paul knows the mind of self-righteous Jews. After all, he was one himself. So in Romans 2, he turns to the Jews and exposes their guiltiness.

Read Romans 2:1–16, 17–24, and then note below how this could apply to Matthew 7:1–5.

How are we to deal with a brother in sin, and not to violate Matthew 7:1? The Word of God clearly teaches that if we see our brother caught in a trespass or straying from the truth, it is our responsibility in love to turn that brother back to a walk of righteousness. Obviously, to do so we have to discern that our brother is straying from the truth.

Read James 5:19, 20.

1. What are God's specific instructions in these verses?

2. How will it benefit the brother who has strayed?

3. In Galatians 6:1 what are we instructed to do?

4. What is to be the spiritual state of the restorer? How is he to restore his brother?

Now then, James 5:19, 20 and Galatians 6:1 cannot directly violate God's command to us in Matthew 7. What then is the answer? Are we to judge or not to judge? The answer is in yourself, the one who is judging. What is your walk with Jesus Christ like? Are you like those in Romans 2 who are judging others and yet practicing the very same thing? Are you like those in Matthew 7 who are going after motes in their brothers' eyes when they have beams in their own? Have you met the qualifications of Galatians 6:1? "Brethren, even if a man is caught in any trespass, you who are spiritual, restore such a one in a spirit of gentleness; looking to yourselves, lest you too be tempted."

Motes can be removed from others' eyes as long as the eye surgery is done in a spirit of gentleness by one who is spiritual, who is not there to condemn but to restore. And there is a big difference! If we will do what Paul says in Galatians 6:1 and look to ourselves lest we also be tempted, this will keep us from an attitude of condemnation. We must realize that we could have fallen also—the flesh is the flesh and any Christian who does not walk in the Spirit will fulfill the lust of the flesh (Galatians 5:16). Therefore, it is absolutely essential that whenever we seek to restore a brother we realize that we could also have been tempted to sin. We cannot have a holier-than-thou attitude. To do so would violate Matthew 7:1 and Galatians 6:1.

Many a time I have sat with dear brothers and sisters who have become ensnared by the devil because they gave in to the lust of their flesh. My heart was grieved over their sin. I winced to think of the blasphemy that it would bring to the name of God. They were wrong. They knew it. And yet, though sometimes I sat in the role of disciplinarian, I wept for them and with them, telling them that I understood for I live in a body of flesh too. As I write this, I cannot help but think of our great High Priest, tempted in all points as we are, yet without sin; the One who did not come to judge but to save (Hebrews 4:15; John 3:17).

The next time, Beloved, that you see a mote in your brother's eye, examine your heart. Is your judgment for the purpose of condemnation or restoration? As you seek to restore, will you go in meekness, gentleness? Answer these questions honestly and you'll know where you stand in your relationship to Matthew 7:1-5.

Many times our judging is wrong because either we don't judge in love or we judge according to our own standard of behavior. This is what we will look at today. Will you come to God with a teachable spirit, Beloved?

The Jews were angry with Jesus. He was not honoring the Sabbath! Obviously, He could not be from God. Jesus sensed their anger so He confronted them, " 'If a man receives circumcision on the Sabbath that the Law of Moses may not be broken, are you angry with Me because I made an entire man well on the Sabbath? Do not judge according to appearance, but judge with righteous judgment' " (John 7:23, 24).

Isn't that the way it is today, Beloved? We look at someone and see that their behavior does not conform to our standards of spirituality. Notice I said "our standards," not God's, for we, like the Pharisees, have added our own traditions to the Word of God. We may rationalize our traditions by saying that God may not have spoken clearly on the issue of our judgment, but surely anyone who loves God wouldn't be doing what they are doing! Or if we don't judge their behavior, we judge their personality. We think they aren't Christlike because they don't seem sober enough, they laugh too much, nobody could be humble and have such authority, such confidence! Or maybe it's their style of dress—it's too contemporary. Now mind you, in all these areas there is no clear or direct violation of the Word of God, but we think surely it could not be spiritual! Could they?

What are we doing, Beloved? The same thing that the Pharisees did in Jesus' day—judging on the basis of appearance. They forgot what God said to Samuel: "God sees not as man sees, for man looks at the outward appearance, but the LORD looks at the heart" (1 Samuel 16:7). It is easy for man to judge according to appearance; it's difficult for him to judge with righteous judgment!

The Jews were judging Jesus on the basis of the interpretation of the Law. And in the process, they became the offenders of the Law. James 4:11, 12 says, "Do not speak against one another, brethren. He who speaks against a brother, or judges his brother, speaks against the law, and judges the law; but if you judge the law, you are not a doer of the law, but a judge of it. There is only one Lawgiver and Judge, the One who is able to save and to destroy; but who are you who judge your neighbor?" The minute you and I sit in condemnation against another, we are speaking against the Law and we are judging the Law. Why? Because the Law finds its fulfillment in love, not judgment. "Owe nothing to anyone except to love one another; for he who loves his neighbor has fulfilled the law. . . . and if there is any other commandment, it is summed up in this saying, 'You shall love your neighbor as yourself.' Love does no wrong to a neighbor; love therefore is the fulfillment of the law" (Romans 13:8–10). How can you tell if you are judging with righteous judgment rather than according to appearance? How can you tell whether or not you are breaking Jesus' command in Matthew 7:1? You will know, Beloved, by your attitude. What is your motivation?

Anytime love of God and love of your neighbor is missing and you're concerned with the mote in your brother's eye in a condemning way, you can know that you are judging the Law and breaking Jesus' commandment not to judge.

So many Christians violate the principle of love and it literally tears the heart out of their Christian testimony. Did not Jesus say, " 'By this all men will know that you are My disciples, if you have love for one another' " (John 13:35)? Judging without love happens many times when we come up with our own code or standard for righteousness. We develop a set of dos and don'ts that determine a man's spiritual status and then we seek to impose these upon others. I think this is what Jesus is warning us against in the Sermon on the Mount. He knows the weakness of our flesh. He knows that as He calls us to this high standard of living it is apt to make us judgmental. How right He is!

In Romans 14 Paul has to address the same problem. "Who are you to judge the servant of another? To his own master he stands or falls; and stand he will, for the Lord is able to make him stand" (Romans 14:4). When Jews and Gentiles were merged into one body, the Jews brought with them their legalism and the Gentiles brought with them their freedom—they had never lived under the Law. This created a major problem. Each had a different standard of holiness and this resulted in judging.

1. Read Romans 14:1–23. What is the problem in verses 1–3?

2. What is the problem in verses 5, 6?

3. According to 14:15, how are we to walk?

4. What are God's instructions regarding judging in this area of differences? Read 14:10–13.

5. What are we to pursue according to 14:19?

6. How are we to walk regarding our own convictions? Read verses 20–23.

Much of our problem in judging is in this area, isn't it? This grey area of dos, don'ts, and differences, all depending on our religious upbringing or lack of it. We need to remember that "the kingdom of God is not eating and drinking, but righteousness and peace and joy in the Holy Spirit" (Romans 14:17). If we walk according to love and pursue the things that make for peace and for the building up of one another, then we need not worry about breaking Jesus' commandment in

Matthew 7:1. "Therefore do not go on passing judgment before the time, but wait until the Lord comes who will both bring to light the things hidden in the darkness and disclose the motives of men's hearts; and then each man's praise will come to him from God" (1 Corinthians 4:5).

O Beloved, go before the throne of grace and ask God to examine your heart. Are you sitting as a judge, speaking against the Law, and therefore judging the Law because you are not walking in love toward your brother? Are you seeking to judge the motives of men's hearts where you can only see their outward appearance? Have you, like the Pharisees, added your tradition to God's Word and then sought to judge another man's walk with God according to your interpretation of the Law?

When you have done eye surgery, have you done it in gentleness? Did you have a holier-than-thou attitude? Or did you realize that you yourself could be tempted also? Do you need to admit that you are wrong? Do you need to go to anyone and to ask their forgiveness? Ask God to show you your heart, Beloved, and then whatever the Spirit of God says to do, do it. You won't be sorry.

## DAY 4

When Jesus said, "Do not judge lest you be judged," was He calling us to a blithe blindness to the unrighteous behavior of others? Was He calling us to close our eyes to sin, to tolerate false doctrines and indiscriminately accept those who teach them? Was He telling us to take the beautiful gems of the gospel and throw them before swine that they might root them in the mud? Was He calling us to share the precious truths of God's Word with those whom we know would only mock and ridicule them, making sport of our beliefs? These are questions to which we need answers and those answers can only come as we look at the whole counsel of the Word of God. So study well, Beloved. Do your assignments. Don't forget to go to your Teacher, the Holy Spirit. Ask Him to lead you into all truth, and as you do, remember He will never contradict what the Word of God has to say. Now then, let's compare Scripture with Scripture.

Read Matthew 7:6 and then answer the questions that follow:

1. What is Jesus warning us about in this verse?

2. Read Philippians 3:2, 3, 17–19. Do these verses call for any judgment or discernment on your part? How?

3. How does Philippians compare with Matthew 7:6?

4. Now, compare what you've learned from Matthew 7:6 and the verses in Philippians 3 with 2 Peter 2:1, 2. Write out your observations.

Swine have no appreciation for pearls, whatsoever. And dogs? The dogs that are referred to in the Bible are not the lovable, well-trained, household pets you and I think of. The dogs of Jesus' day were savage, wild curs that roamed the streets and hills of Palestine, foraging for food and intimidating anyone who would keep them from filling their bellies with garbage. That which was holy meant nothing to them; their god was their appetite. Pigs who lived in the mire could not appreciate beautiful pearls, and dogs who ate their own vomit certainly had no regard for what was holy. Jesus' hearers understood very well what He was saying when He talked about dogs and pigs!

The theme of 2 Peter 2 is false prophets. Although we will study this chapter in greater detail later, I wanted you to see that God compares these false prophets to dogs and sows. Now, the very mention of false prophets ought to take your mind immediately to Matthew 7:15–20 where Jesus, at the conclusion of the Sermon, warns His disciples about false prophets. From 2 Peter 2 and Matthew 7:15–20, it should be obvious that we have to judge who false prophets are! We have to discern who dogs are and who swine are if we are not to put pearls or holy things before them! Then the question becomes, "Do we have the right to pass judgment upon a person's message? Is doctrine important?"

Read 1 John 4:1–6.

1. How does this passage compare with Matthew 7:15–20 and 1 Peter 2:21, 22?

2. What is God's instruction to us in this passage?

3. According to 1 John 4:1–6, are we responsible to discern between the Spirit of truth and the spirit of error?

Doctrine is important, isn't it? The problem is that many won't take the time or the discipline necessary to learn what they believe so they get caught up in false teaching. What have we seen today? Let's summarize. Look up the following Scriptures. Note what each says about wrong doctrine (teaching) and your responsibility, if any.

1. Ephesians 4:14




2. 1 Timothy 1:3, 4




3. 1 Timothy 4:1–3, 6




4. 2 Timothy 4:2–4




Those who belong to the kingdom of heaven are not to sit as censorious judges, but they are to be discriminating about whom they follow. They are also to be discriminating about sharing God's precious truths. To fail to discriminate would mean that truth would be trampled upon and those who hear it would be bent upon the messenger's destruction.

Are we to judge? Yes, we are to judge with just judgment—God's kind of judgment. But you can only know what is wrong by knowing truth. How do you measure up?


## DAY 5


To judge or not to judge, that is the question! Or should I say, that is the confusion? What else, if anything, are we to judge? Let's search the Scriptures so you can see for yourself exactly what God wants you to judge. Look up the verses listed below. As you read, note what you are to judge or discern, and if appropriate, how you are to do it!

1. 2 Thessalonians 3:6, 11, 14, 15

2. 1 Corinthians 5:1–3, 9–13

3. Matthew 18:15–20

4. Hebrews 5:14

5. Titus 3:9–11

6. 1 Corinthians 11:27–32

A careful study of the Scriptures including Matthew 7:1–5 shows that judging is not forbidden. Irresponsible behavior, wrong doctrine, and sin must all be discerned and dealt with. They are not to be swallowed, covered over, or overlooked. Righteousness is to be upheld, the gospel is to be earnestly contended for. No, judging is not wrong if it is done properly. It is fine to correct a brother as long as you do it in a spirit of gentleness, as long as you are spiritual, realizing that you are not above temptation. It is all right to judge as long as the motivation of that judgment is love of God and love of your neighbor. Therefore, the point of judgment is not to condemn, but to restore.

It is all right to judge as long as we judge with a righteous judgment, a judgment that is in accordance with God's Word. We may judge dogs and swine, false prophets, sin, wrong behavior, wrong doctrine— but we cannot judge another man's servants, nor the motives of a man's heart. Above all, Beloved, we must continuously judge ourselves. "But if we judged ourselves rightly, we should not be judged" (1 Corinthians 11:31). Let's make sure the beam is out of our own eyes. This is the message of Matthew 7:1–5.

May our prayer be: "Search me, O God, and know my heart: try me, and know my thoughts: and see if there be any wicked way in me, and lead me in the way everlasting" (Psalms 139:23, 24 KJV).

"Who can understand his errors? Cleanse thou me from secret faults. Keep back thy servant also from presumptuous sins; let them not have dominion over me: then shall I be upright, and I shall be innocent from the great transgression. Let the words of my mouth, and the meditation of my heart, be acceptable in thy sight, O LORD, my strength, and my redeemer" (Psalms 19:12–14 KJV).

# 18 - How to Know You're a Possessor of the Kingdom of Heaven

## DAY 1

Have you ever despaired of being perfect, even as your Father in heaven is perfect, of ever walking on this earth as Jesus walked? Have you ever cried out as Paul, "Who is adequate for these things?" Or with the Psalmist, "It is too high, I cannot attain to it"? Have you ever wondered, "Oh, when will I ever learn, God, when will I learn"? Have you groaned, longing to be clothed with your new body from heaven, sloughing off that flesh that has caused you to stumble? Have you ever feared that someday you will stumble and not get up? I understand.

I understand because I too live in a body of flesh and I know that although my spirit may be willing, my flesh is weak. Jesus understands also, Beloved. He understands because He too lived in a body of flesh. He realized that the spirit is willing but the flesh is weak. He walked where you walk and He sat where you sit. You have a High Priest who can be touched with the feeling of your infirmities. He realizes that He has set a righteousness before you in the Sermon on the Mount that is impossible apart from Him, a righteousness that is high and unattainable except to the poor in Spirit who, in the attaining of the kingdom of heaven, have been indwelt by God's Spirit. Thus, in Matthew 7:7–12, He gives us the Christian's key to abiding righteousness, a righteousness that exceeds that of the scribes and Pharisees.

And what is that key? Godward, it is found in three words: asking, seeking, and knocking (verses 7–11). Manward, it is found in doing for others what you want them to do for you (verse 12). The Christian life is to be lived in total dependence upon God. The greater the dependence, the greater the righteousness. Jesus gives us the key: persistent dependence. You want what is good, Your Father wants you to have what is good. So keep on asking and it will be given to you, keep on seeking and you will find, keep on knocking and it will be opened to you. The source of all that you and I will ever need is found in God. And who is this God? He is your heavenly Father who delights to give what is good to those who ask Him.

Luke 11 sets before us the same truth of Matthew 7:7–12. However, it is preceded by a very pertinent illustration. Read Luke 11:5–13 and then answer the questions that follow:

1. Mark every use of the word *friend* and then record how many times that word is used in verses 5–8.


2. Did the man's friendship have anything to do with giving his friend three loaves of bread?

3. How—or why—did the man get his bread?

4. When Jesus told the story, do you think that He was trying to tell us that even though He's our friend, He is reluctant to give us what we need? Explain your answer.

5. What is the point that Jesus is trying to make in this story? What does He want His children to see?

I think that Jesus wants us to see two things. First, it is the Father's responsibility to take care of His children and meet their needs. Therefore, because He is the Father of fathers, or the epitome of fatherhood, it is His highest pleasure to give us what is good. Earthly fathers, for the most part, seek to give their children good things. How much more will our heavenly Father give us what is good?

You may have noticed that the passage in Luke 11 talks about the heavenly Father giving the Holy Spirit to those who ask Him. I don't want to take off on a tangent, and yet, I want to make sure that you don't go off on one of your own. So, let me simply state some facts that you need to consider. At this point in the economy of God, the Holy Spirit had not yet come to indwell man because Jesus had not yet gone to the Father (John 14:16–18, 26; 16:7, 13). Therefore, they were to ask. However, when it says, "How much more shall your heavenly Father give the Holy Spirit to those who ask Him?" (Luke 11:13), it is *not* telling us, who already have the Holy Spirit through salvation, that we need to ask for the Holy Spirit again. For us, Pentecost has come and gone. We have entered the New Covenant, and as you saw under the New Covenant, the Holy Spirit is given to everyone who believes on the Lord Jesus Christ. Therefore, once you are saved, you don't need to keep asking for the Holy Spirit. But you do need to keep walking in persistent dependence upon God.

What do you need in order to live this life of righteousness that God has called you to? Whatever it is, keep on asking Him for it. Your Father promises that it will be given you. What are you seeking that you need as a child of God in order to please your Father, to do His work?

Keep on seeking it continually and He promises that you will find it. What is closed to you which needs to be opened? Keep on knocking for it to be opened. Keep on knocking, and knocking, and knocking. He promises that it will open. What you need is yours because it is His and as your heavenly Father He delights to give you good gifts. This is why Paul writes, "Now may the God of peace Himself sanctify you entirely; and may your spirit and soul and body be preserved complete, without blame at the coming of our Lord Jesus Christ" (1 Thessalonians 5:23). This is God's desire for us. God's calling is our sanctification, our holiness. Therefore, Paul follows his statement with, "Faithful is He who calls you, and He also will bring it to pass" (1 Thessalonians 5:24). If God calls us to holiness—and He does, Beloved—then He will bring it to pass. Ours is but to pray without ceasing (1 Thessalonians 5:17), continually asking, seeking, and knocking.

Have you ever read the book, *Of Whom The World Was Not Worthy*, by Marie Chapian? I cannot recommend it highly enough. It is a biography that will stir your soul and cast you on your knees, for it is a continual testimony of a life that is spent asking, seeking, and knocking. It is the story of Jakob and Jozeca, simple Yugoslavian peasants—indwelt by the Spirit of God. Jakob and Jozeca had prayed and prayed until God gave them a son. Josip, that son, was to be a man of God. Jozeca was convinced of this. Therefore, when her son, at the age of eleven, was run over by a lorry and pronounced dead, Jozeca threw her body on top of Josip's and began breathing into his mouth, crying, "He is not dead! God did not bring us this far to take his life away! I will not accept it! Never!"

For one hour she breathed into a pulseless body until finally the color came back to his skin. However, Josip was not normal. Although they could find no organic brain damage, for the next five years he suffered approximately 150 breakdowns. He was hospitalized thirty-three times in three different hospitals. Each time Jozeca refused to believe the situation was helpless.

"God gave us this son to train for His glory. Then He raised him up when he had been proclaimed dead. I cannot believe He brought him into this world to be sick in the mind!"

Night after night she remained on her knees by his bed praying until his breathing was regular. The seizures came most often during the night.

In a desperate attempt to do all she could for her son, she slept with him in bed at night and lined her feet up with his so the soles of their feet were touching. That way, she could feel if his nerves twitched and she would leap up and shout, "Josip! Wake up! Come, son, wake up! Praise the Lord, Josip! Wake up! Come, son, wake up! Praise the Lord, Josip! Wake up!" And the attack would be aborted.

When he was hospitalized, she was not allowed to visit him every day so she stood beneath his window and whistled, "God is Love." He could hear her and he knew she was there, near him, and praying for him. And Jakob, who worked in the mine from sunup to sundown often remained on his knees all night in prayer. He would say to his wife:

> "Jozeca, the Bible says, 'Ask and ye shall receive,' and we must believe that."
> "But, Jakob, I have asked and asked and asked."
> "Then ask again."
> "I shall never stop asking, Jakob. Never. I believe God gave us this son to bring glory to His name. I believe He gave us this son to raise to be a minister of the Lord. I believe He will one day serve the Lord. I will never stop praying for this son of ours. Not until either he or I is no longer on this earth."[26]

Several years would pass before that prayer was answered, but answered it was. God sent a believer from Russia to release Josip's body from the grip of the enemy. They had asked, they had sought, they had knocked, and finally they received. The door had finally opened. It was not the last battle that Jakob and Jozeca would fight in prayer for Josip. He would be prayed through rebellion, through impending death, and into a Baptist seminary.

O Beloved, what is *yours* because you are *His?* Pursue it persistently. Ask, seek, knock. This is the Godward aspect of a life of righteousness.


## DAY 2


Yesterday we looked at the Godward aspect of a life of righteousness. Today we want to look at the manward aspect. A righteous walk with God will always manifest itself in its relationship with our fellow man. The two are inseparable.

In Matthew 5:17, Jesus assured us that He did not come to abolish the Law or the Prophets, but to fulfill them. Now He calls us to walk as He walked; as He fulfilled them, so are we to fulfill them. And how do we do this? The answer is in Matthew 7:12: However you want people to treat you, so treat them, for this is the Law and the Prophets.

Here is the Golden Rule that we have heard so much about. "Do unto others what you would have them do unto you." Many a man has sought to live by this rule and yet failed miserably Why? First of all, because he didn't understand that you just can't, of yourself, decide to live by the Golden Rule. At the root of all sin is self-centeredness. True, some men are more self-centered than others and there can be a great and admirable nobility even among sinners. Many wonderful things have been accomplished by people who do not even profess to know Jesus Christ. Numerous humanitarian efforts have been instigated by people whose hearts were filled with compassion even though they were not filled with the presence of the Holy Spirit. Still, for all their good deeds, they did not fulfill the Law and the Prophets. When you look at the Law, you see that the commandments are first Godward and then manward. The commandments begin with loving God and having no other idols before Him, not taking His name in vain, and keeping the Sabbath day holy. From there the commandments turn manward to honoring father and mother, not murdering, not committing adultery, not stealing, not bearing false witness, nor coveting your neighbor's possessions.

It is interesting that the Beatitudes follow the same pattern. First they are Godward in poverty of spirit, mourning, meekness, and hungering and thirsting after righteousness. Then they turn manward in mercy, purity of heart, and peacemaking. What truth is hidden in this order, in this priority toward God? I believe it's the truth of *being* rather than just *doing*. Doing always finds limits when it's done out of its own strength, or according to its own moral code. Doing is limited by what we are. As natural man, we can never fulfill the Law and the Prophets. We will never quite do for others all that we want done for ourselves. But if I can change what I am, if I can be different from ordinary man, if I can be inhabited by God, then I can do for others as I would have them do for me.

Another misinterpretation of this Golden Rule is the motive of doing for others. It has an insidious, self-centered twist to it. The twist is that I *do* in order to *get*. In other words, I'm going to give to you in order to get. I'm going to be kind to you in order to get you to be kind to me, rather than being kind to you simply because I know that you as a human being need kindness. What we should realize is that if I, as a human being, need something, then you, as a human being, have the same basic need. If I need mercy, you need mercy. If I need love, you need love. Therefore, I'm not going to love you in order to get love, I'm going to love you because I know that you need love—because I need it, too. Do you see what I'm saying?

Remember what we saw when we looked at Romans 13? Love is the fulfillment of the Law (verse 10). Therefore, the motivation of doing for others as you want them to do for you is a motivation not of self-centeredness, not of giving in order to get, but of giving out of love. God first loved us and in love He met our needs. Because God is in us, then we will first love men and love will meet their needs.

As I write this, I am distressed with myself and I must admit that I am in somewhat of a quandary. Last night a group of us got together for a covered dish supper here at our house and afterward headed for the Tivoli Theater to see "Bringing Up Baby."

Every now and then, the Tivoli brings good old, wholesome movies to town. The cost is inexpensive; the popcorn used to be a nickel a bag, but is now twenty-five cents! There's a concert on the Wurlitzer organ before the movie starts. We just all go and have a good time. It brings a welcomed relief to our very tight schedules. After the movie, we were laughing at the 1938 antics of Cary Grant and Katherine Hepburn and just having a time of sweet fellowship with other Christians who had also needed a wholesome night out. Jack, my husband, and Clyde Hawkins, the manager of the Tivoli, had a long talk and so we were the last ones to leave the theater.

As we were walking out one door, a man entered the other. His head hung down, as did the paper sack in his right hand. His walk was slow, steady, deliberate, and yet he seemed devoid of life and purpose. He walked past us as if we did not exist. I took my eyes off of him, but I didn't want to. I could not believe his face. It had been beaten and was full of red, raw gashes. It looked as if someone had smashed it up against a concrete wall, leaving him with two horizontal cuts that ran from ear to nose. He walked past us without saying a word and sat down on a bench. Clyde went back and said something to him, which we couldn't hear. The man got up and walked out of the theater just as he had come in.

We walked outside and watched him walk away. Even as I write this, I can see him walking down the street. We stood there and talked about how horrible he looked, how sad he was. We were curious. We hurt. As we walked to the car, I said, "Oh the awful wages of sin." But I never did for that man what I would have wanted done for me. Today, as I thought about him, all I could think of was the statement, "no man cared for my soul." What should I have done? I really don't know. I only know this: I should have done something; in some way I should have reached out to that man. Do you know why I didn't? Because I didn't ask my Father what I should do. To be honest about it, I was so taken aback, so shocked, I never even thought about it. And I am ashamed.

I think I was thrown into a state of inertia because right now my days of service to the Lord seem filled to capacity and overflowing. So when I find myself in a situation like that, I feel stymied by the thought of doing any more. This is when I must go back to what I taught you yesterday—that life of persistent dependence upon God, continually asking, continually seeking, continually knocking. This is when I must remember that if I am to walk as Jesus walked, fulfilling the Law and the Prophets, I must continually keep the highest good of man before me, doing unto others as I would have them do unto me.

What about you? What do you think about what I've shared today? Talk to our Father, Beloved.

## DAY 3

As we come to Matthew 7:13, 14, it seems to me that we have gone full circle. Jesus says, "Enter by the narrow gate; for the gate is wide, and the way is broad that leads to destruction, and many are those who enter by it. For the gate is small, and the way is narrow that leads to life, and few are those who find it."

How small is that gate? It's so small that it causes you to bow in total poverty of spirit.

How narrow is the way that leads to life? It is the narrow way of righteousness, a righteousness that exceeds that of the scribes and the Pharisees. And is it any wonder that those who find it are few?

Before we proceed any further, take a few minutes to read Luke 13:22–30.

1. When is it too late to enter in?

2. What will happen to those who fail to enter in?

Here again, Jesus warns the people to strive to enter by the narrow door, "For many, I tell you, will seek to enter and will not be able." Why? Because they will try to enter under their own terms. They will think that having eaten and drunk in His presence—having listened to Him teach in their streets—will be enough to get them to heaven. There are men who will knock on the door saying, "Lord, open to us"—calling Him "Lord" when He has not been their Lord! And how do we know that He was never their Lord? Because Jesus called them evildoers (Luke 13:27). O, what weeping and gnashing of teeth there will be in that day when they are not permitted to enter into the kingdom of God because they did not come in by the narrow, small gate.

How narrow is the way? It's as narrow as the following Scriptures say it is. As you look up each verse, note exactly what it says about the way to the Father or the way to receive His gift of eternal life.

1. John 3:36

2. John 10:9

3. John 14:6

4. Acts 4:12

5. 1 Timothy 2:5

6. 1 John 5:12

## DAY 4

I don't know about you, Beloved, but I know that the study on the Sermon on the Mount has deepened my concern for the multitudes that sit in church, who call themselves Christians, who say, "Lord, Lord," and yet do not do the will of the Father. Are they not deluded? Have they not been lulled into a sense of false security? Is it any wonder that Jesus next says, "Beware of the false prophets, who come to you in sheep's clothing, but inwardly are ravenous wolves"?

Surely those who call him "Lord, Lord" and yet are walking the broad way have been led astray by false prophets—men who have proclaimed themselves sheep, but are ravenous wolves. They are the blind leading the blind, and both will fall into the pit of eternal destruction. Here are men who claim to speak for God, who claim to have God's message and yet who proclaim lies. Is it any wonder that Jesus cries out "Beware"? The verb *beware* is a present, active, imperative verb. When Jesus used the present tense He was telling us that we must continually beware of false prophets. We can never let down our guard. We must constantly be vigilant lest we be led astray. The mood of the verb is imperative, which signifies that it is a command and because it is in the active voice, the subject (which is implied) is responsible to carry out the action of the verb. You and I are the subject. Our responsibility is to see that we are not led astray.

"But how," you may cry, "can I know a false prophet from a true prophet? What will keep me from being led astray?" Jesus does not leave you in doubt. He tells you how you can spot a false prophet. Read Matthew 7:15–23.

1. Turn to the Sermon in the back of this book. In verse 17, you will notice that the verb *bears* appears twice. Next to each one of these verbs, write PT for present tense. Do the same for the word *produce* in verse 18 where it is used two times; in verse 19 mark the word *bear* PT. (Remember that the present tense indicates continuous or habitual action.)

2. According to this passage, how can you identify a false prophet?

3. What significance does the present tense have in verses 17–19?

4. Do you think that a false prophet would call Jesus "Lord"?

5. According to verse 22, who is going to enter the kingdom of heaven?

6. When it says that you will know them by their fruits, what fruits? Do you think that fruits and doing the will of the Father have any connection at all? Why or why not?

A false prophet will be recognizable because the fruit of his life will not be in accordance with the will of the Father. He may be a hearer of God's Word and may know God's Word, but his life-style will not conform in obedience to the will of God. Therefore, his preaching will *not* call men to that narrow, small gate, and because of this the false prophet will usually gather around himself many followers.

Take a few minutes and look at the life-style of false prophets. Then we will look at their message and the way they care for their sheep. Read the following Scriptures and from them list what you learn about the life-style of false prophets.

1. 2 Timothy 3:5–8

2. 2 Peter 2:1–3, 10–19

It is obvious from these passages that false prophets are controlled by the appetites of their flesh and, therefore, their focus is on earthly things. You will notice that their preaching appeals to man's senses and fleshly desires (2 Peter 2:18). There is almost a flippancy in their walk when it comes to spiritual things. A real arrogancy for "they do not tremble when they revile angelic majesties, whereas angels who are greater in might and power do not bring a reviling judgment against them before the Lord" (2 Peter 2:10, 11).

Their words are arrogant. They hold to a form of godliness, but they deny its power (2 Timothy 3:5). When the chips are down, they are lovers of pleasure rather than lovers of God (2 Timothy 3:4). And what do they speak?

Look up the following Scriptures and then we will discuss it. As you look up each one, take note of what you learn about the message of the false prophets.

1. Jeremiah 6:14,15

2. Jeremiah 8:8–12

3. Jeremiah 23:21–40


4. Ezekiel 22:28


5. Acts 20:29, 30


6. 2 Timothy 4:3, 4


If you have read carefully, Beloved, you have seen that false prophets are those who do not like to disturb people. They come with very smooth words, saying, "Peace, peace, all is well." They heal the brokenness of people superficially. Their preaching usually does not deal with the issues of sin or with the righteousness that conforms to the life-style of Jesus Christ. The Cross and denial of self are seldom heard from their pulpits because their desire is to tickle the ears of those who listen. Oh, their preaching may contain elements of truth, but not the whole counsel of God. The Word of God does not have a prominent place in their preaching unless, of course, it is used out of context. They will lean more toward dreams and vision and prophecies rather than a clear exposition of God's Word. You will find that their preaching does not cause men to see their poverty of spirit, or to mourn over their sins. It does not call them to meekness in the face of disappointment, trials, or suffering. The persecution of the believer will not be exalted as a sign of blessing because, as Paul told us, "they are enemies of the cross of Christ" (Philippians 3:18). How can they call men to a cross that they themselves will not bear or to a life of denial when their god is their appetite?

1. Do they care for the sheep? Read Ezekiel 34:1–6, 14–16, 21–24; then
   list how the false prophets treat their sheep.

2. Now compare what you saw in Ezekiel 34 with 1 Peter 5:1–4. Write down your insights.

Can you understand Jesus' warning for us to constantly beware of false prophets who come to us in sheep's clothing but inwardly are ravenous wolves? Wolves eat sheep.

## DAY 5

Can you believe it? We're almost done! Let me ask you a question that I want you to answer in writing. I want you to write it out because I believe that if you verbalize your answer, God will use it to speak to your heart. Please do not read any further until you answer the question. *How do you know that you are truly a child of God and therefore a possessor of the kingdom of heaven?*

I will never forget the time when I told someone who was very dear to me that I knew that I was going to heaven when I die. He looked at me and said, "I'm not as conceited as you are. I will wait and see what God decides when He weighs the good against the bad." Was I conceited? Can a person know for certain that his is the kingdom of heaven? (Notice I said "is" not "will be.")

I believe the Word of God clearly teaches that you can know that the kingdom of heaven is yours, that you have eternal life, and therefore will never perish. The question is, "How can you know?" I just asked you that question. What did you answer? Did you point back to some past experience? Did you say that, "I know I am going to heaven because:

- I'm a good person and I've lived by the Golden Rule.
- I've been baptized.
- I am a member of the church.
- I walked the aisle and gave my life to Jesus.
- I've been a Christian ever since I was born.
- God is a God of love and He wouldn't send anyone to hell.
- I've invited Jesus Christ into my life, I've believed on Him; therefore, I'm saved.
- I've prayed a prayer and asked Christ to come and live inside of me, and I believe He did.

Now, let's suppose you answered in one of the above ways. Basically, all those answers have something to do with the past—either something that you believed or something that you did. So, let me ask another question. What present evidence is there in your life that shows you and others that you really are a child of God? Take time, Beloved, to answer this question in writing.

Paul closes his second epistle to the Corinthians with this admonition: "Test yourselves to see if you are in the faith; examine yourselves! Or do you not recognize this about yourselves, that Jesus Christ is in you—unless indeed you fail the test?" (13:5). If we could point to a past experience as the evidence of our salvation, then why would it be necessary to test ourselves to see if we really are in the faith? The verb *test* is in the present tense and therefore it talks about a continuous examination of the reality of whether or not Christ is in us. Isn't that something!

According to what I know about the Scriptures, I cannot believe that any true believer can lose his salvation even for a moment. You may disagree with me on this point, but the point I'm trying to make is this: I do believe in the eternal security of the believer, but I believe the only way the believer really knows that he belongs to Jesus Christ and possesses the kingdom of heaven is by his present life of obedience.

I want you to know that on this point, theologically, I'm in excellent company. I consider John MacArthur to be one of the finest Bible teachers in the United States today. He doesn't know me, but I know him. And I admire and appreciate his scholarship. After I wrote our inductive Bible study course on the Sermon on the Mount I discovered MacArthur's book, *Kingdom Living, Here and Now*. It's an outstanding commentary on the Beatitudes. As I told you before, when I found out that he believes the key verse of the Sermon is Matthew 5:20, all I could do was say, "Amen, Brother. I'm with you!" That was the verse I had chosen as my key verse.

As I read on and saw some of the things that MacArthur said about the certainty of our salvation, once again all I could do was say, "Amen." Not because I learned it from him, but because I learned it from God's Word and it was a delight to see that a man of God had the same insight. MacArthur is not the only one that holds this view. A lot of other great and godly men do also.

This quote from *Kingdom Living* is from a passage that is talking about taking communion.

> What is even more serious is to come to the Lord's Table and drink unworthily when you are not a Christian at all. Now do not quickly put this book down, telling me, yourself, and God that this does not apply to you because you have been a Christian for years. The Beatitudes call for a full self-examination. Such an approach Paul calls for in 2 Corinthians 13:5, "Test yourselves to see if you are in the faith." Prove it, he's saying. If it were easy to point to an experience in the past to prove your salvation, why would Paul ask you to examine yourself? There must be something else here.
>
> You might be saying, "Well, I'm a Christian. I believe. I made a decision for Christ." A lot of people point to the past to verify their salvation, but did you know that the Bible never does that? It never points to the past. It always bases proof of real salvation on your life now.[27]

In another place MacArthur writes, "The believer is called to a life of obedience, in which faith is verified by conduct."[28] And still in another place, "The New Testament never talks about making a decision or walking an aisle. It never talks about signing a card. All it says is that you're a Christian if there's present evidence. That's always the issue."[29]

That is the issue in Matthew 7:21–27. According to those verses, those who are continually doing the will of the Father will enter the kingdom of heaven. The verb *does* is in the present tense. Do you see what Jesus is saying? Just because we call Him "Lord" does not mean that we are going to go to heaven. Just because we say that we are Christians does not mean that we are. Just because we have joined the church and sit in church every Sunday does not mean that we are possessors of the kingdom of heaven. You've heard me say it before and it always draws a laugh. It's not original with me, but "sitting in a garage does not make you a car." Yet, isn't this what many believe? Because they sit in church, go through the motions and the rituals—because they have been baptized or confirmed or take communion or try to live by the Golden Rule or because they were born into a Christian family they assume that they are children of God? And yet, Jesus says no. It's not those who say "Lord, Lord" but those who habitually, as a lifestyle, do the will of the Father.

Do you realize that the people in Matthew Chapter 7 had prophesied in the name of Jesus Christ? They had spoken for God. Not only that, but they had cast out demons and even done many miracles. Their lives bore an element of what you and I would call the supernatural. Yet Jesus turns and says to them, "I never knew you; depart from me, you who practice lawlessness" (Matthew 7:23). Did you notice that it's practicing lawlessness, as a way of life, rather than practicing a life of obedience? If Jesus is truly Lord, you will not practice lawlessness.

The essential character of the believer is obedience. The Sermon on the Mount irrevocably links obedience to faith. They cannot be separated. This is why Jesus says in Matthew 7:24, "Every one who hears these words of Mine, and acts upon them. . . ." It is not just hearing, but also acting. Those who hear and act are like the man who built his house on the rock. No matter what comes, it will not fall because it is founded on the rock. But those who hear Christ's words and do not act upon them are like the man who built his house upon the sand—great was its fall.

O Beloved, Beloved, when you examine yourself, is there evidence that Christ is in you? Is your life a life of righteousness; a righteousness that surpasses that of the scribes and Pharisees; a righteousness that is not just external but internal? Do you pursue holiness without which no man will see the Lord? Is there within you a hunger and thirst for righteousness and is it being satisfied? Do you recognize that Christ is in you because the Beatitudes are an expression to one degree or another of your character? Is your character bringing conflict with those who do not know Christ? And what about your conduct? Are you becoming more and more like your heavenly Father?

If you cannot answer these questions in the affirmative, then I invite you to come to that narrow, small gate that brings a man to poverty of spirit and into the kingdom of heaven. Come; you cannot afford not to!

Russians packed the theater in Moscow. It was the premier of a new play, "Christ In a Fur." Alexander Rostovtsev, a convinced Marxist who moved among the highest circles of Soviet life, was to play Jesus Christ.

On the stage was a mockery of an altar. The cross on it was made of bottles of wine and beer. Full glasses surrounded it. Fat "clergymen" said a drunken "liturgy" consisting of blasphemous formulas. In this sham church, "nuns" played cards, drank, and made ugly jokes while the "religious service" went on.

Then Rostovtsev appeared as Christ, dressed in a robe. He had the New Testament in his hands. He was supposed to read two verses from the Sermon on the Mount, then throw away the book in disgust and shout, "Give me my fur and my hat! I prefer a simple proletarian life." But something unexpected happened. The actor read not only two verses, but continued, "Blessed are the meek: for they shall inherit the earth," and so on to the end of the Sermon. In vain the prompter made desperate signs for him to stop.

When Rostovtsev came to the last word of Jesus, he made the sign of the Cross in the Orthodox manner, said, "Lord, remember me when thou comest into thy kingdom" (Luke 23:42 KJV), and left the stage. He was never seen again. The Communists disposed of him. (From *Reaching Toward the Heights,* by Richard Wurmbrand.)

I imagine that at every rehearsal, Alexander Rostovtsev had an opportunity to leaf through the pages of the New Testament. We do not know when God's Word found fertile soil in his heart—but we know that it did. He heard Christ's words and acted upon them. He took the narrow, small gate.

What about you, Beloved?

# Notes

1. Marvin R. Vincent, *Word Studies in the New Testament* (Grand Rapids: Eerdmans, 1976), p. 35.
2. D. A. Carson, *The Sermon on the Mount: An Evangelical Exposition of Matthew Five Through Seven* (Grand Rapids: Baker, 1978), pp. 118, 119.
3. Ibid., pp. 69, 118, 119.
4. W. E. Vine, *An Expository Dictionary of New Testament Words,* Vol. III (Old Tappan: Revell, 1966), p. 56.
5. Lindley Baldwin, *Samuel Morris, The March of Faith* (Minneapolis: Dimension Books), p. 8.
6. Ibid., pp. 10–13.
7. Ibid., pp. 15–17.
8. Vine, ibid.
9. Mrs. Howard Taylor, *Pastor Hsi* (London: OMF Books, 1949), p. 25.
10. Ibid., p. 26.
11. Ibid., pp. 46, 47, 50–52.
12. D. Martyn Lloyd-Jones, *Studies in the Sermon on the Mount* (Grand Rapids: Eerdmans, 1959), pp. 73, 74.
13. Vine, ibid., p. 62.
14. Ibid., p. 60.
15. Ibid., p. 207.
16. Don Richardson, *Peace Child* (Ventura: Gospel Light, 1976), pp. 199–201.
17. Haralan Popov, *Tortured for His Faith* (Grand Rapids: Zondervan, 1970), p. 126.
18. If you would like to pray for and write to those in prison for the gospel's sake, write the Reverend Georgi P. Vins, P. O. Box 1188, Elkhart, Indiana 46515-1188; ask for Prisoner Bulletin.
19. J. Dwight Pentecost, *The Sermon on the Mount: Contemporary Insights for a Christian Lifestyle* (Portland: Multnomah, 1982), p. 112.
20. *The New Testament and Wycliffe Bible Commentary* (Chicago: Moody Press, 1971), p. 717.
21. Pentecost, ibid., p. 127.
22. R. A. Torrey, *The Power of Prayer* (Grand Rapids, Zondervan, 1955), pp. 75–77.
23. James Montgomery Boice, *The Sermon on the Mount* (Grand Rapids: Zondervan, 1972), p. 192.
24. Pentecost, ibid., p. 158.
25. Quoted from "Christmas Eve in Romania," in *A Bible for Russia,* Vol. I, No. 10, Dec. 1983, pp. 3, 4.
26. Marie Chapian, *Of Whom the World Was Not Worthy* (Minneapolis: Bethany, 1978), pp. 156–158.
27. John F. MacArthur, *Kingdom Living, Here and Now* (Chicago: Moody Press, 1980), p. 9.
28. Ibid., p. 8.
29. Ibid., p. 64.

# Appendix A

## The Sermon on the Mount
### (*King James Version*)

### CHAPTER 5

1 And seeing the multitudes, he went up into a mountain: and when he was set, his disciples came unto him:

2 And he opened his mouth, and taught them, saying,

3 Blessed are the poor in spirit: for their's is the kingdom of heaven.

4 Blessed are they that mourn: for they shall be comforted.

5 Blessed are the meek: for they shall inherit the earth.

6 Blessed are they which do hunger and thirst after righteousness: for they shall be filled.

7 Blessed are the merciful: for they shall obtain mercy.

8 Blessed are the pure in heart: for they shall see God.

9 Blessed are the peacemakers: for they shall be called the children of God.

10 Blessed are they which are persecuted for righteousness' sake: for their's is the kingdom of heaven.

11 Blessed are ye, when men shall revile you, and persecute you, and shall say all manner of evil against you falsely, for my sake.

12 Rejoice, and be exceeding glad: for great is your reward in heaven: for so persecuted they the prophets which were before you.

13 ¶ Ye are the salt of the earth: but if the salt have lost his savour, wherewith shall it be salted? it is thenceforth good for nothing, but to be cast out, and to be trodden under foot of men.

14 Ye are the light of the world. A city that is set on an hill cannot be hid.

15 Neither do men light a candle, and put it under a bushel, but on a candlestick; and it giveth light unto all that are in the house.

16 Let your light so shine before men, that they may see your good works, and glorify your Father which is in heaven.

17 ¶ Think not that I am come to destroy the law, or the prophets: I am not come to destroy, but to fulfil.

18 For verily I say unto you, Till heaven and earth pass, one jot or one tittle shall in no wise pass from the law, till all be fulfilled.

19 Whosoever therefore shall

## The Sermon on the Mount
### (*New American Standard Version*)

### CHAPTER 5

1 And when He saw the multitudes, He went up on the mountain; and after He sat down, His disciples came to Him.

2 And opening His mouth He *began* to teach them, saying,

3 "Blessed are the poor in spirit, for theirs is the kingdom of heaven.

4 "Blessed are those who mourn, for they shall be comforted.

5 Blessed are the gentle, for they shall inherit the earth.

6 "Blessed are those who hunger and thirst for righteousness, for they shall be satisfied.

7 "Blessed are the merciful, for they shall receive mercy.

8 "Blessed are the pure in heart, for they shall see God.

9 "Blessed are the peacemakers, for they shall be called sons of God.

10 "Blessed are those who have been persecuted for the sake of righteousness, for theirs is the kingdom of heaven.

11 "Blessed are you when *men* cast insults at you, and persecute you, and say all kinds of evil against you falsely, on account of Me.

12 "Rejoice, and be glad, for your reward in heaven is great, for so they persecuted the prophets who were before you.

13 "You are the salt of the earth; but if the salt has become tasteless, how will it be made salty *again?* It is good for nothing anymore, except to be thrown out and trampled under foot by men.

14 "You are the light of the world. A city set on a hill cannot be hidden.

15 "Nor do *men* light a lamp, and put it under the peck-measure, but on the lampstand; and it gives light to all who are in the house.

break one of these least commandments, and shall teach men so, he shall be called the least in the kingdom of heaven: but whosoever shall do and teach them, the same shall be called great in the kingdom of heaven.

20 For I say unto you, That except your righteousness shall exceed the righteousness of the scribes and Pharisees, ye shall in no case enter into the kingdom of heaven.

21 ¶ Ye have heard that it was said by them of old time, Thou shalt not kill; and whosoever shall kill shall be in danger of the judgment:

22 But I say unto you, That whosoever is angry with his brother without a cause shall be in danger of the judgment: and whosoever shall say to his brother, Raca, shall be in danger of the council: but whosoever shall say, Thou fool, shall be in danger of hell fire.

23 Therefore if thou bring thy gift to the altar, and there rememberest that thy brother hath ought against thee;

24 Leave there thy gift before the altar, and go thy way; first be reconciled to thy brother, and then come and offer thy gift.

25 Agree with thine adversary quickly, whiles thou art in the way with him; lest at any time the adversary deliver thee to the judge, and the judge deliver thee to the officer, and thou be cast into prison.

26 Verily I say unto thee, Thou shalt by no means come out thence, till thou has paid the uttermost farthing.

27 ¶ Ye have heard that it was said by them of old time, Thou shalt not commit adultery:

28 But I say unto you, That whosoever looketh on a woman to lust after her hath committed adultery with her already in his heart.

29 And if thy right eye offend thee, pluck it out, and cast it from thee: for it is profitable for thee that one of thy members should perish, and not that thy whole body should be cast into hell.

30 And if thy right hand offend thee, cut it off, and cast it from thee: for it is profitable for thee that one of thy members should perish, and not that thy whole body should be cast into hell.

31 It hath been said, Whosoever shall put away his wife, let him give her a writing of divorcement:

32 But I say unto you, That whosoever shall put away his wife, saving for the cause of fornication, causeth her to commit adultery: and whosoever shall marry her that is divorced committeth adultery.

33 ¶ Again, ye have heard that

16 "Let your light shine before men in such a way that they may see your good works, and glorify your Father who is in heaven.

---

17 "Do not think that I came to abolish the Law or the Prophets; I did not come to abolish, but to fulfill.

18 "For truly I say to you, until heaven and earth pass away, not the smallest letter or stroke shall pass away from the Law, until all is accomplished.

19 "Whoever then annuls one of the least of these commandments, and so teaches others, shall be called least in the kingdom of heaven; but whoever keeps and teaches *them,* he shall be called great in the kingdom of heaven.

20 "For I say to you, that unless your righteousness surpasses *that* of the scribes and Pharisees, you shall not enter the kingdom of heaven.

---

21 "You have heard that the ancients were told, 'YOU SHALL NOT COMMIT MURDER' and 'Whoever commits murder shall be liable to the court.'

22 "But I say to you that everyone who is angry with his brother shall be guilty before the court; and whoever shall say to his brother, 'Raca,' shall be guilty before the supreme court; and whoever shall say, 'You fool,' shall be guilty *enough to go* into the hell of fire.

23 "If therefore you are presenting your offering at the altar, and there remember that your brother has something against you,

24 leave your offering there before the altar, and go your way; first be reconciled to your brother, and then come and present your offering.

25 "Make friends quickly with your opponent at law while you are with him on the way, in order that your opponent may not deliver you to the judge, and the judge to the officer, and you be thrown into prison.

26 "Truly I say to you, you shall not come out of there, until you have paid up the last cent.

---

27 "You have heard that it was said, 'YOU SHALL NOT COMMIT ADULTERY';

28 but I say to you, that everyone who looks on a woman to lust for her has committed adultery with her already in his heart.

29 "And if your right eye makes you stumble, tear it out, and throw it from you; for it is better for you that one of the parts of your body perish, than for your whole body to be thrown into hell.

it hath been said by them of old time, Thou shalt not forswear thyself, but shalt perform unto the Lord thine oaths:

34 But I say unto you, Swear not at all; neither by heaven; for it is God's throne:

35 Nor by the earth; for it is his footstool: neither by Jerusalem; for it is the city of the great King.

36 Neither shalt thou swear by thy head, because thou canst not make one hair white or black.

37 But let your communication be, Yea, yea; Nay, nay: for whatsoever is more than these cometh of evil.

38 ¶ Ye have heard that it hath been said, An eye for an eye, and a tooth for a tooth:

39 But I say unto you, That ye resist not evil: but whosoever shall smite thee on thy right cheek, turn to him the other also.

40 And if any man will sue thee at the law, and take away thy coat, let him have thy cloke also.

41 And whosoever shall compel thee to go a mile, go with him twain.

42 Give to him that asketh thee, and from him that would borrow of thee turn not thou away.

43 ¶ Ye have heard that it hath been said, Thou shalt love thy neighbour, and hate thine enemy.

44 But I say unto you, Love your enemies, bless them that curse you, do good to them that hate you, and pray for them which despitefully use you, and persecute you;

45 That ye may be the children of your Father which is in heaven: for he maketh his sun to rise on the evil and on the good, and sendeth rain on the just and on the unjust.

46 For if ye love them which love you, what reward have ye? do not even the publicans the same?

47 And if ye salute your brethren only, what do ye more than others? do not even the publicans so?

48 Be ye therefore perfect, even as your Father which is in heaven is perfect.

## CHAPTER 6

1 Take heed that ye do not your alms before men, to be seen of them: otherwise ye have no reward of your Father which is in heaven.

2 Therefore when thou doest thine alms, do not sound a trumpet before thee, as the hypocrites do in the synagogues and in the streets, that they may have glory of men. Verily I say unto you, They have their reward.

3 But when thou doest alms, let not thy left hand know what thy right hand doeth:

30 "And if your right hand makes you stumble, cut it off, and throw it from you; for it is better for you that one of the parts of your body perish, than for your whole body to go into hell.

31 "And it was said, 'WHOEVER DIVORCES HIS WIFE, LET HIM GIVE HER A CERTIFICATE OF DISMISSAL';

32 but I say to you that everyone who divorces his wife, except for *the* cause of unchastity, makes her commit adultery; and whoever marries a divorced woman commits adultery.

33 "Again, you have heard that the ancients were told, 'YOU SHALL NOT MAKE FALSE VOWS, BUT SHALL FULFILL YOUR VOWS TO THE LORD.'

34 "But I say to you, make no oath at all, either by heaven, for it is the throne of God,

35 or by the earth, for it is the footstool of His feet, or by Jerusalem, for it is THE CITY OF THE GREAT KING.

36 "Nor shall you make an oath by your head, for you cannot make one hair white or black.

37 "But let your statement be, 'Yes, yes' *or* 'No, no'; and anything beyond these is of evil.

---

38 "You have heard that it was said, 'AN EYE FOR AN EYE, AND A TOOTH FOR A TOOTH.'

39 "But I say to you, do not resist him who is evil; but whoever slaps you on your right cheek, turn to him the other also.

40 "And if anyone wants to sue you, and take your shirt, let him have your coat also.

41 "And whoever shall force you to go one mile, go with him two.

42 "Give to him who asks of you, and do not turn away from him who wants to borrow from you.

---

43 "You have heard that it was said, 'YOU SHALL LOVE YOUR NEIGHBOR, and hate your enemy.'

44 "But I say to you, love your enemies, and pray for those who persecute you

45 in order that you may be sons of your Father who is in heaven; for He causes His sun to rise on *the* evil and *the* good, and sends rain on *the* righteous and *the* unrighteous.

46 "For if you love those who love you, what reward have you? Do not even the taxgatherers do the same?

47 "And if you greet your brothers only, what do you do more *than*

4 That thine alms may be in secret: and thy Father which seeth in secret himself shall reward thee openly.

5 ¶ And when thou prayest, thou shalt not be as the hypocrites are: for they love to pray standing in the synagogues and in the corners of the streets, that they may be seen of men. Verily I say unto you, They have their reward.

6 But thou, when thou prayest, enter into thy closet, and when thou hast shut thy door, pray to thy Father which is in secret; and thy Father which seeth in secret shall reward thee openly.

7 But when ye pray, use not vain repetitions, as the heathen do: for they think that they shall be heard for their much speaking.

8 Be not ye therefore like unto them: for your Father knoweth what things ye have need of, before ye ask him.

9 After this manner therefore pray ye: Our Father which art in heaven, Hallowed be thy name.

10 Thy kingdom come. Thy will be done in earth, as it is in heaven.

11 Give us this day our daily bread.

12 And forgive us our debts, as we forgive our debtors.

13 And lead us not into temptation, but deliver us from evil: For thine is the kingdom, and the power, and the glory, for ever. Amen.

14 For if ye forgive men their trespasses, your heavenly Father will also forgive you:

15 But if ye forgive not men their trespasses, neither will your Father forgive your trespasses.

16 ¶ Moreover when ye fast, be not, as the hypocrites, of a sad countenance: for they disfigure their faces, that they may appear unto men to fast. Verily I say unto you, They have their reward.

17 But thou, when thou fastest, anoint thine head, and wash thy face;

18 That thou appear not unto men to fast, but unto thy Father which is in secret: and thy Father, which seeth in secret, shall reward thee openly.

19 ¶ Lay not up for yourselves treasures upon earth, where moth and rust doth corrupt, and where thieves break through and steal:

20 But lay up for yourselves treasures in heaven, where neither moth nor rust doth corrupt, and where thieves do not break through nor steal:

21 For where your treasure is, there will your heart be also.

22 The light of the body is the eye: if therefore thine eye be single, thy whole body shall be full of light.

23 But if thine eye be evil, thy

*others?* Do not even the Gentiles do the same?

48 "Therefore you are to be perfect, as your heavenly Father is perfect.

## CHAPTER 6

1 "Beware of practicing your righteousness before men to be noticed by them; otherwise you have no reward with your Father who is in heaven.

---

2 "When therefore you give alms, do not sound a trumpet before you, as the hypocrites do in the synagogues and in the streets, that they may be honored by men. Truly I say to you, they have their reward in full.

3 "But when you give alms, do not let your left hand know what your right hand is doing

4 that your alms may be in secret; and your Father who sees in secret will repay you.

---

5 "And when you pray, you are not to be as the hypocrites; for they love to stand and pray in the synagogues and on the street corners, in order to be seen by men. Truly I say to you, they have their reward in full.

6 "But you, when you pray, go into your inner room, and when you have shut your door, pray to your Father who is in secret, and your Father who sees in secret will repay you.

7 "And when you are praying, do not use meaningless repetition, as the Gentiles do, for they suppose that they will be heard for their many words.

8 "Therefore do not be like them; for your Father knows what you need, before you ask Him.

9. "Pray, then, in this way;
   'Our Father who art in heaven,
   Hallowed be Thy name.

10 'Thy kingdom come.
   Thy will be done,
   On earth as it is in heaven.

11 'Give us this day our daily bread.

12 'And forgive us our debts, as we also have forgiven our debtors.

13 'And do not lead us into temptation, but deliver us from evil. (For

whole body shall be full of darkness. If therefore the light that is in thee be darkness, how great is that darkness!

24 ¶ No man can serve two masters: for either he will hate the one, and love the other; or else he will hold to the one, and despise the other. Ye cannot serve God and mammon.

25 Therefore I say unto you, Take no thought for your life, what ye shall eat, or what ye shall drink; nor yet for your body, what ye shall put on. Is not the life more than meat, and the body than raiment?

26 Behold the fowls of the air: for they sow not, neither do they reap, nor gather into barns; yet your heavenly Father feedeth them. Are ye not much better than they?

27 Which of you by taking thought can add one cubit unto his stature?

28 And why take ye thought for raiment? Consider the lilies of the field, how they grow; they toil not, neither do they spin:

29 And yet I say unto you, That even Solomon in all his glory was not arrayed like one of these.

30 Wherefore, if God so clothe the grass of the field, which to day is, and to morrow is cast into the oven, shall he not much more clothe you, O ye of little faith?

31 Therefore take no thought, saying, What shall we eat? or, What shall we drink? or, Wherewithal shall we be clothed?

32 (For after all these things do the Gentiles seek:) for your heavenly Father knoweth that ye have need of all these things.

33 But seek ye first the kingdom of God, and his righteousness; and all these things shall be added unto you.

34 Take therefore no thought for the morrow: for the morrow shall take thought for the things of itself. Sufficient unto the day is the evil thereof.

## CHAPTER 7

1 Judge not, that ye be not judged.

2 For with what judgment ye judge, ye shall be judged: and with what measure ye mete, it shall be measured to you again.

3 And why beholdest thou the mote that is in thy brother's eye, but considerest not the beam that is in thine own eye?

4 Or how wilt thou say to thy brother, Let me pull out the mote out of thine eye; and, behold, a beam is in thine own eye?

5 Thou hypocrite, first cast out the beam out of thine own eye; and then shalt thou see clearly to cast out the mote out of thy brother's eye.

6 ¶ Give not that which is holy

Thine is the kingdom, and the power, and the glory, forever. Amen.)'

14 "For if you forgive men for their transgressions, your heavenly Father will also forgive you.

15 "But if you do not forgive men, then your Father will not forgive your transgressions.

---

16 "And whenever you fast, do not put on a gloomy face as the hypocrites *do,* for they neglect their appearance in order to be seen fasting by men. Truly I say to you, they have their reward in full.

17 "But you, when you fast, anoint your head, and wash your face

18 so that you may not be seen fasting by men, but by your Father who is in secret; and your Father who sees in secret will repay you.

---

19 "Do not lay up for yourselves treasures upon earth, where moth and rust destroy, and where thieves break in and steal.

20 "But lay up for yourselves treasures in heaven, where neither moth nor rust destroys, and where thieves do not break in or steal;

21 for where your treasure is, there will your heart be also.

22 "The lamp of the body is the eye; if therefore your eye is clear, your whole body will be full of light.

23 "But if your eye is bad, your whole body will be full of darkness. If therefore the light that is in you is darkness, how great is the darkness!

24 "No one can serve two masters; for either he will hate the one and love the other, or he will hold to one and despise the other. You cannot serve God and mammon.

---

25 "For this reason I say to you, do not be anxious for your life, *as to* what you shall eat, or what you shall drink; nor for your body, *as to* what you shall put on. Is not life more than food, and the body than clothing?

26 "Look at the birds of the air, that they do not sow, neither do they reap, nor gather into barns, and *yet* your heavenly Father feeds them. Are you not worth much more than they?

27 "And which of you by being anxious can add a *single* cubit to his life's span?

28 "And why are you anxious about clothing? Observe how the lilies of the field grow; they do not toil nor do they spin,

29 yet I say to you that even Solomon in all his glory did not clothe himself like one of these.

unto the dogs, neither cast ye your pearls before swine, lest they trample them under their feet, and turn again and rend you.

7 ¶ Ask, and it shall be given you; seek, and ye shall find; knock, and it shall be opened unto you:

8 For every one that asketh receiveth; and he that seeketh findeth; and to him that knocketh it shall be opened.

9 Or what man is there of you, whom if his son ask bread, will he give him a stone?

10 Or if he ask a fish, will he give him a serpent?

11 If ye then, being evil, know how to give good gifts unto your children, how much more shall your Father which is in heaven give good things to them that ask him?

12 Therefore all things whatsoever ye would that men should do to you, do ye even so to them: for this is the law and the prophets.

13 ¶ Enter ye in at the strait gate: for wide is the gate, and broad is the way, that leadeth to destruction, and many there be which go in thereat:

14 Because strait is the gate, and narrow is the way, which leadeth unto life, and few there be that find it.

15 ¶ *Beware of false prophets, which come to you in sheep's* clothing, but inwardly they are ravening wolves.

16 Ye shall know them by their fruits. Do men gather grapes of thorns, or figs of thistles?

17 Even so every good tree bringeth forth good fruit; but a corrupt tree bringeth forth evil fruit.

18 A good tree cannot bring forth evil fruit, neither can a corrupt tree bring forth good fruit.

19 Every tree that bringeth not forth good fruit is hewn down, and cast into the fire.

20 Wherefore by their fruits ye shall know them.

21 ¶ Not every one that saith unto me, Lord, Lord, shall enter into the kingdom of heaven; but he that doeth the will of my Father which is in heaven.

22 Many will say to me in that day, Lord, Lord, have we not prophesied in thy name? and in thy name have cast out devils? and in thy name done many wonderful works?

23 And then will I profess unto them, I never knew you: depart from me, ye that work iniquity.

24 ¶ Therefore whosoever heareth these sayings of mine, and doeth them, I will liken him unto a wise man, which built his house upon a rock:

25 And the rain descended, and the floods came, and the winds

30 "But if God so arrays the grass of the field, which is *alive* today and tomorrow is thrown into the furnace, *will He* not much more *do so for* you, O men of little faith?

31 "Do not be anxious then, saying, 'What shall we eat?' or 'What shall we drink?' or 'With what shall we clothe ourselves?'

32 "For all these things the Gentiles eagerly seek; for your heavenly Father knows that you need all these things.

33 "But seek first His kingdom and His righteousness; and all these things shall be added to you.

34 "Therefore do not be anxious for tomorrow; for tomorrow will care for itself. *Each* day has enough trouble of its own.

## CHAPTER 7

1 "Do not judge lest you be judged.

2 "For in the way you judge, you will be judged; and by your standard of measure, it will be measured to you.

3 "And why do you look at the speck that is in your brother's eye, but do not notice the log that is in your own eye?

4 "Or how can you say to your brother, 'Let me take the speck out of your eye,' and behold, the log is in your own eye?

5 "You hypocrite, first take the log out of your own eye, and then you will see clearly to take the speck out of your brother's eye.

---

6 "Do not give what is holy to dogs, and do not throw your pearls before swine, lest they trample them under their feet, and turn and tear you to pieces.

---

7 "Ask, and it shall be given to you; seek, and you shall find; knock, and it shall be opened to you.

8 "For everyone who asks receives, and he who seeks finds, and to him who knocks it shall be opened.

9 "Or what man is there among you, when his son shall ask him for a loaf, will give him a stone?

10 "Or if he shall ask for a fish, he will not give him a snake, will he?

11 "If you then, being evil, know how to give good gifts to your children, how much more shall your Father who is in heaven give what is good to those who ask Him!

12 "Therefore, however you want people to treat you, so treat them, for this is the Law and the Prophets.

---

blew, and beat upon that house; and it fell not: for it was founded upon a rock.

26 And every one that heareth these sayings of mine, and doeth them not, shall be likened unto a foolish man, which built his house upon the sand:

27 And the rain descended, and the floods came, and the winds blew, and beat upon that house; and it fell: and great was the fall of it.

28 And it came to pass, when Jesus had ended these sayings, the people were astonished at his doctrine:

29 For he taught them as one having authority, and not as the scribes.

13 "Enter by the narrow gate; for the gate is wide, and the way is broad that leads to destruction, and many are those who enter by it.
14 "For the gate is small, and the way is narrow that leads to life, and few are those who find it.
15 "Beware of the false prophets, who come to you in sheep's clothing, but inwardly are ravenous wolves.

16 "You will know them by their fruits. Grapes are not gathered from thorn bushes, nor figs from thistles, are they?
17 "Even so, every good tree bears good fruit; but the bad tree bears bad fruit.
18 "A good tree cannot produce bad fruit, nor can a bad tree produce good fruit.
19 "Every tree that does not bear good fruit is cut down and thrown into the fire.
20 "So then, you will know them by their fruits.
21 "Not everyone who says to Me, 'Lord, Lord,' will enter the kingdom of heaven; but he who does the will of My Father who is in heaven.
22 "Many will say to Me on that day, 'Lord, Lord, did we not prophesy in Your name, and in Your name cast out demons, and in Your name perform many miracles?'
23 "And then I will declare to them, 'I never knew you; DEPART FROM ME, YOU WHO PRACTICE LAWLESSNESS.'

24 "Therefore everyone who hears these words of Mine, and acts upon them, may be compared to a wise man, who built his house upon the rock.
25 "And the rain descended, and the floods came, and the winds blew, and burst against that house; and yet it did not fall, for it had been founded upon the rock.
26 "And everyone who hears these words of Mine, and does not act upon them, will be like a foolish man, who built his house upon the sand.
27 "And the rain descended, and the floods came, and the winds blew, and burst against that house; and it fell, and great was its fall."

28 The result was that when Jesus had finished these words, the multitudes were amazed at His teaching;
29 for He was teaching them as *one* having authority, and not as their scribes.

# GOD'S PLAN

### PRETRIBULATION RAPTURE
Or MID-TRIB, POST-TRIB.
Whenever . . . He is coming for His bride!
I Thessalonians 4:13-18   I Corinthians 15:51-58

### JUDGMENT SEAT
OF CHRIST
II Corinthians 5:10     Romans 14:10

### FIRST COMING
OF CHRIST

### ANTICHRIST
REIGNS
Matthew 24:15   Daniel 9:26-27

CHURCH AGE

3½ years      3½ years

John 3:16          Revelation 2-3

### TRIBULATION OR
DANIEL'S 70TH WEEK
Revelation 6-19
Daniel 9:24-27

HADES

ABRAHAM'S BOSOM      Luke 16:19-31   PLACE OF TORMENT
OR PARADISE
(Vacated and taken to the
third heaven after Jesus'
death and resurrection)
II Corinthians 12:2-4

# OF THE AGES

## SECOND COMING OF CHRIST
(Jehovah-shammah)
Revelation 19:11-21

GREAT WHITE
THRONE JUDGMENT
Revelation 20:11-15

BATTLE OF ARMAGEDDON
Revelation 19:11-21

JUDGMENT OF NATIONS
Matthew 25:31-46

FIRE
DESTROYS
EARTH
II Peter 3:10-13

NEW HEAVEN
NEW EARTH
ETERNITY

1,000 YEAR REIGN OF CHRIST
Revelation 20:1-7

Revelation 21 and 22

Satan bound

Satan loosed

## BOTTOMLESS PIT
Revelation 20:1-3

## LAKE OF FIRE
Revelation 20:10, 13-15
Matthew 25:41, 46

# Appendix C

## Discussion Questions

### Lesson 1: A Mask of Hypocrisy?

1. As you read the Sermon on the Mount, what made the most significant impression in your mind?
2. How did it make you feel?
3. What did you learn about righteousness?
4. What did you learn about the Kingdom of Heaven?
5. According to the Sermon on the Mount, who is going to go to heaven? Make sure the class can name the four basic requirements given on p. 18.
6. Have the class discuss the meaning of the word *hypocrite* and how hypocrisy manifests itself. Have they seen it in any form in their own lives? Encourage them to be honest, vulnerable, and willing to grow!

### Lesson 2: What Is the Kingdom of Heaven?

1. Have the class define the four aspects of the kingdom of heaven.
   a. Have them be as explicit as possible in describing these.
   b. Have them share any new insights they gleaned.
2. Have the class share how Revelation 4, 5 can be applied to their lives.
3. Spend time in prayer, praising and worshiping God in short sentences.

### Lesson 3: When Jesus Comes in the Glory of His Kingdom.

1. In Mark 10:17–27,
   a. What aspect of the kingdom of heaven is referred to?
   b. Why couldn't the young man enter it?
   c. What did they learn from this?
2. Discuss the parable of the wheat and the tares, and how it parallels the Sermon on the Mount.
3. Discuss what they learned about the kingdom from Matthew 24, 25.
4. What aspect of the kingdom is the Sermon on the Mount about? Have them support their answers with Scripture.
5. Review the outline of the Sermon on the Mount according to the chapter and verse divisions given on p. 38.

### Lesson 4: Blessing Begins with Poverty of Spirit

1. Define the word *blessed*. How does blessedness relate to happiness?
2. Where does the world think happiness comes from? Why? Where does it come from?
3. Have the class explain what it means to be poor in spirit.
   a. Have them give an illustration from Scripture.
   b. Have them share how a person can come to see his poverty of spirit.
4. How do the poor in spirit live on a day-to-day basis? (Have them share how Jesus is our example.)

### Lesson 5: When Was the Last Time You Wept Over Sin?

1. How would you explain this second beatitude to someone?
2. Why are those who mourn blessed?
3. What are we to mourn over?
4. Have the class discuss how it affects them when:
    a. they sin personally (discuss 2 Corinthians 7, two kinds of sorrow);
    b. there is sin in the church (discuss 1 Corinthians 5; Matthew 18:15–20);
    c. they consider what is going on in our society, our world (discuss Ezek. 9).
5. What place did mourning have in Jesus' life?
6. What impressed them the most about this week's study?

### Lesson 6: Meekness: Knowing God, His Character, His Sovereignty

1. Discuss the sovereignty of God.
    a. Define the term
    b. What is God sovereign over and why?
    c. What problems does this present to men? Why?
2. How does knowing the character of God help you understand His sovereignty?
3. What did they learn about the attributes of God. Review them and define them; then talk about the practical implication to their lives.
4. How does the sovereignty and character of God relate to meekness? Make sure they can define meekness.
5. If God is not sovereign, what then?

### Lesson 7: Meekness: How Does It Behave Toward God and Man?

1. Have the class discuss any new insights they have gained into meekness.
2. Discuss how Jesus displayed meekness. Is meekness weakness? Explain.
3. Where or how does one become meek?
4. How is meekness seen in its behavior toward God? Toward men?
5. Explain the relationship of bitterness and meekness.
6. Have the class share how God has spoken to them this week.

### Lesson 8: Hungering and Thirsting for Righteousness

1. Discuss what it means to hunger and thirst after righteousness.
2. Have the class define and illustrate righteousness. Compare God's righteousness and self-righteousness. Use the Scriptures to do so.
3. Discuss the seven things they can do to increase their hunger and thirst for righteousness.

### Lesson 9: How Can I Be Merciful . . . Pure?

1. How would you define mercy?
2. How does God display His mercy? (Have class review the Tabernacle, discussing what it represented and what function the Ark and the Mercy Seat fulfilled on the Day of Atonement.)
3. Discuss Matthew 18:21–35.
    a. How did the debts of the two men compare?
    b. What was Jesus' purpose in telling this story?

c. What significance does this story have for our lives?

d. How did God speak to you personally?

4. Ask if any are having a hard time forgiving another. If so, take time to pray for them. It is good to have a person pray who has found himself in the same situation.

5. What does it mean to be pure in heart?

6. How does a person get a pure heart?

7. How does he keep it pure? Have the class be very practical, sharing openly the things they do to keep their hearts pure. If people will be vulnerable, it will minister to others.

## Lesson 10: Peacemakers—At All Costs

1. Have the class discuss the true meaning of peace.

2. How can men be at peace with other men?

a. Make sure the class can explain the words *enmity* and *reconcile*.

b. Cover man's *need* to first be reconciled to God.

3. How can man be reconciled to God?

As you discuss this question, you will want them to look once again at Colossians 1:20–22, Romans 5:10, 11, and 2 Corinthians 5:18–21. Have the students explain reconciliation from these passages. Stick to what the Scriptures say. This is a marvelous opportunity to make sure that your class understands salvation.

4. Have the class discuss things that bring disharmony between believers and practical things that Christians can do to make peace.

5. What part does persecution play in the life of a Christian? Explain your answer from the Word.

6. What forms can persecution take?

7. What purpose does persecution have?

8. How are we to handle it when it comes? Be sure you cover Jesus' example in 1 Peter 2:21–25.

## Lesson 11: Salt and Light

1. Discuss why Jesus used the metaphors of salt and light to describe a Christian.

a. Have the class verbalize what they learned regarding salt and its uses. Also discuss the function of light.

b. Cover how salt and light are made ineffective.

2. Have the class compare Lot's life to their own. Discuss ways they have failed to impact their society and why.

3. Discuss 1 John 1:5–7. Have the class verbalize what it is saying and how it compares with John 8:12; 9:5; 12:46.

## Lesson 12: How To Have A New Heart . . .

1. Discuss man's relationship to sin before he is set free. Have your students support their answers with Scripture.

2. Have the class explain how we are set free from sin's slavery by using the passages you studied in John 8 and Romans 6 and 8.

3. Explain 2 Corinthians 5:17. What makes Christians new creatures? How are they new?
   Cover the promises of the New Covenant in Ezekiel 36:26, 27; Hebrews 10:14–16.
4. Review all the things that occur when one enters into the New Covenant. Go back over the passages in Jeremiah 31 and 32, Ezekiel 26, 2 Corinthians 3, Hebrews 10. Have the class verbalize them one by one; it will help seal it in their hearts and minds.
5. Summarize by asking if it is possible to live according to the Sermon on The Mount. How?

### Lesson 13: How Do You Handle Anger, Murder, Lust, Adultery?

1. Why does God judge us when we call someone "Raca" or "fool"?
2. Why is murder wrong? How was it to be judged and why?
3. Why is reconciliation important to God? What beatitude does it parallel?
4. How does Jesus define adultery? How serious is it?
5. Have the class explain the meaning of Matthew 5:29, 30.
6. Discuss how God feels about divorce and why. (This could be a hot issue, so don't lose control of the class. Cover only what the lesson covers.)
7. Finally, discuss making vows. Why are they not needful? Have the class share what God taught them regarding the integrity of their words.

### Lesson 14: What Do You Do When You Get Ripped Off?

1. Discuss the reasons for (or the value of) the Old Testament law of an eye for an eye, tooth for tooth, life for life. Of what purpose were these laws?
2. Is Jesus contradicting these laws when He calls us to turn the other cheek? Have the class explain their answers.
3. Should this principle of turning the other cheek be applied to a nation's judicial system or national defense program? Is this what Jesus intended? Have them *biblically* explain their answers.
4. Discuss how love fulfills the law. Be very practical.

### Lesson 15: Praying and Fasting God's Way

1. Discuss the seven index sentences in the Lord's Prayer.
   a. Have the class cover each topic of prayer and what it means.
   b. Discuss the reason for the order of the sentences.
2. Ask them to share various ways they have applied what they learned. (The book, *Lord, Teach Me To Pray,* also by the author, has become a very effective study book in many churches and Bible classes.)
3. Discuss their problems in private prayer and talk about ways they can improve their prayer life.
4. Discuss the eight reasons for fasting found on pages 217, 218.
   a. Ask them to share what they learned from the Scripture references.
   b. Have them discuss things in their church, community, or nation that might be reasons for fasting.

### Lesson 16: How Do You Handle the Desire for Things?

1. Discuss what it means to lay up treasures on earth and how this affects your relationship with God and His kingdom. Ask the class to be honest and open with the intent of helping one another.

2. Discuss the ways your heart is enticed from heavenly treasure. How do these ways compare with Eve, Achan, and King David?
3. Discuss what it means to seek first God's kingdom and His righteousness. When does this fit in with man's responsibility to provide for his household?

### Lesson 17: To Judge or Not to Judge—That Is the Confusion!

1. Have the class explain what Jesus means by, "Judge not lest you be judged."
2. When is judging permissible? What are we to judge?
3. When we see a brother in error, how are we to deal with that brother? Have the class answer on the basis of Scripture.

### Lesson 18: How To Know You're a Possessor of the Kingdom of Heaven

1. Discuss the two keys given in Matthew 7 whereby we can live righteously before God and before man.
2. Ask the class how they would explain the Golden Rule to another.
3. Discuss how Luke 13:22–30 parallels with Matthew 7. How could it be applied today?
4. What did you learn about false prophets? How are Christians to know and respond to them? Have the class be thorough in their answers, using the Scriptures to make their point.
5. According to Matthew 7, who is going to heaven and why?
6. Ask the class to share the most significant thing God has done in their lives through this study.

For information about Kay's teaching ministry and her Precept Upon Precept inductive Bible study courses, write:

**Precept Ministries of Reach Out, Inc.**
**P.O. Box 23000**
**Chattanooga, TN 37422**
**Attention: Precept Office**
**(615) 892-6814**

Also, if you desire information on audio- or video-cassette teaching tapes that accompany this study on the Sermon on the Mount, write or call the Audio/Video Department. The audio and video tapes are first-quality productions and can be obtained at very reasonable rental costs. They are ideal for Sunday School, church training courses, or home Bible Study.